Argumentation

I would like to thank my wife Jean for her continued encouragement and support. She was invaluable in helping prepare this manuscript. Jean's appropriate vigilance for and exasperation with my periods of procrastination helped focus this effort. It is hard to imagine completing this project without Jean's input. Heather and I appreciate her incisive critical skills and commitment to clarity—although I still flinch a little bit when I hear the phrase "what's that supposed to mean?" Second, I must note what a rare privilege it has been to work on this project with co-author Heather Norton. Our discussions, debates, and occasional revelations during the writing process are among my most significant scholarly moments. Finally, thanks to all the students who have helped shape my thinking on argumentation. It's hazardous to single out any particular individual, but in writing this book, I could not help thinking of two colleagues who embody the qualities of responsible advocacy that we have tried to articulate. So thanks to Mike Bauer (Ball State University) and Sandy McKeown (University of South Dakota); your sense of humor, sense of fairness, and sense of social responsibility, coupled with razor-sharp critical skills, have been inspirational.

—Larry Underberg

I would like to thank my husband Trevor for his constant encouragement of and support for this project and me. Both cheerleader and co-parent, he made sure that I had the time and resources necessary to complete this project. My children Ella and Cade sacrificed many a Saturday with their mother so that we might complete this work, but they gained the joy of knowing Larry and Jean Underberg for it, so they clearly made out well in the deal. My family in Orland provided support from afar, and my parents-in-law did so from close by, and often cared for our children while I wrote. Working with Larry Underberg to put to paper what has been a 25-year conversation on this topic has been the real value and my joy in this journey. The book is a bonus. Fontbonne University awarded me a rare year-long sabbatical to complete the first draft of this text, and the book would not exist without it. For that, and for the moral and material support that the Department of English and Communication and the larger Fontbonne community has afforded me, I am deeply grateful. Finally, I thank the countless students with whom I have learned over the years. Much of our experience together is in this book.

—Heather Norton Davies

Argumentation

The Art of Civil Advocacy

Larry Underberg

Southeast Missouri State University

Heather Norton

Fontbonne University

Los Angeles | London | New Delhi
Singapore | Washington DC | Melbourne

FOR INFORMATION:

SAGE Publications, Inc.
2455 Teller Road
Thousand Oaks, California 91320
E-mail: order@sagepub.com

SAGE Publications Ltd.
1 Oliver's Yard
55 City Road
London EC1Y 1SP
United Kingdom

SAGE Publications India Pvt. Ltd.
B 1/I 1 Mohan Cooperative Industrial Area
Mathura Road, New Delhi 110 044
India

SAGE Publications Asia-Pacific Pte. Ltd.
3 Church Street
#10-04 Samsung Hub
Singapore 049483

Acquisitions Editor: Terri Accomazzo
Editorial Assistant: Erik Helton
Production Editor: Andrew Olson
Copy Editor: Diane Wainright
Typesetter: C&M Digitals (P) Ltd.
Proofreader: Liann Lech
Indexer: Beth Nauman-Montana
Cover Designer: Michael Dubowe
Marketing Manager: Jillian Oelsen

Printed in the United States of America

Library of Congress Cataloging-in-Publication Data

Names: Underberg, Larry, author. | Norton, Heather, author.

Title: Argumentation : the art of civil advocacy / Larry Underberg, Southeast Missouri State University ; Heather Norton, Fontbonne University.

Description: Thousand Oaks, California : SAGE, [2018] | Includes bibliographical references and index.

Identifiers: LCCN 2017008271 | ISBN 9781506345673 (pbk. : alk. paper)

Subjects: LCSH: Debates and debating. | Interpersonal communication.

Classification: LCC PN4181 .U47 2018 | DDC 808.53—dc23
LC record available at https://lccn.loc.gov/2017008271

This book is printed on acid-free paper.

17 18 19 20 21 10 9 8 7 6 5 4 3 2 1

Contents

List of Tables

Preface

This book offers an accessible, practical blueprint for *constructive* dispute resolution through argument. Our inspiration for this project arises from our observation that there has been a coarsening of discourse designed to resolve conflict. Too often, loud voices drown out reasonable voices. Evidence seems to matter less as we afford equal status to opinion and *informed* opinion. Finally, argument is frequently marred by a mean-spiritedness that damages relationships and closes the door to civil interaction. Because conflict and drama sell, we are increasingly exposed to unsavory media models of communication behavior that we may mirror in our own interactions. The consequences of this imitation will not bode well for our ability to effectively work through conflict in our daily lives. In short, it is important to reconsider when, why, what, and how we argue, and this text is designed to answer those queries. We have offered a framework that emphasizes the constructive potential of argument when practiced in a climate of respect, empathy, and recognition of the need to preserve and strengthen relationships.

This text meets the needs of anyone wishing to learn to argue productively, including students in argumentation or dispute resolution classes, practicing advocates, or individuals in search of a reliable means of evaluating persuasive messages.

FEATURES OF THIS BOOK

A variety of features make this text accessible and practical:

- *Issues of process receive a much-needed consideration* without sacrificing attention to the components of a reasonable argument (product). The authors infuse this text with a discussion of *how* we argue (process) to highlight how argumentative demeanor can enhance or diminish opportunities for future dialogue.

- *Full consideration of the many occasions in which we argue* is provided. Traditional concepts tend to focus on formal public exchanges. Such concepts are considered in detail but are also modified and applied to the numerous informal, interpersonal, or community exchanges in which readers will more frequently find themselves.

- *Liberal use of examples clarify central concepts.* Chapters contain an anchor example to illustrate content. Text and endnotes are laced with additional contemporary and historic examples, readily accessible to readers through the Internet, which will allow readers to observe and evaluate exchanges that illuminate textual concepts.

- *Summary textboxes* featured throughout the text provide a convenient outline for readers and useful presentation aids for those teaching from this book.

- *Questions for consideration* at the end of each chapter allow readers to clarify, critique, or extend material covered in each chapter through further investigation and discussion.

- *Easy-to-read supplements on the Toulmin model and logical fallacies* (Appendices A and B) provide convenient guides to the construction of arguments and the identification of reasoning flaws.

LAYOUT OF THE BOOK

The text is divided into three sections, each of which stresses a different component of the argument process.

Section One, "The Nature and Context of Argument," considers the variables of the argumentation process. Chapter 1 offers the philosophy of argument that unifies this text. After defining argument, attention shifts to consideration of the demeanor of the advocate, stressing behaviors that lead to constructive argument while noting circumstances when argument may not be appropriate. Chapter 2 discusses advocate credibility, noting its centrality to the argument process. Ethical strategies for enhancing credibility are a central focus of the chapter. Chapter 3 describes the contextual variables that impact argument and stresses the advocate's need to adapt to audience, field, occasion, and historical context. Chapter 4 describes the importance of adapting arguments to a particular audience. This chapter features discussions of reading familiar and unfamiliar audiences. The uses and limitations of demographic analysis are considered.

Section Two, "Identifying and Making Quality Arguments," addresses the discovery, analysis, and support of arguments. Chapter 5 describes the utility of the narrative perspective in constructing quality audience-friendly arguments. Chapter 6 describes the stock issues that define the burdens of advocates discussing claims of fact, value, or policy. Chapter 7 describes why the use of outside support is essential to reasonable argument and offers general guidelines for assessing support. Chapter 8 extends the analysis of the previous chapter by focusing on specific tests of reliability for examples, statistics, and testimony.

Section Three, "Effectively Presenting Arguments," examines delivery, reinforcing the theme that the *way* we present arguments facilitates constructive engagement. Chapter 9 discusses the role of style in establishing advocate credibility and then examines the impact of word choice on listeners. Chapter 10 focuses on response/rebuttal options available to the advocate. Special attention is given to effective listening and maintaining a positive argument climate.

DIGITAL RESOURCES

https://study.sagepub.com/underberg

Password-protected **Instructor Resources** include the following:

- A **Microsoft® Word test bank** is available containing multiple choice, true/false, and essay questions for each chapter. The test bank provides you with a diverse range of pre-written options as well as the opportunity for editing any question and/or inserting your own personalized questions to assess students' progress and understanding.

- Editable, chapter-specific **Microsoft® PowerPoint® slides** offer you complete flexibility in easily creating a multimedia presentation for your course.

- EXCLUSIVE! Access to certain full-text **SAGE journal articles** that have been carefully selected for each chapter. Each article supports and expands on the concepts presented in the chapter. This feature also provides questions to focus and guide student interpretation. Combine cutting-edge academic journal scholarship with the topics in your course for a robust classroom experience.

Acknowledgments

The authors wish to thank the fine people at SAGE Publishing for their faith in this project and help in bringing it to fruition. We deeply appreciate the confidence and support Terri Accomazzo provided for this project from the very beginning. Andrew Olson, production editor, and Diane Wainwright, copy editor, were superb. Jennifer Jovin gently guided us through the creation of web content. Jillian Oelsen provided important help with marketing. It has been a privilege to work with such a professional and conscientious group of people. A number of reviewers offered incisive comments on early drafts of this text, and we appreciate their help in improving the quality of this work:

Ralph J. Castellanos, Fullerton College

Emily Winters Bergen (Ret.), Tennessee State University

Diana Isabel Bowen, University of Houston–Clear Lake

Myra A. Whittemore, College of Charleston

Susan P. Millsap, Otterbein University

Suzanne J. Atkin, Arizona State University

David C. Bailey, Southwest Baptist University

Carroll Ferguson Nardone, Sam Houston State University

Anthony Ongyod, MiraCosta College

Roy Schwartzman, University of North Carolina at Greensboro

C. Turner Steckline Wilson, University of Louisiana at Monroe

Julie Woodbury, Minnesota State University, Mankato

Beth Zoufal, DePaul University

Lynn Cherry, College of Charleston

Gina L. Jensen, Webster University

James Thompson, Porterville College

Finally, a huge *thanks* to the staff at Six North Café in Ballwin, Missouri, who patiently tolerated our claiming of a corner booth for hours of discussion, debate, and revision of this text.

The Nature and Context of Argument

1 The Process of Argument

This is a book about how we argue. If your initial reaction is to be apprehensive at the thought of arguing, we understand. Popular use of the term *argument* associates it with the loud, aggressive, and unreasonable behavior that we all too frequently witness from politicians, media pundits, or those noisy neighbors working their way toward a disturbing-the-peace complaint. Those are fights, not arguments. We invite you to consider a more productive alternative in which people exchange information or explore alternatives (argue) without malice. We actually engage in argument rather routinely, whether we recognize these interactions as arguments or not. Every day, friends and family members disagree about decisions—big and small—and work it out. Someone proposes a different way to do something at work. Committees deliberate about the best candidate to hire. Students request that professors extend a deadline on assignments or reconsider a grade on a paper. School boards and town councils meet to make policies that will affect the daily lives of their neighbors, who they often invite in to present arguments as well. The list of examples of arguing in our daily lives is endless because every day people work in communities to make sound decisions in ways that do not undermine relationships. These types of exchanges lack the combative features of a TV reality show or talk radio. Often they are not terribly dramatic, and while people argue passionately for their own positions, such disputes tend to bring people together in a shared attempt to forge agreement. Fortunately, such arguments are far more common than their combative counterparts.

ARGUING IS PART OF OUR NATURE

One attribute that separates humans from animals is our reflective nature. We do not respond only automatically or instinctively to situations but instead we consider the reasons for and consequences of our actions. We develop this skill at an early age. One of the most frustrating challenges facing parents is dealing with children who have entered the "why" phase. This is the point where children abandon their tendency to act without reflection to parental commands and adopt a more skeptical stance. Their response to commands is "why?"—as is their response to their parents' explanations. Suddenly, our children are responding to us on a new and often irritating level. Everything seems to be an occasion for debate. Occasionally, these exchanges can be highly productive. Asked *why* they should not talk to a stranger or *why* it is a good idea to wash their hands provides parents with valuable teaching opportunities. Other times they are occasions for parental self-reflection in those situations where they really do not know why they are making a particular demand and have fallen back on that all-purpose "because I said so" response. The *why* phase represents a significant point in a child's cognitive and social development, as he or she becomes reflective rather than merely reflexive. No longer passively reacting to the world around them, children are now trying to understand their environment and behavior. Parents also are communicating on an entirely different level as their child struggles to come to a deeper understanding of their (and their parents') actions, and to understand the role of reason giving in communication and relationships.

Attempting to understand the statements of others through critical reflection and questioning is a natural tendency. As we develop a sense of when it is appropriate to question others and when, instead, arguing is pointless and irritating, we also develop an understanding of the rules of engagement as well as develop the tact and sensitivity that will make our exchanges beneficial learning and teaching opportunities. Additionally, as we respond to questions or reservations voiced by others, we become involved in a process that encourages us to think about what we say—to provide some acceptable justification for our statements. With any luck, we will never grow out of the "why" phase, and as adults we learn to ask increasingly sophisticated and nuanced questions, and become better reason givers as well. In short, we argue.

WHAT IS ARGUMENT?

We define **argument** as *the communication process through which the reasons that inform our statements are explored.* There are a variety of definitions for the term *argument*, and each of them suggests particular ways in which to view, study, or practice the activity. A number of definitions draw attention to the elements that constitute an argumentative statement, noting that an argument consists of an assertion (claim) that can be supported with **reasons (grounds)**. For a more detailed account of product-centered definitions, consult the discussion of the Stephen Toulmin model of argument contained in Appendix A. Our definition casts argument as a *communication process.* This notion is important in that it focuses on **argument as process** (as in "they are *having* an argument") in addition to **argument as product** (as in "that is a good argument").[1] In this book, our attention is focused primarily on how we might productively argue (the process of argument) while understanding that making good arguments (product) is a part of that process, but the quality of the product depends heavily on the reputation of the advocate, the nature of the audience being addressed, and the context in which argument takes place. In short, you can make the case that an argument must contain particular elements, but those formal requirements are often altered by circumstances.

Labeling argument a communication process suggests the social/public nature of argument. Granted, we may engage in the kind of reflective activity by which we think through our statements—internalized argument. However, our concern is with those occasions where our judgments, and the foundation upon which those judgments are based, are shared with others. Examples could include a variety of exchanges or discussions with romantic partners, family, and friends; presenting an idea at a parent–teacher conference, city council meeting, classroom, or civic club; to the more formal and stylized exchanges that characterize judicial or deliberative bodies. Confining our attention primarily to communication exchanges is critical to understanding that argument has social consequences and that the process functions best in a climate where information is freely shared with and evaluated by others.

Finally, argument involves the evaluation of the *reasons* that inform our statements. When others ask us to explain our positions, we are invited to engage in argument. The process works best when we are willing to clearly explain ourselves and are open-minded enough to consider the other points of view that emerge as part of the process. Our definition provides the beginning of an ethical perspective on argument—behaviors that discourage the examination of reasons are at best poor argument and at worst an exercise in propaganda or coercion. To effectively engage in argument, one should observe the attributes that facilitate reason giving, such as clarity, empathy (understanding other perspectives), and open-mindedness.

WHY SHOULD WE ARGUE?

To answer the question "Why should we argue?" it is important to recall our definition of argument as the communication process through which the reasons that inform our statements are explored. Embracing argument as a form of communication carries with it some vital assumptions about the way we interact with the world around us. First, we believe that our opinions and actions should not be random or arbitrary. We believe and act only after we are satisfied that our decisions are based on good reasons. We are constructively critical of the messages to which we respond: Why should we buy a particular product? Why should we vote for a particular political candidate? Why should we grant or withhold our support for a ballot initiative, school board proposal, or community project? Why should we donate our time and resources to a particular civic or charitable organization? On a more personal level, how should we respond to the challenges and decisions that we confront on a daily basis? The short answer to all of these questions is that we respond after weighing the alternatives available to us, examine the foundation upon which these options are based, and make the best choice possible given the information we possess or are able to acquire. Much has been written about the value of being an informed citizen. Clearly, there is a degree of personal satisfaction and empowerment as we do not simply act, but act *wisely*. The critical and inquiring mind that makes informed action possible is a result, in large measure, of our willingness to embrace argument. It is the communication equivalent of taking off the blinders.

A second benefit of argument is that it is a path to productive citizenship. Our democracy is based on notions of informed consent of the governed, or in other words, we are to be participants in, rather than mere spectators of, public decision making. Admittedly, at times our impact may be limited, but often we underestimate the influence we can exert. The alternative is an apathetic posture where we are content to defer to others as they make decisions that may dramatically affect us, our friends, or the society in which we live. We may rationalize our inaction with the comforting yet dangerous belief that decision makers, being well intentioned, would not act in ways that run contrary to our interests or the interests of society. Yet how would they know those interests if no one bothers to speak up? Particularly at the local level, individuals can make constructive contributions, but they have to be willing to express themselves.

Being an engaged citizen is not easy. The task is complicated by the fact that all too often we must wade through misleading statements, exaggerations, misinterpretations, and occasionally outright lies. As we become accustomed to evaluating the reasons that inform statements made by others, we rehearse the critical habits of mind that enable our informed judgment. These skills go well beyond the persistent *whys* of a child as we learn to listen critically, evaluate fairly, and present our own positions with clarity while at the same time cultivating an environment that encourages the exchange of informed opinions that constitute the basis for sound judgment.

ARGUING PRODUCTIVELY

Arguing can be one of the most productive and informative methods of communication. It can also be destructive. The quality of the outcome depends heavily on the outlook of those participating; we refer to them as advocates. We can choose to imitate talk-show ideologues who make a career out of browbeating and embarrassing guests who do not share the host's point of view or who only engage those with whom they really already agree, turning discussions into opportunities for mutual venting and self-praise rather than critical reflection. We can choose to model our behavior after what we have seen on televised political debates where all manner of verbal contortion is used to avoid directly answering meaningful questions from a moderator. We can take a page from the politician's book and respond in vague but nice-sounding generalities that are unlikely to elicit any meaningful scrutiny. We can accept as "normal" friends or families whose constant bickering and fighting seem the default position for conflict resolution. Finally, we can copy the demagogue and rely on fear, intimidation, or our apparent power advantage to ensure that our ideas prevail. Publicly, we can lament the lack of civility in public discourse even while our own actions contribute to the condition. We can, however, choose more productive and humane ways to communicate. A central premise of this book is that argument is a productive activity, and with the proper outlook on the part of the participants, argumentative discussions can work to the mutual benefit of those involved in the exchange and to the advantage of those who will be required to live with the decisions.

Keeping Our Ego in Check

Anytime we engage in an exchange that is argumentative in nature, we take a significant risk. The essence of argument is that ideas are clearly expressed and tested or modified in a thoughtful discussion. Of course, nobody likes to "lose" an argument, but if we engage in an argument believing that any result short of receiving a ringing endorsement of our stance constitutes a loss, then we are in no position to make productive use of the exchange. Advocates should enter arguments with more of an open mind. What if we were to define "winning" as mutually reaching a wise decision? This does not mean that we are not passionate about our opinions but does demand that we willingly and honestly reflect on them and are receptive to other points of view. We afford to those with whom we communicate the same consideration we expect in return—a fair hearing. This implies a dual burden. As advocates, we are mindful of the fact that the exchange is not about us but is instead about our ideas. This degree of detachment allows us to keep our egos in check. We are not offended by questions like "Why do you believe that?" We fully expect our ideas to be evaluated and recognize that critical evaluation by another is not an assessment of our worth as a person. Recognizing that it is our ideas (not ourselves) under consideration, we feel less compelled to wow onlookers with our dazzling display of skill. Obviously we speak with conviction, but ultimately we realize that the product of the argument process is what matters, not simply showing off to gain personal recognition. We approach the exchange with humility and shun notions that the humiliation of other persons is a worthy goal. Beyond our responsibilities as advocates, we also have obligations as listeners. Are we truly listening in an attempt to understand the other, or are we listening strategically in an effort to find a weakness and pounce on it? If we do find a weakness in another's position, do we exploit it in an attempt to make ourselves look superior rather than address it in an attempt to improve the final product of the argument process?

Hardball, MSNBC's political interview show hosted by Chris Matthews, provides an interesting example of an ego gone awry. Matthews has a keen analytical mind and a deep passion for politics. Unfortunately, his passion can trump his sense of argumentative decorum. Matthews's interrogation style is aggressive as he asks his guests complex questions (often six to eight questions in a single burst) and continually interrupts them to ask additional questions as they attempt to respond. Guests rarely are given time to provide a coherent response and are easily derailed by the persistent questioning that interrupts or redirects their responses. The tragedy of this tactic is that informed participants are seldom afforded the luxury of formulating a coherent line of argument, much less resolving controversial points via reasoned debate. Such antics deny viewers the opportunity to learn as our judgments are reduced to simply determining who came out looking the best after the ordeal. We might point to Matthews's poor listening skills and attempts to dominate discussion as being responsible for creating a climate that prevents a meaningful exchange of ideas. One of Matthews's most famous exchanges involved his coverage of the keynote address of Democratic Senator Zell Miller at the 2004 Republican National Convention.[2] Miller had just delivered a hostile, incendiary speech, and his assertions deserved scrutiny. Enter Chris Matthews. With his characteristic aggressive style of inquisition, Matthews pressed Miller, who only became more agitated as the interview progressed. Finally, in an "I dare you to say that to my face" type moment, Miller expressed his regret that it wasn't the old days where he could challenge Matthews to a duel. The interview concluded and Matthews shared an "I can't believe he just did that" moment with the remaining panelists. He should not have been surprised. Given Miller's already agitated state and Matthews's relentless "you can't possibly believe that" line of questioning, the results were predictable. Matthews's apparent dismay was reminiscent of a basketball player intentionally delivering a vicious nose-fracturing elbow to an opponent and then raising his hands in an innocent "what did I do" gesture as the referee prepares to make the call and his bloodied opponent prepares to respond.

Who doesn't like to be the smartest person in the room? Often it is not enough that we know it; we want everyone else to know it as well. This is where our egos can be a major impediment to productive argument, as we see an argument as a performance that will convince others of our superiority. Any retreat from our original position is viewed as a personal failure. Under such circumstances, we have misunderstood the process of argument. Argument should be viewed as a learning opportunity in which we test our opinions and, if necessary, modify our judgments as a result of what we learn in the exchange. A willingness to change our mind or to question positions we once took as unassailable is not a sign of weakness but rather an indication that we are open-minded and willing to listen and learn. While we should have confidence in our opinions and should advance them as clearly and persuasively as possible, we should also be willing to alter our views when circumstances warrant. A healthy argumentative perspective assumes that thoughtful deliberation yields superior results. How often have we dismissed decision makers as "wishy-washy" or indecisive when in fact they are reflective? How often do we express admiration for leaders who "go with their gut" only to later regret decisions that were made absent a thoughtful consideration of alternatives or consequences? The key is to trust the process, to engage others with an open mind, and to the extent ego enhancement is our goal, to tie personal satisfaction to how well we are able to create an environment that produces a quality outcome rather than to engage in a spectacle where we posture or show off.

An example of how argument can devolve into a clash of egos and deprive the audience of a genuine opportunity to learn something is provided by an interview of actor Tom Cruise by NBC's *Today* morning show host Matt Lauer.[3] The focal point of the interview was the potential worth of antidepressants as a treatment option. Actress Brooke Shields (who was not present) had just been prescribed Paxil for post-partum depression and, like many who have taken such medications, was sold on the drug's benefits. Cruise questioned the validity of Shields's experience, claiming "there is no such thing as a chemical imbalance," taking the position that anyone embracing "mind-altering antipsychotic drugs" as effective was uninformed and, worse, irresponsibly promoting their use to a naïve public. Lauer countered that a number of people had taken antidepressants and found them to be helpful and asked Cruise to concede that for at least some people in some circumstances there could be medical benefits. Sidestepping the issue, Cruise informed Lauer "[y]ou don't know the history of psychiatry; I do" and offered an impassioned critique of psychopharmacology. When it appeared neither was willing to give any ground, Lauer offered an olive branch, telling Cruise, "It's very impressive to listen to you because clearly you've done the homework and you know the subject." Dodging this compliment, Cruise used it as ammunition to assert that it would be nice if Lauer had bothered to do a little homework because he "should be a little more responsible." It would be charitable to call this exchange an argument—it was more like a verbal fight. Both ended the conversation where they had started, with Lauer asserting that he knew people who had been helped by antidepressants, and it was a bit arrogant for Cruise to discount the validity of his experience by simply responding "you don't know; I do."

To appreciate why this exchange went off the rails, consider the ways in which the communicators were constrained. Cruise was a strong believer in Scientology and, as such, a believer in the group's theological stance on the causes of human suffering. Scientology continues to devote considerable resources to debunking the psychiatric profession. Framed this way, Lauer's doubts are easily construed as attacks on Cruise's deeply held religious convictions. Since Cruise is seen by many as a high-profile spokesperson for the church, reluctance to publicly defend the faith was simply not an option for him. Lauer, on the other hand, had his own experiences with people who had benefited from antidepressants and was unwilling to tolerate having those experiences treated so dismissively. In short, we have two people unwilling to admit they might be wrong becoming stridently inflexible in a public exchange. Had this been a private conversation, both might have been more flexible, but with a national television audience looking on, neither wanted to endure the embarrassment of being "bested" in an argument. The whole interaction comes down to proving you are the smartest person in the room.

Both men had a lot to lose if they were the one who ended up looking uninformed. The treatment of mental illness is an extraordinarily important and controversial issue, and most unfortunately, the viewers of the Lauer/Cruise interview learned little. Judging by viewers' comments on YouTube, it was perceived as the argumentative equivalent of a professional wrestling match. In other words, the interview was an exaggerated, sensationalized imitation of the real thing.

Controlling Competitive Juices

Our knowledge, beliefs, and understanding of the ways the world does and should work are often called into question during argument, so it is easy to see why we feel our egos are on the line. Moreover, in Western culture, arguments are "won" or "lost," meaning that our skills as advocates are at issue as well. Too often, competitive success is our yardstick. Competition is so ingrained in our society that we often are unaware of its adverse consequences. We compete for grades, popularity, and financial success. We measure our accomplishments by asking ourselves if we are viewed as "better off" than others. We look over the fence at our neighbors and ask, "Do we have a nicer house, prettier yard, or flashier automobile?" Our society embraces the notion that competition encourages excellence and achievement, and we carry that assumption into nearly all of our activities.

Although we are conditioned to compete, it is not necessarily an inherent part of being human. It does not necessarily help us to live better together or solve the problems of our communities. Psychologist Alfie Kohn has written a number of thought-provoking, though controversial, critiques of competition. His book *No Contest: The Case Against Competition* asserts that there are limited grounds for viewing competition as an inherent part of human nature. According to Kohn, competition does not enhance performance or motivation, does not build character, and undermines relationships. Kohn laments the fact that "[l]ife for us has become an endless succession of contests" and implores his readers to "look at what it really means to try to beat other people, a careful investigation of this arrangement that requires some people to fail in order that others can succeed."[4] Kohn describes **structural competition** as a situation "that is characterized by . . . mutually exclusive goal attainment. This means, very simply, that my success requires your failure."[5] This may be a result of simply following decision rules that demand win/lose decisions as in a court of law. We suggest that in argumentative exchanges norms requiring **zero-sum** results, while not always stated, are binding on participants. A second type of competition might be termed **intentional competition**, which is more a question of individual attitudes reflecting one's "proclivity for besting others"[6] and may operate in a variety of circumstances.

Consider the advantages that would result if one views argument as a cooperative search for truth. We find Kohn's advocacy of cooperation rather than competition to be compelling, and while we may not agree with all of his claims, we certainly find his approach to learning and conflict both liberating and rewarding. A more cooperative process of argumentation, we believe, provides a more productive path of problem solving. Kohn cites the observations of Morton Deutsch and outlines what we believe to be an enlightened approach to conflict:

> A cooperative process leads to the defining of conflicting interests as a mutual problem to be solved by collaborative effort. It facilitates the recognition of the legitimacy of each other's interests and of the necessity of searching for a solution that is responsive to the needs of all. It tends to limit rather than expand the scope of conflicting interests. In contrast, a competitive process stimulates the view that the solution of conflict can only be one that is imposed by one side on the other . . . through superior force, deceptions, or cleverness. . . . The enhancement of one's own power and the minimization of the legitimacy of the other side's interests in the situation become objectives.[7]

In the realm of argument, the difference in a **competitive** or **cooperative mindset** can be seen in behaviors that seek control over compromise, humiliation of others rather than humility, or combat over compassion.[8] Given the choice, what type of individual would you rather engage in conversation? If our objectives in argument are strictly competitive, we sacrifice opportunities for productive cooperative problem solving, jeopardize relationships, and most likely convince ourselves that ethical and humane considerations are secondary to winning. Imagine the benefits for our relationships and the greater opportunities for continued productive dialogue with others if we were to devote more attention to openness, compromise, and empathy. Yes, there will always be conflict since argument assumes some level of disagreement over ideas; but how we deal with conflict is vitally important.

TABLE 1.1

Suggested Rules of Engagement

• It is not about me, it is about my ideas.
• I could be wrong.
• I am not diminished by changing my mind or compromising.
• I am not interested in humiliating others.
• I am community-centered rather than self-centered.
• I value cooperation over competition.
• I will communicate in a way that creates and maintains a positive argumentative climate.

WHEN NOT TO ARGUE

The circumstances under which we should not argue, given the way we have defined the term, are rare. After all, the statements or claims we make are based on reasons, and an argumentative perspective simply means we are willing to give voice to those reasons. On the other hand, even if one follows the "rules of engagement" listed in the previous section, there is no guarantee that the person with whom you are communicating shares that commitment. He or she may view the exchange as threatening, aggressive, or a waste of time. The skilled advocate will recognize this and consider the disposition of the audience and their overall receptiveness to argument. The skilled advocate will recognize when the environment would be conducive to constructive and robust discussion, and strive to create a more favorable climate for argument. Common sense dictates that advocates should select their opportunities to engage carefully. There are a number of variables to consider as you assess the potential benefit of engaging in argument.

When You Are Not Sufficiently Prepared

You should know what you are talking about. Admittedly, there are occasions when one argues without significant prior preparation. For instance, we may attempt to help others better understand their positions by playing **devil's advocate** (intentionally taking an opposing position whether we believe in it or not) or suggest alternatives to a position that is conditional or not well thought out in hopes we might reason together. There is value to these interactions, but we believe they should be rather rare. Remember, it is a fine line between being a devil's advocate and being a contrary pest. The "let me just throw this out there" advocate may come across as ill prepared or intellectually lazy. It might be fine to ad lib in informal or spontaneous interactions, but the practice is hazardous in more formal forums or when decisions of great consequence must be made.

You (and your audience) will gain more from argument if you do your homework. You will be better prepared to explain your positions and better equipped to evaluate counterpositions. Your level of preparation also conveys a sense of respect for your audience. Teachers and professional speakers, for example, might be able to occasionally "wing it," but that approach gets old fast as your listeners expect you to leave them with something of value. A common example of arguing while unprepared involves public response to newly released and potentially controversial art, books, and movies. It is not uncommon that individuals will voice strident condemnation of a work's so-called politically objectionable or socially irresponsible content. Unfortunately, frequently the critic's answer to the question "have you seen/read it" is "no, I don't need to" or "I won't support trash like that by paying attention to it." Here, people are expressing their opinion but they are not offering an *informed opinion*. Judgments such as this simply regurgitate condemnations heard elsewhere or are *a priori* judgments based on suspect assessments about the motivation or mind-set of the work's creator.

When Argument Will Not Make a Difference

Is arguing simply a waste of breath because your audience is so stridently committed to a position that they will not give you a fair hearing? If so, you should consider choosing *not* to engage. However, we believe these occasions are infrequent and in subsequent chapters will demonstrate that there is usually an opportunity to establish common ground with your audience. The alert advocate is aware that even in those instances where an audience is unlikely to totally embrace a competing point of view, they may be receptive to more modest requests. For example, members of the National Abortion Rights Action League would likely reject any proposal that limits reproductive choice from a pro-life advocate, but the two may find some common ground on the issue of preventing unwanted pregnancy.

Consider the recent national debates—and stalemate—over raising the country's debt ceiling. Congressional votes on the debt ceiling, which are normally routine and simply mean the United States will not default on its debts, were for the first time mired in controversy in 2005 as a number of politicians insisted that the ceiling should not be raised until we got our national debt under control. The debt crisis can be addressed through spending cuts or revenue enhancements, yet a number of key players in the controversy entered the negotiations with notions about how some options, such as raising taxes, closing corporate tax loopholes, or making cuts to Medicare and Social Security, are "off the table." Constrained by signed pledges to never raise taxes or bound by commitments to powerful lobbies or voting blocs, negotiations seemed to be at an impasse. As a result of this impasse, the credit rating of the United States was downgraded. Significantly, Standard and Poor's referenced the poor prospects for constructive problem solving by our elected officials as partially responsible for their decision:

> The political brinksmanship of recent months highlights what we see as America's governance and policy making becoming less stable, less effective, and less predictable than what we previously believed. . . . The statutory debt ceiling and the threat of default have become political bargaining chips in the debate over fiscal policy. . . . In our view, the differences between political parties have proven to be extraordinarily difficult to bridge. . . . [9]

Until participants adopt a mature argumentative perspective that allows for compromise and values-competing perspectives, the issue will be difficult to resolve.

When the Issue Is Not Worth Arguing About

Pest is one pejorative term we apply to individuals who will argue aggressively and unproductively about virtually anything. Much like the youngster who responds to every statement with "why," the routine gets tiresome and irritating after a while. Adults (who should know better) may offer argumentative challenges that seem trite or unwarranted by the nature of the issue being considered. All ideas deserve exploration, but argument should, when possible, involve matters of consequence. In short, it is probably best not to argue when the issue is trivial while keeping in mind that what is trivial to you may be a matter of great consequence to others.

Decisions have to be made and matters settled, and the notion of **burden of proof** illuminated by Richard Whately can help an advocate appreciate the status of a decision.[10] You are likely familiar with the concept from the many legal programs on television. The notion is that existing ideas, laws, etc., are assumed to be fine (or enjoy **presumption**) absent compelling reasons to believe otherwise. The presumption of innocence is central to our judicial system. Those who would question established wisdom assume the responsibility to present a compelling case for their position. In other words, though perhaps everything is negotiable, we cannot renegotiate everything. Some sense of stability is needed. Imagine enrolling in college and expecting to graduate in 4 years only to find that the graduation requirements change each semester. You would never graduate. By the same token, how would one even make long-range decisions if we could not assume agreement over "settled" matters rather than having to renegotiate at every encounter? Sometimes we do not argue because we respect prior decisions. Other times we simply weigh the risks of argument and determine the issue is not big enough to justify the effort and potential damage discussing it might entail.

When Arguing Could Jeopardize Important Relationships

Arguments can injure relationships. If the person involved in discussion with you is likely to view even innocent questions as aggressive threats, then you might want to modify your approach or simply avoid engaging in argument. This involves some sensitivity on your part as you attempt to understand your audience and determine the most appropriate means of reaching them. We will discuss that in more detail in Chapter 4.

The term *relationship* is used here in an expanded sense. On one hand, you may not want to jeopardize personal friendships through your discourse. On the other hand, we refer to a **communication relationship** and are concerned with whether or not our actions diminish the possibility of future productive argumentative encounters. Ask yourself if your response patterns make it more or less likely that your friend will engage in open, honest communication with you in the future. Will someone risk expressing themselves if they perceive that your default position is to question and criticize unnecessarily?

Real Housewives of New York (and New Jersey and Orange County and Beverly Hills . . .) is a popular television series. Watching the show is a lot like viewing an interpersonal train wreck. Gossip, petty jealousy, and fights are a standard feature of the program. One of the most compelling parts of the drama is the private "heart-to-heart" talk between friends. It goes like this: One of the housewives invites another out for lunch or a drink and a "talk." The premise of the talk is that because the housewife is such a firm believer in open, honest communication and wants a better relationship with her "friend," it is important that they meet in conversation so that the housewife can explain why she thinks her friend is such a hideous human being. It goes downhill from there. The point of this example is that the results are predictable. Could you reasonably expect someone to sit passively as you dig up some real or imagined slight from the past and explain to your friend why it was all her fault? The exchanges are dramatic but unproductive and help to perpetuate the conflict that evidently makes the show so popular.

Sometimes, even when you "win," you lose. The phrase *pyrrhic victory* is derived from the actions of Greek King Pyrrhus, born in the third century BCE. Considered a great general, Pyrrhus defeated the Romans at Heraclea in 280 BCE and Asculum in 279 BCE. His victory, however, came at a great cost—an unacceptable loss of life and resources—which would render his ability to continue his military campaign doubtful. Pyrrhus considered the carnage and is reported to have said, "If we are victorious in one more battle with the Romans, we shall be utterly ruined." The term *pyrrhic victory* is now used to refer to any situation in which victory is gained at too great a cost.[11] Applied to the field of argument, a pyrrhic victory might refer to a situation where the advocate "scores a point" but in the process ruins relationships, loses the trust and goodwill of others, achieves capitulation rather than commitment, or so contaminates the communication environment that chances for reasoned discourse in the future are undermined.

In summary, some arguments are important to have. Often, we need to argue to sort through options and make good decisions. We do not suggest avoiding difficult conversations or standing up for one's beliefs simply out of deference to all relationships. Carefully considering one's approach is important, however, if the goal is to both maintain the relationship and have someone important to us understand and appreciate where we are coming from. But there also are times when the benefits of arguing just might not be worth the potential damage that can come to a relationship.

TABLE 1.2

When Not to Argue

- I am unprepared to participate constructively.
- There is no possibility of resolving the issue.
- The issues are trivial.
- Arguing unnecessarily jeopardizes a relationship.

CONCLUSION

You may be thinking that the approach to argument advanced here is nice in theory but naïve in practice. After all, isn't it a jungle out there? In the "real" world, aren't people out for blood? You might even agree that we have a nice aspirational goal but consider it to be impractical. In response, we encourage you to look around at your own interactions with friends and family, in the classrooms in which you learn, the social clubs in which you gather, and the workplaces in which you negotiate responsibilities. There you see a more cooperative version of argumentation in action every day. The fact that media are focused on conflict and see limited ratings value in reasoned discourse and cooperative problem solving does not mean that the spectacles they present are the norm.

As teachers, we see constructive argument used effectively in classrooms where students question assumptions held by others in a respectful and open-minded manner. It is much more rare—though not unheard of—that class discussions are derailed by students whose argument behavior alienates and intimidates others. The same is true in boardrooms, public meetings, and a host of other forums where important decisions are facilitated by cooperative argument.

There are other encouraging signs. That people are becoming increasingly disenchanted with leaders who would rather posture and score political points than solve problems is evidenced by the fact that public approval of and confidence in Congress is at an all-time low.

In your own experience, consider the conversations you have with others where you explain your feelings and opinions or seek guidance. These enriching exchanges are examples of argument, even though you may have never considered them as such given the negative associations conjured up around the way the term *argument* is frequently portrayed.

QUESTIONS FOR CONSIDERATION

1. Locate a video example of an unproductive argument. Which "rules of engagement" explain why the argument was unproductive? What adjustments could the advocates make to render the argument more constructive?

2. Find a video example of a productive argument. What was it about the advocate's behavior that made the exchange productive?

3. Find an example of an argument in which you think the wiser course of action would have been not to argue at all. Explain why it would have been better not to have had the exchange.

In your opinion, under what conditions (if any) could the argument be made productive?

4. View the movie *Fail Safe* (1964). In what ways does the negotiation between the president (Henry Fonda) and the Soviet premier illustrate or contradict the "rules of engagement" discussed in this chapter?

5. View a video of one of the presidential debates. Does the debate reflect what you would consider quality argument? Why or why not?

6. Social media platforms (Facebook, Instagram, Twitter, etc.) give us a nearly infinite number

of opportunities to engage (or not) in argumentation with "friends" online. Consider the implicit rules that you have developed that help you determine when to argue and when not to argue. Do they align with the reasons provided in the text? Do those implicit guidelines work well for you?

7. Given the situation as you understand it, what were Matt Lauer and Tom Cruise's argumentative alternatives in the situation described? Was it inevitable, or were there other choices available that they could have made to make the interaction more useful for the viewers?

KEY TERMS

Argument as Process 3
Argument as Product 3
Argument 3
Burden of Proof 13
Communication Relationship 13

Competitive Mind-Set 10
Cooperative Mind-Set 10
Devil's Advocate 11
Intentional Competition 9
Presumption 13

Reasons/Grounds 3
Structural Competition 9
Zero Sum 9

Credibility: The Foundation of Responsible Advocacy

In February of 2015, NBC suspended Brian Williams, managing editor and anchor of top-rated *NBC Nightly News*, for 6 months without pay for "embellishing" his experience while covering the Iraq War. On his newscast and in other settings, Williams had dramatically discussed how the helicopter in which he and his crew were flying nearly a decade earlier was hit by a rocket-propelled grenade and forced to land. The problem is that the helicopter he was flying in did *not* take a direct hit—another helicopter in the same group did. Despite Williams's repeated apologies and professed uncertainty as to how he could have been mistaken on such a significant detail, Steve Burke, CEO of NBC Universal, wrote to NBC employees announcing the suspension, indicating "Brian has jeopardized the trust millions of Americans place in NBC News."[1] Williams would tell you that he is a *newscaster*, not an *advocate*. However, NBC knows that credibility is paramount when people are turning to you for information. The network had learned this lesson half a century earlier when anchor Walter Cronkite's credibility helped turn public opinion against U.S. involvement in the Vietnam War.[2]

In this age of the Internet and social media, when virtually anyone can publish an opinion and have it read by people across the world, we can too easily forget that *who* offers an argument matters. All advocates are not equal. The success of an argument is largely dependent on the ethos/credibility of the advocate offering the claim. In interpersonal interaction as well as in more public forums, credibility is crucial. There are people in our lives whose opinions we just take more seriously. We attach more value to their advice. Advocates (and friends and family, for that matter) who demonstrate appropriate knowledge of the subject, goodwill, sound character, and dynamism are far more likely to be taken seriously. In trying to make sense out of this complex process of argument, we begin with credibility, since it is perhaps the most important variable in effective and responsible advocacy.

TYPES OF CREDIBILITY

What Aristotle termed *ethos* is now generally discussed as **credibility** or the related notion of reputation.[3] Both terms refer to the audience's assessment of the advocate as deserving of trust, ultimately rendering the advocate's ideas worthy of serious consideration.

Credibility is not inherent within an advocate but is ascribed to the advocate by those who assess the arguments. Like reputation, credibility can be difficult to build and easy to lose, and is tightly tied to our ability to persuade others.

To every encounter, audience members bring a sense of how much they can trust an advocate to be knowledgeable, have their best interest at heart, and be honest. The esteem that the audience holds for the advocate at the beginning of the encounter is commonly referred to as **initial credibility**. In interpersonal terms, initial credibility is what sends us to particular people for advice—we believe them to be knowledgeable and reliable sources.

Often, reputation precedes advocates, and their audience has formed an opinion of them and their potential arguments before they even speak. Audience members may have heard about them through friends, read something that they have written, or heard reference made to them in other contexts. The information that they have may or may not be accurate or fair, but it still influences the expectations that they bring to your comment. When listeners are impressed with an advocate's reputation, they tend to give that person the "benefit of the doubt" and are more receptive to their ideas.

In the event the audience is unfamiliar with the advocate, they still hold preconceived notions based on the "type" of person that they believe holds a particular opinion or position, or speaks in a particular type of forum. Stanley Milgram called this **background authority**.[4] For example, an audience might expect a speaker to be very good if he or she has been invited to speak at a prestigious event. When audiences attend or tune in later for TED Talks, they tend to expect high-quality, interesting ideas that are presented well. Not all presentations meet that criterion, but the series has gained enough of a reputation that the expectation persists. Generalizing from this limited information helps us to simplify and make sense of our world. For example, we hold conscious and unconscious beliefs that particular "types" of people just *are* a particular way until they show us differently. This cognitive shortcut sometimes serves us well, but can also pose significant difficulty. Used-car salespersons and lawyers both, for example, can face difficulties with initial credibility due to this type of logic. The reputation of those professions makes some suspicious. Are we wrong to be suspicious? It's hard to say. But even if this suspicion is misplaced, it requires the advocate's attention. This initial assessment leads us to give some people the benefit of the doubt based on their position or role. If you recognize this as the logic that underpins stereotyping, you are correct (and hopefully sensitive to its hazards). The term **halo effect** is frequently used to describe a tendency to assume that because one is credible in one area, he or she must also be credible in others. If you have siblings older than you who teachers or other authority figures like, you may have benefited from a halo effect. If you followed siblings who were "troublemakers," you may have been greeted with suspicion or trepidation, also a type of halo effect. Understanding the audience's preconceptions based on the categories to which they might assign you (woman, college student, Latinx, liberal, etc.) will allow you to more effectively craft your message and overcome (or capitalize on) the reception that might initially greet you.

Credibility is dynamic. Audience members adjust their assessment of advocates based on the advocate's performance. The esteem that one holds *after* the interaction is **transaction-based credibility** and a result of the person's initial credibility as it is adjusted during their performance. Sometimes we are pleasantly surprised when a presentation that we have been required to attend (or class we have been required to take) turns out to be especially compelling—and we leave a new fan of the speaker. For example, few Americans had heard of Barack Obama, then a candidate for the U.S. Senate from Illinois, in 2004 when he delivered the keynote address to the Democratic National Convention. He had little initial credibility because few people in the national audience knew him. The credibility that he derived from that speech, however, was monumental as he went on to launch a successful bid for the presidency 4 years later. Advocates have the opportunity to increase their credibility with an audience but also risk damaging it by the choices that they make. Consider the number of times you have been excited to hear someone speak and left disappointed because he or she somehow didn't live up to your expectations. In general, when we understand and meet or exceed the audience's expectations, we tend to gain credibility, and when we misunderstand the disposition of the audience or somehow prove ourselves to be unworthy of the audience's trust, we tend to lose credibility.

FACTORS AFFECTING AN ADVOCATE'S CREDIBILITY

We have established that our initial credibility can be improved or damaged, so we now turn to those specific factors that affect audiences' perceptions of advocates. They fall into three categories: an advocate's perceived level of knowledge, sound character and goodwill toward the audience, and dynamism.

Knowledge

All opinions are not equal. *Informed* opinion trumps uninformed opinion. Knowledge in the subject area under discussion is critical for advocates hoping to persuade an audience that their judgment is sound. An adequate level of knowledge and understanding could easily be considered an ethical imperative for advocates hoping to influence attitudes and behavior. We are certainly inclined to see knowledgeability as an ethical issue. Most actions and beliefs are not based on direct experience but are forged by the information obtained from other sources. Therefore, advocates bear responsibility for the consequences of inaccurate or misleading statements. Of course, audiences should critically assess the information that advocates present, but the onus for accuracy remains on the advocate.

Knowledge-based credibility, as it relates to argument, generally comes from two important sources: experience and research. We will explore each of these in turn and then discuss how advocates can best present that knowledge to increase their credibility with audiences.

Knowledge Based on Experience

Advocates often possess knowledge and expertise based on life experience. Physicians who speak about health care reform based on their years of work with health maintenance organizations bring this type of knowledge. Parents of children with special needs who lobby school districts for increased resources for their children's classrooms also carry a type of experiential knowledge. This type of knowledge is deeply personal, and the resulting first-person accounts often provide very powerful testimony. The value that we place on hearing from someone who has "been there" is substantial. People who are not technical experts in the area being discussed but who have personal experience with the issue are often asked to testify about their experience in congressional hearings and are favorite subjects of feature news stories. Experiential knowledge, then, can be a compelling way of persuading. As advocates, we should draw on our own experience and carefully make our audience aware of it as well. When conveyed without appearing to be bragging, arrogant, or self-absorbed, experience usually enhances an advocate's credibility.

When considering experiential knowledge, it is important to remember that experience in one area does not necessarily qualify an advocate to speak on *all* areas. We sometimes mistakenly assume that an advocate's personal experience qualifies him or her to credibly speak about the entirety of an issue or topic. Although they might have opinions that we need to take into consideration, smart and ethical advocates will respectfully assess those areas of personal experience that lend them (and listeners) special insight, realizing that such experience has boundaries. Actor Michael J. Fox, struck in the prime of his career by Parkinson's disease, provides a useful case study. Fox has used his celebrity to bring significant attention to the ways in which the disease affects the daily lives of those living with Parkinson's. His personal experience (not to mention his likability) serves him extraordinarily well in that effort. However, when advocating for his foundation and discussing the potential avenues for treatment and a cure for the disease, Fox studies, relies on, and refers to the research conducted by leading physicians in the field—not his own experience.[5] He recognizes that his experiential knowledge of Parkinson's is as a patient, not a doctor or a researcher, and bolsters his knowledge accordingly to be a credible advocate.

Experience in an area can certainly increase an advocate's credibility if that experience is viewed by the audience as typical, relevant to the topic at hand, and not oversold.

One risk of drawing *too* heavily on personal experience is that personal experiences differ so dramatically that, though genuine, they are not necessarily typical. One student's experience with a professor or in a class may or may not be what most students usually experience, for example. That's why often we consult with those that we trust before determining what to believe. If our experience is not truly the norm but is represented as such, use of it is disingenuous and unethical. Audiences may easily dismiss it—and perhaps the rest of your claims as well. One of the authors listened to a speech by a student who had a relative that was involved in a head-on collision. He was not wearing a seat belt and as a consequence was thrown from his convertible and sustained only minor injuries. The officer on the scene informed him that had he been wearing a seat belt, he would have been killed. The student speaker argued against mandatory seat belt laws based on her own experience. That experience was so atypical that the audience rejected it. In fact, it appeared to listeners that the student's experience made her incapable of considering the countless studies that contradicted her opinion.

Advocates do not always have direct experience on which to draw. Lack of personal experience with an issue, however, need not be an impediment to effective advocacy. Many advocates are attracted to an issue because it relates to their core values or beliefs. Bono, the lead singer of the band U2 and tireless advocate to eliminate the scourge of AIDS in Africa, is not African, nor does he have HIV or AIDS, yet he still has raised millions of dollars in his quest. When actual experience doesn't provide us with all of the knowledge that we need to generate compelling arguments (and sometimes even when it does), research can prepare us to speak responsibly and credibly on a subject.

Knowledge Based on Research

There are a number of avenues available for someone wishing to acquire expertise on a particular topic. Subject-area books are often widely available at the local public library, bookstore, or electronically. Newspaper coverage of a topic of interest can provide invaluable background information and supply an advocate an excellent sense of the multiple perspectives and players in a controversy. Depending on the controversy, there may have been studies published in academic journals or governmental reports produced, both of which may be available on the Internet or through a university library database. Finally, conversations with people who *do* have experience with the topic are incredibly valuable for personalizing the issue for the advocate and audiences who will later benefit from the information.

The subject of choosing additional support to bolster your credibility and your arguments is treated much more thoroughly in chapters to come. For now, it is enough to know that experience and research are essential ways of coming to understand a topic and of establishing a credible place from which to speak. You *can* achieve a high level of credibility through demonstrating your comprehensive understanding through well-prepared and clearly presented research.

Signaling Your Preparation (Without Being Annoying)

Simply possessing knowledge is insufficient—advocates need to be able to make it clear to their audience that they are knowledgeable. But how does one do that without bragging, reciting your résumé or a list of facts, or boring the audience with the worst imitation of a college lecture? There are a few ways. Consider these strategies to signal your preparation to the audience without appearing condescending or self-absorbed. First, open the presentation with a quick discussion of your interest in the subject, which also indicates the research you have done on the topic. Public speaking professors call this the "credibility step" of an introduction and recommend its use in many contexts. Such a recitation might be strange in an interpersonal exchange, but we often engage in argument with others where we refer to what we have heard, read, or experienced to indicate to them why our ideas should be taken seriously. You may, for example, try to convince friends that the movie they want to see with you is not the best choice given what you have heard from others or the review you saw in the newspaper. Second, weave your research into your presentation to support your points. When you do, cite your sources when appropriate. In other words, tell your audience where you found your information. Also, tell them a little about the source so that they will be reassured that your ideas are based on credible people and research. Finally, when necessary, admit where there are gaps in your knowledge and do not falsely take advantage of your listeners' trust. Pretending to know things that you don't will undermine your audience's confidence in your presentation. Even if you could get away with the deception, remember that responsible advocates respect their audiences and argue in a manner that respects the process—there are simply some things you should not do to "win" an argument. These basic steps will boost your credibility by helping your audience understand that a lack of direct experience with an issue does not indicate a lack of relevant knowledge.

As members of an argument community, we need to establish credibility in ways that encourage rather than discourage engagement. Too many advocates believe that they are the *only* ones who can speak with authority on a particular subject. This level of disregard for the process of argument implies contempt for the audience, resulting in unproductive and pointless communication. We do not want to dissuade others from engaging with us because we have presented our experiential or other knowledge as unassailable. Moreover, advocates who present their knowledge in a manner that intimidates co-arguers risk not only undermining the opportunity to engage in productive dialogue but often end up damaging their reputations.

Finally, while having and demonstrating knowledge of their subject benefits advocates, *failing* to have or demonstrate that knowledge can significantly hurt their credibility. Audiences simply expect that advocates have done their homework and are well informed. It is helpful to remember the dramatic lessons provided by Secretary of State Colin Powell's speech to the United Nations in 2002 to gain support for military action in Iraq.[6] At the time, Powell carried a very high level of credibility with the American people and the world, based in part on his role as a joint chief of staff during the first Gulf War and his clear knowledge of foreign and military affairs. So when he spoke on behalf of the George W. Bush administration and based his plea for an aggressive response to Iraq given the "fact" that Iraq's Saddam Hussein had acquired weapons of mass destruction, his statements carried substantial weight. Later, however, it was revealed that Hussein indeed did *not* have weapons of mass destruction. Powell's credibility was damaged heavily. The fallout came not only because he brought faulty information before the United Nations but because his knowledge, experience, and position would indicate that *he should have known* that the information that he was providing was false. Audiences are fairly generous when speakers are wrong for understandable reasons. Bush was forgiven by many for his "mistake" about the existence of weapons of mass destruction because people believed that *he* believed it and was relying on the (faulty) intelligence provided to him. People expected more out of Powell. His background and position suggested that his intellectual curiosity should have compelled him to dig a little deeper to verify the information instead of just repeating what was provided to him by the intelligence community. Advocates are held responsible for the information that they proffer—be they Colin Powell or anyone else.

TABLE 2.1

Assessing Your Knowledge

- Do I claim knowledge in excess of what I possess?
- Do my knowledge claims prevent others from engaging me out of deference?
- Do I have a sufficient level of knowledge to advocate effectively?
- Is my personal experience sufficient?
- Is my personal experience typical?
- Do I need to supplement my existing knowledge with research?

Sound Character and Goodwill

Quintilian, a teacher of rhetoric in ancient Rome, believed that the ideal orator was not only skilled at speaking but also possessed good character.[7] He believed that being a *good person* was inseparable from being an effective advocate. Being of sound character and goodwill still matters in advocacy. Consider those people in your own life who you respect and trust to give you sound advice. Now consider those whose opinions you trust less fully. What is the difference in these two groups? You probably have noted several distinctions, and we anticipate that those differences come down to your assessment of each person's character.

Although each of us might have different understandings of what it means to have good character, it is important to remember that the particular audience determines what constitutes good character, and who possesses those qualities. Openness, good humor, loyalty, or family might be important aspects of being a "good person" to some audiences. Other audiences will consider academic training and intellectual preparation to be more important. Thus, demonstrating your own alignment with a particular audience's values (to the extent that you *do* align with them) is an important step in building credibility. Establishing credibility is especially important with a skeptical or hostile audience. If you find yourself unsure of what those markers of good character might be, identify those people that the community trusts and looks to for guidance. They might be community members themselves or more public figures and opinion leaders. In either case, coming to understand what they bring to the community and how they do that will go far to helping you discover what a community considers to be a good person.

One trait that most audiences expect from an advocate is **trustworthiness**. Indeed, effective advocates, according to our definition, *are* honest in their advocacy. It is important, then, that advocates not only are trustworthy but that they somehow convey that to the audience. With close friends and associates, you have probably developed (or failed to develop) a reputation for being trustworthy, which in turn determines the degree of skepticism with which your arguments are greeted. You know which people in your life you can most trust, as well as those you can't. When encountering public audiences, we have less to go on. Audiences need to believe that they can trust the validity of the advocate's information and the advocate themselves to represent that information honestly. There are some subtle ways to communicate your trustworthiness to an audience without beseeching them to trust you. As we discussed earlier, providing sufficient background information from reputable sources as well as explaining your own reasoning process (as opposed to simply offering conclusions and demanding that someone accepts them based on a leap of faith) helps to demonstrate your honesty and increase your believability.

Part of the appeal of such populist political speakers as Senator John McCain, former Governor Sarah Palin, and President Donald Trump is the consequence of their carefully cultivated images as truth-tellers. Naming his campaign bus "The Straight Talk Express" during his failed 2008 presidential bid, McCain presented himself as an honest man who told voters the truth no matter the consequences. The campaign's "America First" slogan highlighted McCain's sincerity. His reputation as a maverick in the Senate—one who told truth to power and did the right thing for the people without regard for its political fallout—supported his image as someone that the voters could trust. His running mate, then-governor of Alaska Sarah Palin, brought a reputation for cleaning up Republican politics in her home state and continued to cultivate the image of herself as a "straight talker" through admonitions to what she termed the *gotcha media* to stop corrupting her message with their own liberal agenda. The McCain/Palin campaign ultimately lost to Barack Obama, a candidate with a very different speaking style that we will explore a bit more in the next section, but not necessarily because the voters didn't believe them or find them to be good people. Donald Trump's 2016 presidential campaign provides an interesting parallel. Famous for "speaking his mind," Trump was, in many circles, infamous for not knowing when to stay silent and arguing in ways that cultivated an environment hostile to reasoned discussion. Because he violated important tenets of argument, his style resonated with angry, disenchanted voters who praised his often vituperative rhetoric as "telling it like it is" and expressing what "others are afraid to say." He rode that wave to the presidency.

Audiences do hold some advocates to higher standards than others. People who have made a reputation based on their personal morality and by calling out others who have, in their minds, failed to adhere to the appropriate moral code tend to be held to especially high standards. Religious leaders, some politicians, and "moral" leaders such as teachers might be in this category depending on their role in a particular community. They tend to fall especially hard if it is discovered that they have violated one of the tenets about which they have crusaded because audiences generally do not consider hypocrisy to be consistent with "good character." Consider, for example, the extensive list of ministers and politicians who have preached or campaigned on "family values" and yet have been brought down by sex scandals. Their fall often is especially damaging given the height of the particular pedestal on which they have perched.

Identification as an Instrument of Credibility

We tend to believe those people that seem to be like us in a way that matters. Advertisers, for example, count on this when they use "moms" to sell us peanut butter and cleaning supplies, and when they align the race of their models in print advertisements to match the demographic of a magazine's readers. In short, we most trust and believe those people with whom we identify. *Identification* is a way the advocate demonstrates an understanding of what is important to listeners by indicating they are *very much like* the audience in some fundamental manner.[8] We tend to assume that if advocates are like us in one way that they also share other important characteristics with us—like our values and beliefs. Watch political advertisements in any state with a significant rural population and you will see a politician wearing a brand-new plaid flannel shirt and blue jeans standing next to a tractor, even if they've never set foot on a farm or ranch. They are trying to identify with rural voters. Similarly, it is nearly comical how quickly politicians in Missouri switch the pronunciation of the state depending on their location. They know that citizens in the cities—primarily St. Louis and Kansas City—will look askance if their speakers talk about Miss-ourah, while their rural counterparts will become more skeptical of them if they proclaim to be from Mis-ouree. There is no quicker way to stake an ideological claim in the state than how you pronounce its name. Identification is not limited to politicians, however, and is especially important to bolstering your credibility when an audience is likely to be unreceptive to your ideas.

Similarity to one's audience can often be found in shared personal background, social roles, or general interests. If you want your audience to begin to accept you, point out similarities as a means of creating common ground. Beginning your presentation by emphasizing the overlap in your beliefs, values, and goals is extraordinarily useful with an audience who is not already committed (or is even overtly hostile) to your perspective. Perhaps a representative from the Coalition to Stop Handgun Violence has, at first glance, little in common with an audience filled with National Rifle Association supporters. Still, it is likely that they share an interest in decreasing the death of children due to gun violence. If they can begin their conversation with that shared interest in mind, discussions might be more productive. Representative Gabrielle Giffords, who survived a gunshot to the head fired by one of her constituents at a meet-and-greet in Tucson, Arizona, in 2011, for example, has become an icon in the gun control community, yet she and her husband Mark Kelly rarely miss an opportunity to remind audiences that they are "proud gun owners." In doing so, listeners who might otherwise dismiss them as gun control "fanatics" who don't understand gun culture or the value of firearms have a reason to listen and engage with their arguments.

The key to efforts at identification is that they appear—and are—genuine. When not natural, efforts to generate identification can come across as desperate, artificial, and even insulting. It is also worth noting that in this age of digital recording via ubiquitous camera phones and recording devices, it is easier than it used to be to spot someone who is trying to identify too closely with (perhaps) too many audiences. Mitt Romney, the 2012 Republican nominee for president, learned this the hard way. Romney had worked hard in an effort to gain the trust of working- and middle-class Americans by demonstrating his understanding of their plight. Romney's attempts to relate to average listeners were made more difficult by the visible trappings of his success, such as his wife Ann's appearance at the 2012 Olympics in London to watch her expensive German horse compete in the high-class sport of dressage. He further undermined his effort to identify with the working American when a recording of him speaking with wealthy benefactors at a high-priced fundraiser surfaced. In it, he said that he could not worry about the 47% of voters who did not pay taxes and who were "dependent on the government" and who feel "entitled to health care, to food, to housing, to you-name-it." They would inevitably vote for the incumbent, Barack Obama, he lamented. "I'll never convince them they should take personal responsibility and care for their lives," he said.[9] Hardcore Romney followers likely did not take this personally, but "Main Street Americans," especially those who collected Social Security, and disability, and many others who qualified for the social programs that he had included to come to the astonishing figure of 47% of Americans who were "dependent" on the federal government, had reason to question his understanding and appreciation of their everyday lives and challenges.

There are limits to identification. We *do* like people who are like us, but audiences may also appreciate people who demonstrate dispositions and abilities that they themselves value but may not possess. Therefore, holding public officials, judges, police, teachers, or ministers to a higher standard is common, understandable, and probably a good idea. We want them to understand us but also need them to complement our weaknesses with their strengths. This might mean showing strength or resilience, for example, when we are feeling weak or defeated, or resolve and courage when we are fearful. In these cases, we need them to be *better* than we think we are. These circumstances, while not atypical, illustrate how role or status influences identification. Done well, building common ground still may not overcome all objections, but it will demonstrate that one is coming to the group with goodwill and intentions, and can work to opening the audience to considering the advocate's message even if they are initially resistant.

Considering the Audience's Perspective

In the opening chapter of this book, we stressed the value of empathy, open-mindedness, and perspective-taking as traits of responsible advocacy. Speakers also demonstrate their good character and goodwill toward the audience when they show that they have familiarized themselves with and seriously considered the various perspectives represented by their audience. Like interactions with our friends and family that are best when we have considered what it means to have "walked in their shoes," taking the perspective(s) of the other is not merely an effort to pander to our listeners but a prerequisite to productive engagement. Audience centeredness creates a climate for productive engagement by listeners. Advocates wish to appear well prepared and respectful, attributes that not only contribute to a productive decision-making environment but also demonstrate personal features that audiences are likely to appreciate. We will address how to assess and respond to the audience's beliefs and perspectives in the next chapter. For now, it's enough to note that audiences bring a set of values, beliefs, and knowledge to each interaction and that it will find advocates to be more credible when those are taken into consideration.

Appropriate Self-Interest

Advocates wishing to demonstrate their goodwill make clear how they are working on behalf of the larger good (and perhaps on behalf of the audience) and not just looking out for their own interests. People who can't, or won't, look past their own self-interest are difficult to deal with and we tend not to trust them—which is why many are skeptical of that salesperson working on commission who tells us how fabulous we look in the pricy dress or shoes we have tried on. Advocates who are largely free of vested interests, or are honest about the interests that they do hold, are likely to be more trusted and have their arguments considered more carefully by their audience than those for whom an audience holds suspicion. For example, one of the authors, when faced with a maternity policy that did not work well for her and her colleagues, decided that she would be a more compelling advocate if she waited until after completing her family before taking up the issue with her employer. No matter the approach, it seemed likely that she would be too easily dismissed as a pregnant woman complaining about not having enough time off if she advocated a change in policy that so obviously served her personal needs. In other words, the effort risked seeming too self-serving to be taken seriously, so because she could manage with what was available, she chose to wait and address the issue as one who had experience with the policy but less self-interest in having it changed.

Advocates who suspend self-interest tend to be especially compelling because audiences assume that the speaker's positions are *other*- as opposed to *self*-centered. Advocates who stand to lose something significant by their advocacy, for example, are often taken quite seriously by audiences. Much like the testimony in courts of law of reluctant or hostile witnesses, the audience's concern about the advocate's motivating interest is diminished if the advocacy is not tied exclusively to the advocate's self-interest. This is why whistleblowers tend to be such compelling figures. They often tell their story at considerable risk to their jobs, personal reputations, and sometimes their lives. Unless we sense that they somehow stand to personally gain from public revelation of their insider knowledge, we tend to give their stories considerable credence because we believe that it would be easier, and safer, for them to have remained quiet and not assumed the personal risk that accompanies their revelations.

The power of reluctant advocacy was made apparent when finance guru and billionaire investor Warren Buffett made news in 2011 during the national budget crisis. He famously proclaimed the unfairness inherent in the fact that he paid a smaller percentage of his annual income in taxes than did his secretary. He argued that the wealthy do not pay their fair share of federal taxes and that their tax rate should be increased. President Obama recognized the rhetorical power of the second-richest man in the world's comments and put the "Buffett Rule," to increase taxes on the very wealthy, into his budget reduction plan. Buffett's statements were compelling because they seemed to go against his self-interest—he wanted to pay *more* taxes, not less—so his ideas were taken more seriously.[10]

Finally, consider the use of "jailhouse snitches," who often have something to gain (for example, a reduced sentence, greater privileges, etc.) from testimony they give in court. Attorneys remind jurors that the benefits such witnesses will enjoy from their testimony renders their reliability suspect. While not always fair, advocates who gain something substantial by their advocacy (particularly money) often need to work especially hard to establish a credible place from which to speak.

TABLE 2.2

Assessing Your Character and Goodwill

- Have I made an honest self-appraisal to determine if I am the best advocate for this argument, or would my personal disposition make it difficult to engage in effective argument?
- Might my audience automatically dismiss me before I am able to present the arguments due to their assessment of my character?
- Is my goodwill genuine or simply a contrivance to win over an audience?
- Am I self-righteous to the point that I am contemptuous of others or see their disagreements as indicative of a character flaw or ignorance?
- Have I made a legitimate effort to see things from another's perspective?
- Am I demonstrating the characteristics that my audience would associate with a "good person"?
- Have I avoided knowingly deceiving my audience?

Dynamism

The final element of speaker credibility is **dynamism**. Effective advocates inspire audiences with their presentational styles. Argumentation scholars Chaim Perelman and Lucie Olbrechts-Tyteca viewed style as critical to credibility, noting that "a speaker should inspire confidence. . . . Without it his speech does not merit credence."[11] Sound arguments are critical, but the style in which they are presented can determine their impact on an audience. Speaking style is not everything—but far from irrelevant.

For some advocates, dynamism comes quite naturally. It is an extension of their personality and reflected in their natural speaking style. They draw us in simply by how they project their ideas. Presidents Bill Clinton, Barack Obama, and Ronald Reagan are modern political examples of dynamic speakers, and exemplars also abound in popular culture. We all know otherwise retiring people who seem to "come alive" when talking about their particular passions. Advocates need to share that passion with their audience to be credible representatives of their cause. Former President Jimmy Carter was not known as dynamic but is quite impassioned when speaking about his humanitarian work since leaving the office. Unfortunately, that same passion seemed absent in his presidential speeches, which were often uninspiring. In a nutshell, the audience asks, "Does the advocate believe what they are saying?" and the advocate's manner—in particular their level of dynamism—is taken as a sign of conviction.

Dynamism requires a degree of finesse by the speaker but advocates sometimes go over the top. Politicians seem especially unable to resist these demonstrations of enthusiasm, despite the fact that failures in this effort often become legendary. Howard Dean, who ran for the Democratic nomination for president in 2004, is more renowned for his "Scream Speech" designed to rally supporters after a disappointing third-place finish in the important Iowa Democratic caucus than for almost anything else in his substantial political career. A fiery guy but not always a dynamic speaker, Dean apparently got caught up in the moment when delivering his concession speech to an enthusiastic crowd of supporters and when his voice broke into a croaky scream after declaring that "we're going to take back the White House!"[12] Red-faced and swinging a clenched fist, Dean picked up his volume and pace as he offered a list of states he would soon win, then ended with a resounding "AAAARRRRGGG." The "crazy, red-faced rant,"[13] as Dean himself later referred to it, was replayed endlessly in the news and entertainment media, and an embarrassed but "not apologetic" Dean was publicly ridiculed.[14] A week later, when he came in second to the likewise dynamism-deficient John Kerry in the New Hampshire primary, Dean withdrew from the race.

Vice President-turned-environmental-activist Al Gore provides another useful example of both (1) a naturally reserved speaker who tried to increase his own dynamism level with embarrassing results and also (2) a speaker whose inherent style worked particularly well once he found his natural forum. Criticism that Gore was stiff and unapproachable was not a terrible detriment to his career as President Bill Clinton's vice president throughout the mid-1990s. Clinton had enough charisma to buoy them both. However, as the Democratic nominee for president in 2000, Gore's aloofness was causing difficulty with his campaign and threatening to keep him from winning the White House. The Democratic nominating convention gave him a national stage on which to demonstrate that he was ready for the spotlight, and he emerged for his acceptance speech energized to seize it. He strode from backstage on his way to the podium and stopped to share a long, lusty kiss with his then-wife Tipper, presumably to publicly demonstrate the "passion" that he had been accused of lacking. The moment, however, is remembered less for Gore's passion or enthusiasm than for its awkwardness. He lost the race (though few would blame the kiss) and returned to the private sector. The less dynamic, more lecturing style that hindered him in the political arena, however, eventually served him well in his new role as a leader in the environmental movement. His explanation of the dangers of climate change, and the passion and enthusiasm with which he speaks about it, is engaging and appropriately dynamic. Given the serious nature of the subject, Gore's professorial style was an asset. Touring the country with his Academy Award-winning film *An Inconvenient Truth*, the plywood political approximation was replaced by a vibrant, powerful speaker whose message was taken much more seriously than almost any other environmental activist. The subject matter clearly made a difference in Gore's "transformation," but so did the fact that his presentational style and level of dynamism more closely matched the audience's expectation for the situations in which he spoke.

TABLE 2.3

Questions Based on Your Dynamism

- Do I project a confidence in myself and my position that is appropriate?
- Does my level of dynamism represent my position strongly, or does it go beyond that to exaggerate the worth of my position?
- In my effort to demonstrate my passion about the issues, might my performance and persona be described as artificial or "over the top"? In other words, am I trying too hard?
- Do I use dynamism as a weapon to deny others a fair hearing?

As you can see, the components that affect credibility are complex and interrelated. Audiences want to be sure that advocates have done their homework, considered the issues carefully, and represented the information and themselves truthfully. They need to be able to believe and respect an advocate. Being able to identify with an advocate facilitates all of these things, as does honesty, a healthy dose of humility, and some carefully calibrated dynamism.

THE ADVOCATE/LISTENER RELATIONSHIP

Advocates gain credibility with audiences when they argue in ways that are respectful of the audience. Wayne Brockriede, scholar of argument, provides a useful metaphor for quickly assessing one's relationship with other advocates and considering the consequences of the argumentative posture from the perspective of the audience. He suggests that interactions can be broken down into three types of encounters.[15] Arguers as *abusers* structure situations so that they have more power than their opponents, and use that power to silence those who attempt to engage them.[16] They are contemptuous of their argumentative counterparts and intend to victimize and dominate instead of engage with others. Arguers as *seducers*, in contrast, attempt to get their way through the use of "charm or deceit."[17] Like the abuser, the seducer has little interest in reason-giving as a means of making better decisions, and sees audiences as vulnerable to trickery or charm. Finally, we believe that Brockriede's arguers as *lovers* best represents the ideal stance of public advocates. Arguers who engage as lovers view argumentation not as a means of domination but as a road to good decision making and productive relationships. They do not view listeners as potential victims to be dominated, silenced, and/or tricked but as equal partners in a balanced relationship.

It is not difficult to see how engaging in these three different argumentative stances might influence an advocate's credibility. Abusers, and seducers once they are recognized, tend to violate most audiences' ideas of character and goodwill. They frequently use knowledge as a weapon instead of the basis of good reasons. These tendencies might be temporarily obfuscated by charisma or dynamism, but a thoughtful audience will see through such advocates fairly quickly. Arguing as lovers allows advocates to interact on more equal footing, bringing knowledge to bear in ways that increase understanding and high-quality decision making, arguing from a place of truthfulness and goodwill. Dynamism encourages likability and, properly used, will encourage thoughtful and interesting interaction. Finally, arguing from the position of lovers instead of as abusers or seducers not only benefits the audience but, Brockriede argues, it makes the arguers themselves better people: "Since only lovers risk selves, only lovers can grow, and only lovers can together achieve a genuine interaction."[18]

The responsibility that comes with advocacy is profound, so it is imperative that advocates engage in behaviors that encourage rather than stifle discussion. Considering credibility as we have here suggests that advocates can conduct themselves in ways that encourage the types of discussions and reason-giving behaviors that lead to good decisions. Besides making our efforts more credible and persuasive, cultivating an argumentation style that encourages rather than discourages engagement helps to maintain the types of relationships that will continue to make difficult conversations possible and will help to support high-quality decision making.

CONCLUSION

We suggest that responsible advocates exhibit qualities designed to encourage productive engagement. To that end, the following guidelines will help advocates assess if their arguments will benefit their own credibility and their efforts to support good decision making or if their behaviors instead prove risky to those efforts. Let's consider those behaviors in light of the factors that affect our credibility that were discussed earlier in the chapter.

Responsible advocates only claim as much knowledge as they possess. They do not downplay their level of knowledge and always should be well prepared, but they do not claim more expertise than they legitimately possess. Similarly, they do not promote their own knowledge in such a way as to discourage others from engaging them in conversation. Scaring people away from argument is not an appropriate way to engage in argumentation. As we mentioned previously, however, advocates need a sufficient level of knowledge to effectively make decisions and to facilitate good reason-giving behavior. The question of "how much research is sufficient" often arises. In short, the advocate should do sufficient research to feel prepared for the exchange. Generally, when one has read enough of the public conversation so that he or she is not encountering any new information, the territory has been covered sufficiently. Finally, the question of personal experience comes into play. A responsible speaker will give personal experience its proper place by representing it accurately, understanding if the experience is typical or unique, not relying on it exclusively if the arguments that he or she chooses to make are outside their immediate experience, and supplementing it with outside research to strengthen experience-based claims.

Responsible advocates make an honest appraisal of their own character and disposition toward the audience to determine if they are indeed the best person to represent a point of view. As well intentioned and prepared as one might be, if an audience is unlikely to give an advocate a hearing, the message will be lost. The difficult but most useful decision might be to find a suitable substitute and help him or her to state the positions effectively. Furthermore, audiences can tell the difference between genuine goodwill and contrivance. They appreciate it when you are accurate and genuine. Having attempted to see your arguments from the perspective of another will make you a believable advocate by establishing credibility with those you engage. All of the issues delineated earlier in the chapter will be easier if you understand what attributes your audience takes to be indicative of a person of sound character.

Responsible advocates project an air of confidence in themselves and their positions, and represent their positions strongly. Responsible advocates are as dynamic as they genuinely can be but do not use that dynamism to overshadow the ideas of their less dynamic co-arguers, silence others, or substitute a dynamic style for genuine substance.

Argumentation and advocacy take place within the very real communities of which advocates are a part. Helping those communities make decisions based on the best information available requires that advocates actively cultivate a reputation, manner of engagement, and environment where constructive argument can take place. Understanding the various types of credibility that you do (or don't) have, and how the elements of knowledge, sound character, goodwill, and dynamism influence others' perceptions of you and your message, therefore, is critical. The qualities of a credible and ethical advocate that arise from these elements will help to guide your efforts as well. In the end, the arguments that you offer are *your* arguments, and their effectiveness will depend in large part on the reputation that you cultivate.

QUESTIONS FOR CONSIDERATION

1. Investigate the background and knowledge of the leading spokespersons in the antivaccine movement. Are their positions based on careful research, personal experience, or both? Jenny McCarthy and Jim Carrey are two celebrities actively involved in the antivaccine movement. Does their celebrity status help or hurt their cause?

2. How, if at all, are our notions of credibility altered by the apparent popularity of political candidates who campaign as political "outsiders"?

3. Locate examples of celebrity endorsements of products or ideas. Is their use as spokespersons appropriate or diversionary?

4. Locate examples of public controversy in which calls to "trust the experts" have discouraged public participation in dialogue over public policy.

5. Think of a friend or acquaintance who you view as a "know-it-all." How has this claim to knowledge affected the way you interact with him or her?

6. Consider a time that you changed your opinion for the better about someone. What made you inclined to like or respect him or her more than you did initially? Conversely, when did you start out liking or respecting someone (perhaps a public figure) only to change your opinion of him or her? What factors led to their loss of your esteem?

KEY TERMS

Background Authority 18

Credibility 17

Dynamism 29

Halo Effect 18

Initial Credibility 18

Knowledge-Based Credibility 20

Transaction-Based Credibility 19

Trustworthiness 24

External Factors Influencing Argument

Imagine that you are a parent who is participating in a school board forum where the issue under consideration is adoption of a biology text that gives equal weight to the Bible's book of Genesis and Charles Darwin's *Origin of the Species* as explanations for the origination of life. People are likely to approach the issue from a variety of directions. Teachers may see the controversy as an issue of academic freedom; administrators may be concerned with the impact text selection will have on the school's conformity with state accreditation standards; parents may view this as an issue of local control over public schools or be concerned that their children will be taught concepts that violate their own deeply held convictions; and local religious and civil libertarian organizations will demand a hearing as well. To complicate matters, your ability to make your case is constrained by rules regarding who is to speak, when, and for how long; norms (both formal and informal) dictating decorum; what types of presentations are acceptable; and what types of arguments and support are appropriate. All of this will take place in a room that will be constructed in a particular way, which may facilitate or discourage interaction. And oh yes, this controversy will play out against the backdrop of a national conversation about the teaching of evolution. That's a lot to think about, and perhaps enough to make a thoughtful advocate want to let someone else do the talking.

Such **rhetorical situations**, as some scholars refer to them, are daunting in their complexity, but that doesn't mean important or difficult argument opportunities should be avoided.[1] Productive participation demands that advocates consider how arguments might be structured and supported to merit consideration by those with whom they are in conversation, since the audience's disposition causes them to readily accept particular points of view while dismissing others as irrelevant or diversionary. This chapter will highlight the external factors that should be considered when preparing to engage in argument. Understanding the **external constraints** posed by the audience, the field, and the environment is critical to effective and responsible advocacy.

THE AUDIENCE

Audience matters. Knowing to whom we are speaking is not as obvious as it might first appear. Of course, the audience in attendance is important. People who hear the message firsthand or read or view it later constitute the **actual audience**. They may be in attendance to hear a particular speaker, but they may also be in attendance as a function of circumstance—that is, because there was something else going on that they are interested in at the event at which you are speaking. Although it is important to consider who will be listening, it is equally important to consider who *needs* to hear the message. In other words, who must consider and accept the advocate's arguments in order for the advocate to achieve their goal? That is the **target audience** and may be more limited than the actual audience. There may be several groups of people addressed simultaneously. We will consider the audience in detail in the next chapter but include an abbreviated discussion here to indicate how audiences (as well as speakers) are constrained by situational factors.

Audience members have expectations regarding appropriateness, style, and content when they consider arguments put before them. Understanding and meeting those expectations increase an advocate's persuasiveness. It is impossible to parse every individual audience member's expectations, but fortunately the advocate does not really need to. One can gain a solid understanding of the obstacles and the opportunities likely to emerge by considering the **forum** and occasion, the audience composition, and the larger conversation about the issue at hand.

FIELD AND OCCASION

One way to begin to think about the external constraints on argument is through the concept of **argument "fields."**[2] *Field* refers to the type of argument community (in a philosophical sense) in which an argument takes place. Different fields have different norms dictating the appropriate content and style of argument. The critical notion to keep in mind is that field strongly influences the audience's expectations about argument.

Considering the Field in Which You Argue

Expectations of argument vary widely in fields such as science, religion, art, business, and law. An advocate's chances of being persuasive are increased when their ways of arguing match those expectations. For example, in the legal field, there are rigid procedural rules, criteria for the admissibility or appropriateness of evidence, time-honored concepts like presumption of innocence, burden of proof, and proof beyond reasonable doubt. Alternatively, science embraces the scientific method in its search for answers and explanation. A hypothesis (a proposition offered as explanation for phenomena) is rigorously tested, usually through experimental means, and results are published so the scientific community can further evaluate the adequacy of the hypothesis. In this latter stage, a hypothesis can be confirmed, denied, or appropriately modified. Religion is a belief system concerned primarily with spirituality and human values.

A religious perspective implies a belief system that guides and explains human behavior. Faith is a central tenet of religion, and actions and arguments are evaluated in terms of their consistency with established religious doctrine. Recall the example from Chapter 1 where Tom Cruise's commitment to Scientology influenced his belief about the causes of mental illness. This listing is but a brief sampling of how field (or argument community) dictates standards of judgment.

So how can the advocate know what fields govern argument in a situation? A good place to start is to consider the roles of the advocates involved. Are they speaking from their expertise as clergy? As a field expert? As a politician? Likewise, consider the audience members. What is the core element that has brought them together—their concern as citizens, representation of a religious body, concern as members of a profession? Finally, the best clues as to what field someone is arguing from are the arguments themselves—the basis of the advocates' appeals.[3]

Advocates may not be absolutely proficient in areas outside their area of expertise, but using common sense, asking the right questions, and demonstrating some sensitivity to the preferences and expectations of others makes productive argument more likely.[4] The same type of logic that informs our understanding of the influence of technical argument fields can be applied as one attempts to appreciate the nontechnical constraints governing everyday interaction (i.e., conversational norms, civility, empathy, etc.).

Commitment to or training in a particular set of field-specific concerns can act as perceptual blinders that hinder interaction with other communities. Consider the popular comedy *The Big Bang Theory* where Sheldon's complete immersion in the conventions that govern scientific dispute have made it impossible for him to converse in other fields or to productively engage in nontechnical interpersonal exchanges. It is easy to misunderstand or ignore arguments made by those outside of our argument communities when we do not share the assumptions or understand the conventions. Advocates and their listeners share the responsibility for adapting to field-specific concerns.

The same logic that helps us understand the influence of fields may be applied more broadly as a means of understanding the conflicting personal agendas that make argument difficult. We are conditioned to argue in predictable ways or to privilege certain approaches based on our familiarity with particular argument communities. One of the authors was involved with the planning of an annual downtown music festival. The process turned out to be frustrating. Our planning meetings were characterized by posturing and conflict that was unproductive to the point of alienating some of the committee members. Once the festival concluded and the dust had settled, awareness dawned (too late) as to why so many of the meetings were problematic. There were conflicting agendas. Bands were secured by a musician who was concerned that performers be respected and well paid, placing him at odds with club owners who wanted cheap entertainment and, as a consequence, higher profits. Stage technicians did battle with event sponsors, whose primary concern was prominent placement of their product banners on stage. Event planners envisioning a giant party atmosphere encountered resistance from law enforcement officials concerned with crowd control and local merchants who thought blocking streets would drive away "regular" customers or worried that inclusion of heavy metal or punk would attract the "wrong element." A local music store that generously provided technical support for the festival saw the value of focusing on local and regional entertainment (mindful of future equipment sales), while some event planners insisted on national acts as a means of enhancing the reputation of the festival. The artist who designed the poster for the event could not understand why his beautiful work should be cluttered with mundane information like event descriptions, a schedule, or directions, much to the dismay of the promotions committee. What disrupted the planning was a near universal failure to understand competing perspectives among the dedicated and talented individuals involved. A little common sense and sensitivity would have dramatically improved the climate. Would there have been conflict? Certainly. But the chances for cooperation, compromise and, yes, occasional concessions would have been far more likely had participants taken the time to understand the perspectives of others. There is a world of difference between leaving a planning session frustrated at the "unreasonable" positions of others and leaving the meeting knowing that those who disagreed with you had predictable reasons for doing so. To address this, consider seeking out common ground through a thoughtful consideration of the viewpoints of others, acknowledging how their viewpoints also have been shaped by past experience and affiliations.

Considering the Occasion

Understanding *why* the audience is in attendance helps advocates make better decisions about the tone and content of their arguments. When people gather to hear a speaker, the **occasion** generally implies a specific purpose to (1) celebrate, (2) render a judgment, or (3) formulate a plan of action.[5]

There is a long tradition of using public address as a means of commemoration as people gather to celebrate or memorialize a person, place, thing, or event. Aristotle referred to these occasions for **epideictic speaking**, and graduations, weddings, and funerals are common epideictic situations. Audience members have particularly rigid expectations of appropriate and inappropriate communication in ceremonial occasions. If asked to deliver a funeral eulogy, for example, a speaker might already know the types of comments that are expected based on attendance at other funerals: a message that highlights the character of the deceased; acknowledges the sorrow all in attendance feel for the loss; and looks toward the future, urging others to carry on and perhaps highlights the value of the contribution or character of the deceased that may guide our future actions. These basic themes have been rigidly adhered to since the time of the ancient Greeks.[6] Often, advocates can use their experiences with various epideictic occasions to determine what types of comments are appropriate under the particular circumstance.

Deviation from audience expectations in epideictic situations is risky. Consider, for example, the differences in the responses made by President Barack Obama and 2008 vice presidential candidate Sarah Palin after the shooting in Tucson at a 2011 political gathering where Representative Gabrielle Giffords was seriously wounded and six people were killed. Deemphasizing traditional eulogistic requirements, Palin used the occasion to diffuse charges that her own recent political statements had fed the uncivil climate that critics charged had contributed to the tragedy.[7] Clearly, Palin needed to address the accusations, but that she chose to do so at a time that called for mourning the deceased made her attempt at image restoration seem callous. Obama's tribute followed traditional eulogistic requirements and was widely praised as a moving and appropriate response.[8] Although the two very different public figures hold distinct roles in American society, the expectations that audiences held for their comments were largely the same. Who they were mattered little because they were responding to a situation where the appropriate response is steadfastly prescribed.[9]

The second type of situation advocates encounter are those in which the audience needs to make a judgment on a past (or current) action. These are occasions for **forensic speaking**, and since the term *forensic* generally means "pertaining to legal trials,"[10] it is understandable that the most easily recognized forum in which such advocacy takes place is in a court of law. But courts are not the only place where judgments are rendered—people routinely argue about what happened (or did not happen). We might argue whether the latest blockbuster movie is good or not, if the university was wise to close due to inclement weather on a day when final exams were scheduled, or if our favorite team should have done more to keep its star around longer. Grievance committees consider whether an employee was wronged, supervisors evaluate employee performance, and political candidates ask us to judge their record.

Occasions for **deliberative speaking** invite listeners to render a decision that a particular course of action should (or should not) be taken. If you want to "get something done," you will likely need to convince a deliberative body to act. Congress is a deliberative body—it argues about and ultimately makes policy. City councils hear and make decisions about local policy, and school boards make policies to govern everything from bus schedules to curriculum and textbook choice. Additionally, deliberative bodies are often acting on behalf of larger communities to which they answer. Providing them with reasons that are persuasive to both the decision makers and their constituencies is important.

Labeling an argument as deliberative in nature does not always suggest the degree of formality the previous examples imply. Much of the discourse that marks interpersonal interaction is actually deliberative in nature: Should we see a movie tonight (which one)? Should we order wine with dinner (red or white)? Should we move to a larger apartment? Should we tell our parents about our relationship? All of these questions set the stage for argument because they ask us to make a decision.

Considering Relationships

Content and style of argument are influenced by the relationship between the participants. A meeting with friends may call for a more informal style of interaction. Groups that are recreational or social in nature sometimes shy away from weighty or controversial issues. On those occasions where we find ourselves working on task-based projects with friends and close associates with whom we usually socialize, there can be uncertainty about how we should communicate. Under such circumstances, it is a good idea to set some ground rules that let group members know how to interact, lest our friendly chatting interfere with getting necessary work done or where a rigid task orientation strains friendships because interpersonal needs are not appropriately considered.

If you are invited to participate in an argument, it is appropriate to consider why *you*, in particular, were extended an invitation. Does the group want to take advantage of your experience and expertise on a particular issue, or does it have significant disagreement with a position with which you are associated? In the former circumstance, your chief objective might simply be to share information, while the latter circumstance is likely to require you to more fully justify or defend a position.

The advocate's relationship with the audience and subject dictates whether they should assume an equal, superior, or subordinate role. In a job interview or employment evaluation, the interviewee's behavior will be marked by a degree of deference. In other circumstances where advocates possess acknowledged credibility on the subject under consideration, their deference is likely to be viewed with disappointment. When dealing with friends or romantic partners, the need to preserve the relationship obviously informs our argumentative stance and probably limits posturing for dominance. Whatever the circumstance, one's relationship with the audience dictates appropriate communication options. Many of us have left meetings with negative impressions of participants that result from their inability to discern their relationship to others involved in the discussion. Consequently, some come off as aloof, overbearing, and aggressive, while others seem withdrawn, uninterested individuals who have little of value to contribute. In any case, the potential for productive future interaction is diminished by behavior that seems inappropriate. Past interactions with a particular audience will provide insights into relationships and expectations. If advocates lack a shared history with listeners, attentiveness to their reactions is absolutely critical during our interactions with them.

THE LARGER CONVERSATION

Ongoing controversies have argument terrain that is already established and quite clear. Entering such a conversation without having a clear understanding of the issue as it has unfolded is akin to entering a private conversation partway through. Advocates need to do their homework before wading into such unfamiliar waters. Without the benefit of a recap, we risk offering arguments that are redundant or irrelevant. Additionally, listeners will likely resent having to bring an advocate up to speed on issues with which they should already be familiar. Assessing the arguments on all sides and taking them into consideration when formulating a plan of advocacy is essential not only to making the strongest case possible for a particular audience but also to establishing credibility as an advocate.

Credibility as an advocate requires familiarity and engagement with the larger conversation. On occasion, being the first to identify an issue and bring it to the attention of others will mean that there is not an ongoing conversation on this issue. However, even if that seems to be the case, it remains a good idea to look around, especially if you are new to the community (or new to paying attention to its business). Check with locals who you trust to be knowledgeable to see what they've heard about the issue, and do some digging (research!) into the history of the issue by looking at local news reports and minutes of relevant meetings or engaging in conversation.

Skilled advocates are sensitive to external events that might affect their audience and seek to respond appropriately. Understanding central concerns keeps the advocate on track. For example, a routine school board meeting about the high school curriculum will take on an added urgency if, prior to the meeting, it is discovered that student achievement tests indicate underperformance or if the group becomes aware that projected state budget shortfalls will necessitate deep cuts to public education. You would appear foolish if you were to say, "I know we are facing a financial emergency, but before we get to that, would you all mind giving me your views on these color samples so we can repaint the teachers' lounge?"

Similar issues in neighboring communities are also worth considering. It is likely that the audience has heard about that as well. Applying the same questions listed previously to prepare to address why the issues raised *there* are (or are not) relevant *here* can be instructive. Disregarding the history of analogous situations will make you appear ill informed at best and arrogant at worst, as if other points of view are not worthy of your attention.

Finding the larger conversation that informs a local issue will often provide advocates with additional resources on which to draw, and elevates the importance of their arguments by linking them to national concerns. Pay special attention to issues and themes that keep arising. When you find them, you've probably found the heart of the conversation. Although national news outlets might not be reporting on the specific community with which you are concerned, they are likely reporting on the issue in some manner. Communities having conversations about local watersheds or preserving natural habitats, for example, will find conversations about those same issues in the national discussion about environmental protection. Furthermore, people interested in the local controversy will be making decisions informed by the broader conversation as well, so it will be useful to understand their assumptions, positions, and decisions. Reviewing regional and national news outlets, browsing books on the subject at local bookstores, or searching the Internet quickly provides the information that advocates need.

When advocates demonstrate an appreciation for what has been said previously on both sides of an issue, they enhance their credibility by demonstrating their serious preparation to listeners. Credible advocates are better positioned to have their arguments receive serious consideration.

TABLE 3.1

Argument and Historical Context

• Do I know enough about the history of this controversy/issue? Is there research to be done?
• What are the arguments that have been offered? Where did they succeed or fail?
• How do the new arguments that I want to offer fit into the conversation?
• Do those on the other side of the issue bring up questions or concerns that I have not considered? How does that change my thinking? How might I best answer these concerns?
• What does tracking the conversation tell me about where (what forum and to what target audience) my arguments are best directed?
• Is there a larger (regional or national) conversation surrounding the issue about which I should be concerned?

Atmosphere/Mood/Climate

Many of us have had the experience of walking into an unfamiliar restaurant and being struck with the realization that we might be inappropriately dressed. We may decide that the place is not what we had in mind and look for a different eatery. After dinner, we may head out to a club to listen to some music and after looking around, make some judgments about what is in store. A Goth motif or chicken wire protecting the stage would alert us that the venue was not one for "easy-listening" music. Alternatively, candles and champagne on the tables occupied by people in formal attire would quickly suggest that heavy metal is probably not in the offing.

Argument environments also contain important physical cues indicating the kind of interaction likely to take place there. There is plenty of information available to the alert speaker. How are people dressed? Is the mood of the audience prior to the speech relaxed or tense? Has the way the event was promoted created expectations from the audience that the skilled advocate should satisfy? Did that high-tech support system for your PowerPoint presentation arrive, and does it work? Who else is on the program? Does the room appear elegant or informal? Consider these factors and others that stand out to you as indicative of what might be expected, and adjust your presentation to take advantage of the environment.

Physical Setting

We have sat through many large lectures in opulent surroundings with the speaker at a podium front and center who proclaims, "I am a pretty informal person and invite you to ask me questions at any time during my speech." There are mixed messages here. In reality, the layout does not lend itself to relaxed conversation. These speakers have failed to adapt and will frequently interrupt their speech to "chat" with a fortunate few in the front rows as they ask questions or make comments that nobody else in the room can hear. For the majority of listeners, this proves frustrating.

Degree of formality is often indicated by the layout of the room, providing cues as to expected style and behavior to both speakers and audience members. Like the speaker, audience members pick up on physical cues and usually behave according to their assessment of the environment. A podium or stage facing an audience arranged in orderly rows suggests that the speaker will be doing most of the heavy lifting and that the presentation likely will resemble a lecture. Microphones (with attendants) at the front of the room or in the aisles for audience questions signal that the organizers expect the questioning process to be orderly. Alternatively, the room may not facilitate audience interaction at all and consequently call for a higher degree of speaker formality.

If a speech takes place in a room where all chairs are arranged in a circle and there is nothing to convey an elevated status to the speaker (i.e., podium, bigger chair, nameplate, etc.), a more free-flowing discussion is probably expected. A more relaxed or plain style is generally in order in such a room. Likewise, having the audience seated at round tables suggests that interaction with each other (and the speaker) is the expectation, inviting a more participative atmosphere. Multiple unattended microphones scattered around the room might indicate more of a "town hall" atmosphere, where the audience is expected to be vigorously participating. Highly formal and scripted presentations tend to suffer if not altered for these types of interactions.

Speakers should adapt to their environment but need not be completely passive. They can have a lot to say about the room setup and event promotion as they strive to create a situation that is an appropriate fit to the style and content of their remarks. Asking a few questions prior to the event and visiting the venue in advance helps speakers to avoid most unpleasant surprises. Too many speakers fail to maximize their chances of success by neglecting to do simple things like move the podium and visual aids to a visible spot, get the audience to move so that they can easily see them, or adjust their volume and presentational aids to fit the size of the room. In short, speakers should work to control the environment rather than being undermined by it.

The care with which one can manage their performance environment is evident in the work of actor/singer/songwriter Ronny Cox. Cox was one of the lead actors in the film *Deliverance* (the guitarist in the "Dueling Banjos" scene), and his frequent appearances as a character actor (*Star Trek: The Next Generation, Beverly Hills Cop II, Robocop, Dexter*, etc.) have made him one of Hollywood's most recognizable faces. Singing is his second career path. A promoter for one of his concerts in a small community made the most of his high profile in posters used for the event. Additionally, the promoter knew this appearance was a rare treat, so he secured an elaborate light rig, agonized over the music to be played through the house public address system before the show and during breaks to "create a proper mood," came up with a room arrangement that would "enhance the credibility of the event" (tables with candles and tablecloths), and labored over how to introduce the guest. The promoter was a bit frustrated when Cox suggested that the house lights remain on and there be no stage lighting because he wanted to "minimize the distance between himself and the audience." Cox discouraged the use of music before the show or during the break, arguing that it would send the message that music was simply "background noise that the audience could talk over" and as a consequence would provide a rehearsal for behavior that he wanted to discourage during the show when the audience's full attention should be on the performer. Cox requested a very early sound check so he would be free to visit with everyone as they came in the door to see the show because establishing an intimate relationship suited the reflective and personally revelatory nature of his music and encouraged more involvement from his audience. The idea of a grand introduction was dismissed as impersonal since Cox preferred to introduce himself. These were not typical requests to a promoter who was used to performers storming the stage after a glowing introduction and playing to a darkened room under stage lights that not only "look cool" but would illuminate all the fancy equipment that had been borrowed for the event. Despite his disappointment that the plan was not to be followed, the promoter honored the requests and noted afterward that though the staging was a bit unorthodox, it created a perfect listening environment for Cox's heartfelt songs. This arrangement would not have worked for most other artists but turned out to be highly appropriate under the circumstances. The lesson to be learned is do not hesitate to make your environment work for you.

CONCLUSION

Effective advocates realize that constructing arguments is a complex undertaking that is more likely to succeed when they are mindful of the audience and adapt their statements to the context in which the argument takes place. Understanding the field(s) of argument and occasion will help advocates to prepare for their presentations. While we have discussed each of those elements in turn, it is useful to remember that there tends to be a degree of overlap between field and forum since specific locations are predictive of the types of arguments to be made. For example, legal arguments are common in courts of law and scientific or academic arguments are often found in universities, professional conventions, academic or scientific literature, etc. This overlap is not total, however, since an exchange with a friend, in a small group or a community gathering, may involve field-specific norms that are tempered by the unique personal nature of the forum. You might have a deliberative exchange with a friend as you decide where to eat dinner, but the formal norms that would mark parliamentary deliberation would certainly be out of place.

As we noted at the beginning of this chapter, the "best" arguments in any given situation are those that consider the rhetorical situation in its full complexity. Good arguments are well supported and logical, but such attributes are a product of consideration of the audience, the field in which they are being argued, and the historical and physical environment. Attention to these factors helps ensure that sound arguments are transformed into persuasive arguments.

QUESTIONS FOR CONSIDERATION

1. View *Inherit the Wind* (1960), a movie about the Scopes monkey trial. In what ways do the arguments made by Clarence Darrow and William Jennings Bryan represent their misunderstanding of or willingness to ignore the constraints of the field (legal)? Was this a wise decision on their part? From which fields do Darrow and Bryan argue?

2. View the film *Twelve Angry Men* (1957). How do the experiences/perspectives of the jurors influence their positions?

3. What norms govern argument in a classroom? Do these norms facilitate or undermine productive argument? How are these norms similar to/different from norms governing argument in the workplace?

4. Identify a recent or current controversy on your campus or in your local community. What field(s) are represented by the advocates involved? How does that influence the types of claims they are making and how the interaction/argument plays out?

5. Is it possible to violate the dictates of the occasion and still be received favorably? When might that happen?

6. Listen to or read Robert F. Kennedy's Remarks on the Assassination of Martin Luther King, Jr. Consider: What is/are Kennedy's purpose(s)? What type of occasion does this speech address? Does Kennedy make an argument? Does his message constitute a fitting response to the situation?

KEY TERMS

Audience-Based Argument

In an ill-advised decision to speak, Democratic National Committee Chairman Debbie Wasserman Schultz chose to address her home-state delegation immediately prior to the start of the 2016 Democratic Nominating Convention. Her decision to resign her position immediately after the convention over which she was to preside had just been made public. "The controversy erupted when a series of leaked emails confirmed that party officials had conspired to sabotage the campaign of Senator Bernie Sanders of Vermont."[1] The revelations aggravated the already aggrieved Sanders delegates who had long suspected that the Democratic establishment had supported Hillary Clinton despite the expectation that it would not play favorites during primary contests.

Perhaps it was an attempt by Schultz to test the waters with a friendly audience while considering her convention role that led her to address a breakfast meeting of fellow Floridians. Schultz seemed unprepared for the angry Sanders delegates in the crowd who were so vocal in their protest that it was difficult to hear her speech. Schultz finished her presentation and made a hasty exit with the help of a security detail. She would later decide to resign immediately (no doubt with some gentle prodding) rather than endure the disruption that her presence at the convention was sure to cause.[2]

Schultz had just gotten a lesson in audience analysis. Letting her ego get in the way of sound judgment, Schultz was unwilling to step aside in the face of criticism, and she seriously underestimated the outrage of Sanders' delegates. Lesson learned, Schultz reasoned that the honor of chairing the national convention would be overshadowed by the media spectacle of an angrily divided convention, which would provide a clear counterpoint to the Democrats' proclamations of party unity.

Audience analysis skills are essential to effective persuasion. Effective advocates modify their messages based on what they discover about their ability to identify with the audience, their credibility, and their chances at successful persuasion. This is a lesson that many politicians have learned the hard way.[3]

An advocate's ability to understand and adapt to the disposition of his or her audience is critical. Identifying areas of common ground helps advocates adjust the content of their arguments to the needs of listeners. We do not suggest pandering but do recommend that you find ways to adapt to listeners in order to increase the chance that your arguments receive a fair hearing.

INTERACTING WITH FAMILIAR AUDIENCES

Most of the arguing we do involves interaction with **familiar audiences**, including friends, family, coworkers, and the like. In such cases, we have the advantage of knowing something about their interests, attitudes, and response patterns. We know which coworker is more likely to be receptive to our request to cover a shift for us, we know which parent is most likely to overlook a curfew violation, and we know which of our teachers is likely to be more receptive to our request for an extension on an assignment. The behavior of familiar audiences is somewhat predictable because we enjoy a degree of knowledge as a result of our long-standing relationship or frequency of interaction with them. This knowledge provides several important advantages.

Your Credibility Is Known

If you are arguing with someone with whom you have an established relationship, chances are you will have a fairly accurate notion of the credibility you bring to the discussion. As you may recall from Chapter 2, credibility refers to the image of the speaker held by the listener, and when you know your audience well, you will have a pretty good idea of where you stand with them. If you have a good relationship, your credibility is probably high. You likely wouldn't maintain a relationship for long with someone who did not trust you, saw you as selfish or self-serving, or viewed you as intellectually inferior. In situations of positive familiarity, speakers are often afforded the benefit of doubt.

Relationships run the gamut from close and intimate to the minimal association in relationships of necessity or circumstance (you serve on the same civic commission, you are coworkers, you are neighbors, etc.). In each of these situations, you know when you are likely to be persuasive or likely to be ignored. Most of the time, there is a need to preserve the relationship by arguing in a way that provides a basis for future productive interaction. In instances where you lack credibility, it's probably a good idea to do some image restoration to make future communication more positive and productive. When your credibility is low, it is advisable to use respected outside sources to support your claims. In this way, you are saying, "Don't take my word for it . . . look at what other knowledgeable sources have to say on the issue."

Knowing When to Defer

Closely akin to the concept of credibility is the idea of **deference**—recognizing when it is wise to say, "Okay, you know more about this than I do, let's go with your idea."[4] Unless you are a masochist, being in a relationship that demands continual deference will probably be unfulfilling and short lived. However, there are a number of occasions where deference might be expected (for example, employee and boss, parent and young child, or student and teacher). If you have ever watched movies or television shows focused on life in the White House, you have seen deference in action. Good presidential leadership involves listening to diverse voices, so it's not out of the question that cabinet members will voice their reservations about issues, but at the end of it all, they respond, "Yes, Mister President," and the discussion ends. If they are confident their objections have been heard, White House staff gets on board, even if the decision made is not the choice they would have made—simply having a voice in the decision-making process is valued. On the other hand, absolute deference should not be the default position since such a stance denies the president necessary counsel. Consider the frequent criticisms of presidential judgment where decisions are made in the comfortable "bubble" of affirming subordinates.

There are a number of situations where, after discussing an issue, we defer to another's point of view because we think that they are in a better position than us to make a decision. One of the authors continually defers to his wife on matters of managing the bank account (or anything mathematical) but is less likely to defer when it comes to making a decision about what colors will look best when the bathroom is repainted. This is not an admission of defeat but the product of knowing and respecting another's credibility on a given subject.

Ability to Rely on Shared Experiences

If you have played a board game where your success depends on getting your playing partners to correctly guess an answer based on the clues you provide, you have undoubtedly noted that teams consisting of longtime friends, spouses, those belonging to the same occupational group, people the same age, or those who shared the same environment have a considerable advantage. That is because clues offered are often based on shared experiences. Teams consisting of relative strangers are less successful with their generic clues. The advocate is in a similar position when communicating with a familiar audience. Because of their shared history, the advocate is able to support arguments using examples to which the audience can relate—in fact, the listener has often shared the experience. In cases where the listener, because of his or her own history with a subject, is likely to be repelled by an idea or example, the advocate is often aware of the situation and can avoid inappropriate statements. In short, an intimate knowledge of your listeners' experiences allows the thoughtful advocate the opportunity to select topics and construct arguments that will be relevant to the listener.

Predictability of Listener Response

Having a clear understanding of your audience adds predictability to the exchange. For example, the advocate can generally make a pretty good guess as to how the listener will respond to an idea. In those instances where a negative response seems likely, one can either avoid the subject or, better yet, adopt a presentational style and adjust argument content to achieve a more favorable hearing. We consider how we can present arguments without seeming condescending, rude, insensitive, or arrogant. Content, especially outside support, can be adjusted given the advocate's knowledge of the kinds of proof that the listener will find compelling.

Greater knowledge of the listener allows the advocate to plan ahead. For example, you may think to yourself, "If I say this, she will say that," and you can have a response ready to go or can argue in a way that addresses potential objections. Use caution here and remember this is not a contest. Having a prepared response for every objection is not necessarily a bad thing as long as it doesn't prevent you from listening and responding thoughtfully and genuinely. Overly prepared responses can also seem overly aggressive, sometimes eliciting responses such as "you are being pretty contrary" or "you have an answer for everything, don't you?" That type of interaction rarely moves the argument forward in a productive way.

Reduced Areas of Ambiguity in Language

Shared experiences with familiar audiences means we are able to avoid some of the pitfalls of ambiguous language. We will discuss language and style in detail in a later chapter. For our purposes here, it is sufficient to note that words mean different things to different people, both on denotative (the object to which a word refers) and connotative (the emotional content of particular words) levels. The Fourth of July, for example, denotes the Independence Day holiday celebrated in the United States that commemorates the signing of the Declaration of Independence and generally connotes patriotism, fireworks, and barbecues. But connotations are personal and situated, as Frederick Douglass's famous oration "The Meaning of the Fourth of July to the Negro" reminds us.[5] Emergency services workers often have connotations of trauma-filled shifts spent responding to injuries associated with inebriated and reckless behavior. For pet owners, the holiday connotes long evenings managing frightened animals as neighborhood pyrotechnics erupt seemingly at random. Familiarity with a person means we often know exactly what they mean when they use a particular term. Our understanding is more complete and nuanced given our shared history. In a moment of clarity, a man once noted that when his wife says, "The trash is getting pretty full," that statement is not just a call for agreement on a factual level. Action is required since to her the statement means, "Take out the garbage."

In essence, we have a greater chance of productive argument with familiar audiences because we can more readily determine the intended meaning of their statements. We are able to express ourselves more clearly given our shared understanding.

Greater Awareness of Potential Communication Hazards: Knowing When Not to Argue

Chapter 1 describes a number of situations in which it might be best not to argue. When addressing familiar audiences, the advocate is in a good position to spot these potential hazards. Consider the number of times you have reconsidered arguing because your listener was not in the mood to give you a sympathetic hearing. On other occasions, you don't argue because you understand that your listener "has things under control," so arguing would only shake his or her confidence or raise debilitating self-doubts. You are also aware of hot-button issues where you decline engagement. Talking politics with your in-laws may not be a good idea, for example, if you are aware of significant differences between you. On those and many other occasions, we avoid topics because chances of reaching agreement are remote or we know that it is not worth placing a relationship at risk. Finally, we are alert to trivial issues that are probably not worth arguing about. Knowledge of the other helps us determine those nonissues.

The advocate clearly enjoys a number of advantages when the audience is familiar. We believe that in long-standing, mutually satisfying relationships, preserving a constructive communication climate (and consequently the relationship) becomes a dominant concern that influences what we argue about and the manner in which we argue.

The potential for productive interaction with familiar audiences is extensive given our shared experiences and mutual understanding. Particularly with respect to the positive argumentative stances outlined in the opening chapter, it is easier to engage in perspective taking, arguing without malice in a manner that maintains our relationship, while cultivating a climate that makes further exchanges more likely. In short, we can avoid those behaviors that push the others' buttons.

TABLE 4.1

Advantages Enjoyed With Familiar Audiences

- Our credibility is firmly established.
- We know when deference is wise.
- We can rely on shared experiences.
- Audience response is predictable.
- Ambiguity in language is reduced.
- We have a greater awareness of when not to argue:
  - Aware when your contribution would be minimal
  - Aware when chances of resolution are remote
  - Aware when another's mood would prevent positive interaction
  - Aware of the primacy of preserving a positive communication relationship

Unfortunately, these advantages fade when we are meeting someone for the first time or are arguing in more formal public forums where our knowledge of our listeners is (at least initially) limited.

UNDERSTANDING UNFAMILIAR AUDIENCES

On occasion, advocates encounter **unfamiliar audiences**. When confronted with listeners with whom the advocate does not have a personal relationship, or in more public forums where the audience is likely to be both unfamiliar and diverse, some homework is necessary. The strategies used by corporations marketing a product can inform the speaker wishing to market ideas. Corporations use a demographic analysis in which they isolate characteristics of an audience that might be predictive of the audience's needs and purchasing preferences. For this reason, MTV viewers will see advertisements for products that will likely appeal to a young audience, ESPN will carry ads stressing sports and fitness (and beer) that will appeal to the network's likely viewers, and episodes of *Masterpiece Theater* will be sponsored by companies targeting audiences that are inclined toward cultural events. In each instance, generalizations will be made about the listening audience that guide advertisers' notions about what products are likely to be appealing to the listeners. Additionally, the style and content of each advertisement is influenced by audience analysis. Humorous or irreverent advertisements that resonate with certain viewers could be seen as tasteless or offensive to others. MTV ads seem a bit more edgy and humorous than sponsorship announcements on *Masterpiece Theater*. Undoubtedly, the generalizations made through a consideration of demographic factors are laden with exceptions, but they provide a starting point for product promotional strategies. Marketing strategies are further refined by ongoing consideration of indicators of audience receptivity (e.g., product purchases or angry boycotts).

The **demographic composition** of the audience supplies the advocate with good clues as to what listeners might find compelling. Although understanding the demographic composition of our target audience cannot tell us definitively what someone has been through, or exactly what their value structure is, understanding audience composition can help us to make argument choices that likely are more relevant and compelling to that audience. Since audiences consider arguments in light of their own knowledge, values, and experience, it is useful to consider age, knowledge, status, geographic factors, gender, cultural factors, and group affiliations as you construct an audience profile.

Age

Age is one possible indicator of audience disposition. The common cliché that "with age comes experience" has merit. The notion that "wisdom comes with age" is more suspect. New experiences and information can broaden our horizons if we can embrace them as a means of intellectual and social development. On the other hand, experience can bring on a degree of intellectual stagnation if we seek information that confirms our existing opinions or prejudices and as a result become inflexible and set in our ways. Research suggests that younger audiences tend to be a bit more open to new ideas, while older audiences are cautious and resistant to change.[6] The advocate is advised to be mindful of the fact that some audiences are more resistant to persuasion than others and as a consequence have a high need for information (support) to offset entrenched ideas.

Selecting support for your arguments is often driven by consideration of the age and experience of the audience. As we discuss the use of outside support (statistics, testimony, and examples in later chapters), we stress that outside support should be relevant to your listeners. This is particularly true with examples that can be more or less effective depending on audience age. We were both in the airport waiting for a flight to a professional conference when Timothy McVeigh bombed the Murrah Federal Building in Oklahoma City in 1994. We watched the events unfold on televisions in the passenger waiting room carrying a continuous news feed of the tragedy. The incident had a lasting impact on us and as a result became a go-to example for class discussions of terrorism. Despite our own vivid recollection, we found that over the years the event becomes less recognizable to our students—most of whom were not born when the event took place. If we continue to use the example, we are able to do so only when we first provide a great deal of background information. More current examples of terrorist activities, because students have direct knowledge of them, work far better as an instructional tool. In this text, we use current examples but rely heavily on older (we call them classic) examples. When using the latter, we consistently have to provide substantial background information and often references that allow the reader to explore them further.

Consider, for example, a discussion of the nation's sluggish economy to note how age may influence receptivity or interest in particular arguments. Older listeners will be more energized by arguments that address the impact of the economic downturn on their retirement savings, while younger audiences will probably become more engaged when the discussion emphasizes the bleak prospects of gainful employment after graduation. While such arguments are a good way to identify with the audience, do not let your use of targeted examples communicate to the audience that you think they are incapable of appreciating the big picture or are unwilling to think beyond their own narrow self-interest.

One needs to be cautious with generalizations based on age. If the speaker's message projects the attitude that the audience is old-fashioned or out of touch (older audiences), or naïve and inexperienced (younger audiences), the audience tends to quickly recognize the stereotyping and object to it, and even to the speaker.

Knowledge and Experience

Knowledge and experience with a subject come from a number of sources. If the issues to be discussed are completely new and foreign to your audience, there is some groundwork to be done—some background information provided in an audience-friendly (easily understandable) way is probably in order before the advocate even gets to the central argumentative claim he or she wishes to raise. Advocates in these situations also need to be especially vigilant not to speak over the heads of their audience members, which risks having an argument dismissed because it is incomprehensible to listeners. On the other hand, one must not go too far in simplifying ideas lest the audience feel that their intelligence is being underestimated. Providing relevant background information—and avoiding jargon—is especially important when advocates introduce an audience to a new area of concern.

Alternatively, an audience may have been living with the issue in their community for a while and have come to have a "felt," or experiential, understanding of the issue being discussed. These audiences believe that they know about the issue—and they do. Their experience, however, might differ from that of the advocate, or might conflict with the premises on which the case is to be made. Knowing the listener's experience is important; acknowledging that experience is imperative. It is exceedingly difficult to argue with someone's experience. They lived it. They felt it. Dismissing those experiences will only alienate listeners. Responsible advocates respect the experiences of the audience even as they offer an alternative interpretation. Respecting audience members' varied experiences does not mean accepting them as the truth—but instead acknowledging them as *their* truths—about a situation. From there, the advocate can find common ground, work to redefine or reinterpret where necessary, and move forward with the arguments.

Not all audiences have personal experience with an issue. Some are interested because it is an issue that they care about based on principle or that has the potential to affect them or their community. Often, these audiences know the broad strokes of the controversy and have been following the issue in the local or national news. Following the reporting on the issues that you are addressing is an important way of not only familiarizing yourself with the conversation (and knowing where to enter it) but also of understanding what your audience already likely knows. A review of local news coverage (often found in a local newspaper's searchable online archives), as well as the popular news magazines of the day, will quickly give an advocate a sense of what the audience may have read and expect to hear you address in some manner.

We believe that an audience's direct knowledge on a particular issue is important. It is also true that the listeners' formal education level might be relevant when it comes to the expectations that an audience has about how arguments are constructed. Uniformly, audiences expect arguments to be clearly stated and supported, but high school graduates, those with college coursework, and people with postgraduate degrees have all likely been trained a bit differently as to what it means to make a good argument. Colleges and universities tend to stress academic writing and argumentation, perhaps making such audiences more prone to require more traditionally structured and supported arguments than their peers.

Understanding the education and knowledge level of the audience helps an advocate know where to pitch his or her argument. Over- or underestimating an audience's knowledge, or failing to take their experience into account when crafting messages, are common pitfalls of advocacy.

Status

We use the term **status** in a broad sense as referring to one's position in a social system (i.e., parent, child, teacher, student, etc.) and also as an indication of relative prestige.[7] Status tends to imply roles and expectations. For the advocate, knowing something about how a listener perceives his or her own status relative to the speaker can provide vital information about how to approach a situation. In interacting with an audience of higher status, the speaker is cautious, lest their arguments seem disrespectful or insubordinate. Conversely, absolute deference to an audience could put the speaker's credibility in question. Advocates may enjoy a higher status than their audience, in which case they will likely receive a degree of deference from listeners, yet to shamelessly exploit this advantage can make speakers look arrogant. To be sure, it can be a delicate balance to maintain.

Violating status-derived role expectations can be problematic. Children often face limitations delineating how they can effectively argue with their parents in the same way that employees are limited in terms of what areas are negotiable with their boss. Lawyers can object to a judges' rulings, but arguing risks securing a contempt of court citation if they are too persistent. Undoubtedly, you argue differently based on your understanding of relative status. Your demeanor with a friend or romantic partner is dramatically different from exchanges with others where there is an apparent difference in status.

In our society, there is a connection between income and status. Knowing something about the economic position of a listener not only gives clues to status but indicates areas of interest. One whose income is devoted primarily to meeting survival needs (food, rent, utility bills) probably isn't going to be moved by sales pitches about buying gold or trips to the Bahamas. However, making generalizations based on income carries risks. A colleague recalled how a number of students were offended by the way they were treated by salespersons who they believed made correct but *insulting* assumptions about their economic status based on their age or the way they were dressed. As one student reported, "Yeah, I didn't have a lot of money to spend, but I was mad that she immediately took me to the bargain rack as if I couldn't possibly afford anything in her store."

Geographic Factors

General **geographic factors** also may define an audience. Often, you can make some generalizations about audience interests based on where they live. For example, don't expect your plea for a shift to clean alternative energy sources to be enthusiastically embraced in the mining communities of West Virginia; snowmobiles will be a tough sell in Florida; and your suggestion that online activity stunts our socialization will not play well in Silicon Valley. The topics you select and the examples you use to support them should be adjusted to reflect the interests of your audience.

Earlier in this chapter we suggested the need to do your homework as you try to uncover what a particular issue means to a region and community. A consideration of geographic factors can help you avoid being perceived as insensitive to or out of touch with your audience.

Gender

Considering the place of **gender** in analyzing one's audience is tricky. Certainly, the old generalizations about women being primarily interested and rooted in the private sphere while men take interest in the business of the public are tired and often erroneous. Likewise, assuming that sports and war metaphors will instantly win over your male audience or that your female audience is primarily interested in shopping and hair care likely will get you shown the door quickly. Yet certain issues may be more resonant with women or men. It depends on the subject; just be careful. A long history of having their concerns and opinions minimized and dismissed by a patriarchal culture has made women sensitive to generalizations, and it behooves us to remember that men are not a monolithic group either.

Research into communication differences between men and women do, however, indicate that there might be reason to at least consider how gender affects or reflects how men and women approach argumentation. Deborah Tannen's work in genderlect suggests, for example, that men tend to be more concerned with status than women, which often manifests itself in greater competition with the direct confrontation and one-upmanship that marks the argumentation style that we often see reflected in the public conversation. Women's desire for connection and concern for relationships, however, is often reflected in a communication style that emphasizes the finding of common ground.[8] We have argued that a noncombative stance is generally more productive. An astute advocate might keep these factors in mind when anticipating listener response.

Advocates should consider gender one of the aspects of audience demographics and give appropriate weight to the larger situation. Responsible advocates work to make the argumentation environment one that welcomes engagement and does not shut down conversation because of insensitive or inappropriate argument choices. Understanding the gender of the audience can help one to strike the appropriate tone and balance.

Cultural Factors

It is easy to make the mistaken assumption that everybody thinks the way we do. That is seldom the case since everyone is the product of their own experiences, which in turn has a dramatic influence on their values and behavior. This is especially evident as the advocate considers the **cultural factors** that influence listeners. Race and ethnicity exhibit a strong influence. Consider how the experience associated with race and racism often influences opinions on affirmative action or immigration reform. With respect to ethnic variables, one can easily see how customs and ethnic pride vary from one group to the next. Wars are waged and international agreements thwarted because of the cultural insensitivity or intense nationalism that makes cooperation difficult.

Beyond the global implications, it is obvious that regions have their own traditions and preferences. For example, there is often a degree of truth in some of the clichés and commonplaces we use to describe the views and lifestyles in different regions of America (e.g., Deep South vs. Northeast, urban vs. rural). It is inevitable that your listeners will come from diverse cultural backgrounds. Exchanges with diverse listeners expand our opportunities for learning only if we are aware that it would be ill advised to assume that the perspectives gained through our own cultural experiences are shared or superior. We should keep an open mind and be aware that perspective taking can be very difficult in intercultural exchanges.

Advocates can easily offend a diverse audience if they are wholly oblivious to important differences. An actual exchange may illustrate this most clearly. Six individuals who evidently belonged to a study group of some type had just finished their meal at a Pan-Asian restaurant and engaged in a conversation about the "decline of America." The group was distressed that there were so many "foreigners" in "our" country, and to make matters worse, "these people" did not even bother to adopt "our" customs and many did not speak "our" language. An observer from a neighboring table was conflicted about how he should react. He violently disagreed with the point of view. The fact that the study group had chosen to dine in an international restaurant owned and staffed by individuals who had recently moved to the country and enriched the community in many ways seemed a potent rebuttal to their argument (the discussants were oblivious to the irony). Should the observer have intervened? On one hand, it was doubtful that he would be able to alter the opinion of the study group (one of those occasions when we suggest argument will not be productive). On the other hand, the cultural insensitivity of the study group was magnified by the fact that their discussion was conducted in a public place and the group appeared incapable of understanding how offensive their remarks were to the restaurant staff and the diverse group of diners who were overhearing the conversation. Under these circumstances, the observer thought intervention might be warranted, not because he felt he could change the group's opinion but he might at least get them to show a little sensitivity to the impact their conversation was having on the unintended audience (many of whom simply held their tongues given their hesitancy to insult their customers). All too frequently, advocates lose sight of the need to consider the impact of cultural factors on our listeners and counteract their best arguments by demonstrating their own closed-mindedness.

Group Affiliations

People tend to socialize with others who share their interests. These connections can be occupational in nature since sharing a similar job also implies shared experiences. Some groups are social or recreational. Sports teams, book clubs, the Kiwanis Club, writers' groups, fan clubs, fraternities, and sororities are examples of social groups (though admittedly motivation for membership may vary). Finally, we may be involved with groups that reflect our political interests. Local or campus political party organizations or issue-oriented groups such as the National Rifle Association, Greenpeace, the Tea Party, and a host of others allow us to interact with those who share our opinions.

The advocate should investigate the **group affiliations** that may be held by members of the audience. Understanding these affiliations helps the speaker determine areas of interest or preexisting stances on issues that help with argument construction. Presentations on the need for handgun regulation delivered to Second Amendment enthusiasts, a defense of offshore oil drilling made in the presence of environmental activists, or a speech extolling the benefits of Obamacare to an audience distrustful of the expansion of federal government powers, while not impossible, are incredibly difficult. Astute advocates take care to acknowledge and not belittle the competing points of view held by the audience. Usually, the persuasive objectives of the speaker are made more modest in light of possible audience resistance. More modest goals of persuasion are often required as we seek out areas of agreement and slowly build on them rather than offering positions that would be dismissed as extreme absent shared understanding and trust.

Group affiliation can also dictate our style of interaction—we would certainly be less formal and probably more entertaining when addressing individuals who have gathered for recreational or social purposes. This "light" style would seem out of place in task-oriented groups who would likely see such an approach as diversionary or more likely one that trivialized the importance of the issues that unify the group.

LIMITS OF DEMOGRAPHIC ANALYSIS

The effective advocate learns something about his or her audience and adapts accordingly. It is important to recognize that the generalizations derived from demographic analysis, while generally accurate, can be dangerously erroneous, in which case advocates adjust by monitoring the reception that greets their ideas and modifying their approach given the immediate feedback.

TABLE 4.2
Demographic Categories

- Age
- Knowledge
  - Formal Education
  - Subject-Specific Knowledge and Experience
- Status
- Geographic Factors
- Gender
- Cultural Factors
- Group Affiliations
  - Occupational Groups
  - Social and Political Groups

There will be rare occasions where you have very little information about your audience. In such cases, your best strategy is to monitor reactions carefully during your conversation as you look for indicators of affirmation, rejection, or disinterest (head nods, lack of attention, applause or lack thereof, and other nonverbal indicators).

In short, the effective and sensitive advocate seeks to understand the audience. In those instances where the advocate faces an audience with whom they are unfamiliar, it is wise to make some generalizations about listeners to serve as guidelines. Remember that there are bound to be exceptions to the assumptions made on the basis of a demographic analysis, and the analysis of the audience is an ongoing process subject to modification as our conversation progresses.

CONCLUSION

We frequently find ourselves in situations where there appear to be no obvious clues that guide our way of arguing. Unlike the rigid expectations that govern well-established fields or genres of discourse (for example, courts of law, Congress, a funeral oration), most of our everyday exchanges require us to construct our own argumentative map as we attempt to adapt to specific situations and audiences.

Shared experience or history provides needed insight when you are dealing with familiar audiences. On the other hand, when an audience is unfamiliar you can often predict response patterns based on a demographic analysis of listeners that considers age, knowledge, status, geography, gender, cultural influences, and group affiliations. The generalizations possible through demographic analysis should be used with caution since there are always going to be exceptions. Nonetheless, a general understanding of your audience provides an appropriate starting place, and advocates will modify their assessment as the discussion unfolds.

QUESTIONS FOR CONSIDERATION

1. How do you find that you approach argument (or conversation) differently when talking to your boss, a professor, a friend, or a roommate? If you have supervised others at a job or maybe a residence hall, what expectations did you have about how people communicated with you? Why?

2. Is it easier to argue/engage with familiar or unfamiliar audiences for you? Why?

3. One of the most dramatic cultural shifts in recent memory has been on the issue of legal marriage for same-sex couples. If you were to speak to a group on the issue, which of the demographic characteristics would be the most important to consider? The least? Why?

4. If, as Tannen contends, men are more inclined to be concerned with status and women more concerned with connections, how might that influence your arguments if you are presenting to a skeptical audience of all men, all women, or a mixed group?

5. How might the age of your audience members affect your arguments on technology in the classroom?

6. What messages does it send to our audience when a speaker fails to adapt to them?

KEY TERMS

Age 52
Cultural Factors 57
Deference 48
Demographic Composition 52

Familiar Audiences 48
Gender 56
Geographic Factors 56
Group Affiliations 58

Knowledge and Experience 54
Status 55
Unfamiliar Audiences 52

Identifying and Making Quality Arguments

5 Discovering Arguments: Narrative Approaches

In what was termed the "buzziest blockbuster of the winter," FX's 2016 *American Crime Story* recounts the events of one of America's most riveting trials.[1] Nicole Brown Simpson and her friend Ron Goldman were brutally stabbed to death in the courtyard of her Brentwood, California, home on June 12, 1994. NFL football hero-turned-actor O. J. Simpson (Nicole's estranged ex-husband, with whom she had shared an abusive and stormy relationship) was quickly identified as a suspect. He was arrested later that week after a nationally televised slow-speed chase in a now-infamous white Ford Bronco. Simpson engaged high-profile lawyers Robert Shapiro, Johnnie Cochran, and F. Lee Bailey to lead his defense team and pled "absolutely 100 percent not guilty" to two counts of first-degree murder.[2]

The trial lasted a staggering 11 months. The prosecution, led by Marcia Clark and Christopher Darden, presented what it believed was irrefutable physical evidence (including DNA evidence) implicating Simpson. Referring to their "mountain of evidence," both seemed confident that a guilty verdict was inevitable. The "Dream Team," as the media dubbed Simpson's defense counsel, countered by working to undermine the credibility of key witnesses and offering a counternarrative that posited that the defendant was framed—the convenient victim of a racist and inept police force that would stop at nothing to close the case and again punish a successful black man for daring to love a beautiful blond white woman.

The jury deliberated for only 4 hours before acquitting Simpson on all charges. The verdict was controversial. For some, it was inconceivable that the jury would be unmoved by the substantial evidence against Simpson. For others, the verdict rightly acknowledged a rush to judgment by a corrupt and incompetent system. How can we account for such divergent responses to the trial and verdict? We believe that the key to understanding both the verdict and the public's reaction lies in the *choice* of arguments made by the attorneys involved and the story they told to the jury.

ARGUMENTS AS NARRATIVE

In this chapter, we offer the *narrative paradigm* as a perspective that can help identify why audiences find some arguments more compelling than others. As any advocate or trial lawyer will attest, having all of the facts on your side does not guarantee that the judge or jury will see things your way. Most of us have experienced the same thing in arguments with friends and family. We are "right"—and can "prove it"—but our listeners just won't come around. Effective advocates identify the most central issues in a controversy and address them in a cogent and compelling manner—they don't just overwhelm their audience with facts but present arguments with which the audience can identify.

It is tempting to consider argumentation exclusively as an exercise in formal logic, unclouded by emotion, past experiences, and feelings about the advocate. However, people are indeed exercising reasoned judgment when their conclusions are influenced by considerations such as an argument's coherence or consistency with their own experiences and beliefs, and factors that seem to go beyond just the facts. While there are particular audiences and fields that expect a strictly analytical approach (the scientific community, for example), an audience-centered style of argument is more inclusive and appropriate in many cases. Furthermore, it is no less valid. With that in mind, we offer that audiences experience advocacy as narratives. Stories (often dramas) play themselves out complete with an unfolding plot, heroes, villains, and all of the other elements that a good tale contains, and we make judgments and decisions based on these stories. It is only natural, then, that we consider narratives as arguments.

Your reaction to the narrative perspective may be similar to ours when we first encountered the model: We were skeptical. Our initial reaction was that arguing is a serious business; we are not telling stories or spinning yarns here! We viewed arguments as claims supported by evidence—a process we thought was made predictable and manageable because of formal rules of logic and inflexible standards for evaluating support. Trying to recast arguments into narrative terms seemed inappropriate and even a bit silly.

We began to see the error of our ways on those occasions where we offered brilliant, logical, and well-supported arguments only to have our point of view dismissed with statements like, "That's a really good point *but* . . ." These rebuffs would often be offered by those we admired as thoughtful individuals. This happened often enough that it became clear we couldn't dismiss these reactions as the misguided responses of "unreasonable" people. We knew otherwise but were at a loss to explain their decisions. The narrative paradigm brought a moment of clarity. Most people haven't memorized a complex system of formal logical rules. Generally, we interpret arguments in a way that allows them to make sense to us, and that means viewing arguments as narratives.

The narrative approach does not demean responses that don't follow formal debate rules but embraces them and accounts for them by allowing us to discover what constitutes "good reasons" for an audience. Consequently, we were able to form more persuasive arguments and get a better hearing from our listeners. That does not imply that formal rules and tests of evidence are irrelevant (we have quite a few of them in this text) but rather that they could be incorporated as part of a narrative perspective. Our attempts to cast arguments in terms of plot, characters, setting, and narrator seemed awkward at first, but it was really pretty similar to the *who, what, when, where,* and *why* that is standard in journalism. Finally, and not insignificantly, the narrative approach respects an audience's contribution and thus seemed a more comfortable fit with the mutual respect theme we outlined for advocates in the opening chapter. We hope you will agree.

Good arguments have much in common with good stories. Both are told from particular points of view by advocates (narrators) who relate their "story" to an audience and who are believed to a greater or lesser extent depending on the credibility ascribed to them by that audience. In both, the people or organizations (characters) involved are carefully rendered to act consistently with their motivations. Descriptions of the issue at hand and its unfolding (plot) are carefully described to be clear, well organized, and free from internal and external contradiction. The situation (scene) serves as the backdrop for the argument and gives it a meaningful context. In a sense, good arguments *are* good stories.

Admittedly, as advocates, we are not telling traditional, literary stories. We are offering **rhetorical narratives**. Rhetorical narratives are designed to persuade the audience to think and act differently and are distinct from literary narratives, which exist primarily for the purpose of exemplifying or entertaining. For example, rhetorical narratives may not reach the formal stage of plot resolution.[3] The audience interprets and completes the story. However, rhetorical narratives are like literary narratives in that they feature rising action and turning points where characters must make important decisions.

If we want to be persuasive, we can help our case by paying close attention to those traditional narrative elements that seem so natural to our listeners. The advocate who understands the many ways that people process arguments in narrative terms can more readily see the controversy from the audience's perspective. When we understand *how* people are persuaded, we are better prepared to engage our audience productively and persuasively.

NARRATIVE ELEMENTS

Narratives have predictable elements: plot, characters, setting, and narrator. Astute advocates not only take note of how they can best present these elements to further their case but also consider how their listeners are doing the same as they process and evaluate the narrative.

Plot

If advocates are to have a story worth listening to, *something* must happen in it. The **plot** of the narrative from the point of view of the advocate, then, is the description of *what happened.* Think of it as the story line. The plot is often what first interests us in a controversy and compels us to seek out information and perhaps take action. "They did *what?*" might be the cry of someone who is responding to the pull of a narrative's plot.

In a rhetorical narrative, a well-rendered plot will often bring the audience to the brink of embracing the desired conclusion while allowing the audience to fill in the blanks on its own, giving the audience a role to play in the story and empowering it to act in the actual controversy. Of course, the advocate doesn't leave the audience's conclusions to chance. Instead, they construct the plot in such a way that there is a narrow range of acceptable conclusions that the listener can draw. In other instances, the advocate presents conclusions overtly, hoping the audience will see the claim as the inevitable destination of a particular story line.

The most persuasive plots often are grounded in cultural or universal myths that are familiar to the audience and are presented in a manner that the audience finds to be logical.[4] Popular myths include celebrated story lines such as "pulling yourself up by your own bootstraps," triumph of the underdog, good triumphs over evil, and a litany of others. Such cultural anchors render the plot recognizable and relatable to the audience.

As you can imagine, the narratives of the prosecutors and defense counsel in the O. J. Simpson trial presented very different plots. Although they did it badly, the prosecution told the culturally well-known story of a jealous, rage-filled, physically abusive ex-husband who brutally murdered his ex-wife and the man who was accompanying her and then began immediately working to avoid arrest. As the story went, the man then boarded a plane to Chicago to evade suspicion, provide himself with an alibi, and dispose of evidence. When his arrest was imminent, he wrote a suicide-like note, enlisted a friend to drive, and climbed into the back of a white Ford Bronco with a gun. When the police tried to apprehend him to serve the warrant for his arrest, the nation watched a live television news helicopter report as the pair led them on a slow-speed chase to his residence, where he ultimately surrendered to police. The defense team denied that Simpson had committed the murders and offered an alternative (and also well-known narrative within the local community) in which racism and incompetence in the Los Angeles Police Department had led to the wrongful arrest and prosecution of a grieving man.

Issues and events most of us face are seldom so dramatic. Still, plot is important in the arguments that we make every day. Consider the conversations that you have with family and friends when you return from a weekend or vacation that you want them to understand was "the best vacation ever." Plot often is central when you are justifying your assessment. The support for these arguments might start with the quality and events involved in the initial travel ("We were late getting to the airport and barely made it through security—but got to the gate just before they closed the doors and got bumped to first class for the cross-country flight!"). Other reasons the vacation was terrific perhaps centered on the experiences at your destination ("We spent the first day relaxing at Seal Beach, had lunch at a wonderful cafe nearby, and got into the hottest new club in town that night. The next day, we drove up to L.A. and caught a taping of *The Price Is Right*, where Bob Barker made a special appearance!"). If the reasons that you cite for evaluating the trip center on *what happened*, you've focused the rhetorical narrative on plot.

Characters

Characters are central to all stories, and as such, are often the most obvious component of a rhetorical narrative.[5] Usually, we can readily point to the major players in any controversy. In most narratives, particular character types are easily recognizable. At least three basic character types are generally presented in argumentative narratives: heroes, villains, and victims.[6] Audiences become invested in the narrative through the characters, so they must be able to, at minimum, recognize the characters as realistic and, ideally, identify with and cheer for the heroes, be repelled by the villains, and empathize with the victims. While characters are often human, other entities such as organizations or corporations can be treated as characters as well.[7]

Knowing the disposition of the audience helps with the casting of believable characters in the rhetorical narrative. An example might make the use of characters more clear. When we argue about raising taxes on the wealthiest Americans, the characters are central. Depending on the advocate's perspective, the wealthy are depicted as either heroic, innovative job creators; self-absorbed villains interested only in their accumulation of wealth; or victims of big government, taxed and overregulated by those jealous of their success. Our perspective clearly dictates the direction of the arguments and the casting of characters as either heroes, villains, or victims. The extent to which the audience embraces the advocate's characterizations influences the narrative's believability.

Generally, heroes embody classic virtues, as well as those that the advocate/narrator finds to be important. American heroes tend to be adventurous and daring, and infused with particular American ideals such as individualism and achievement, as well as being visionary and worthy of the status of legend.[8]

Villains attempt to block the path or otherwise work against the goals of the heroes. Depicting someone as a freedom fighter as opposed to a terrorist, for example, deeply affects our opinions of a character's motivations and actions. For a discussion on paralanguage (vocal behavior) in his Nonverbal Communication course, one of the authors played the postgame interview with Carolina Panthers quarterback Cam Newton after the Panthers' disappointing loss to the Denver Broncos in the 2016 Super Bowl.[9] The clip displayed a dejected Newton, who pouted and offered nearly inaudible one-word responses to questions before walking out of the interview after only two and a half minutes. Anxious to offer a bonus life lesson, I argued that Newton's demeanor revealed much about his maturity. In my narrative, Newton was a villain of sorts—a spoiled brat who wouldn't pull himself together to do the requisite interviews or maintain even an appearance of good sportsmanship. In what proved to be an embarrassing misread of my audience, I was made aware of the large number of football players in my class. They saw Newton (the character) differently—as a gifted competitive football hero whose poor behavior was further confirmation of his heroic competitiveness. "Of course he is disappointed," they said, and noted that his competitive nature as revealed in his ill-mannered interview only proved him to be more heroic since if you are not passionate, driven, or ultracompetitive, you have no business in the NFL.

Victims have been harmed or suffered in some manner, usually at the hand of the villain. Sometimes, the advocate/narrator takes the role of victim and speaks from that vantage point. To be persuasive, audiences must be able to empathize with victims and perhaps identify with some aspect of their personality or circumstance. They do not necessarily need to find the victim to be likable, although that often helps. In the Simpson case, the defense succeeded in adding O. J. Simpson to the list of victims (i.e., Ron Goldman and Nicole Simpson) presented by the prosecution.

If you want to understand what values an advocate holds dear, look at those embodied by the heroes or the types of injustices visited on the victims. The same holds true for the values that they reject, or at least find to be much less important; look at the values embodied by the villains in their narratives. The characters in the Simpson trial were one of the reasons that the defense narrative was so compelling. A legendary football hero-turned-actor is accused of murdering his beautiful ex-wife and her friend. A freeloading party boy who was living in Simpson's guest house *may* have heard something, and a racist cop with questionable professionalism handled some of the important evidence in the case.

The Simpson defense team encountered some challenges in rendering their characters in ways that would support their narrative. One of the difficulties that the prosecution in the Simpson trial had to overcome was Simpson's status as lovable American sports hero. Heroes don't murder their ex-wives, though they can become victims themselves when they are accused of doing so. The defense was able to turn a police officer (Mark Fuhrman) into a villain, and did so by playing damning recordings of the officer's racist rants.

The most believable characters act consistently with their ascribed values and their past behavior.[10] In other words, heroes are heroic, villains are obstructive or destructive, and victims have truly been harmed. People, however, are not always consistent, so the characters who represent them in the narrative may appear inconsistent as well. Narratives that offer characters who act contrary to type (like those discussed previously) encounter more skepticism and require more careful rendering. In such cases, the narrator has an added burden of helping the audience to understand the inconsistency, whether the reason for it is based in a personal transformation, a unique circumstance, or some other factor, if the audience is to find the character to be compelling and the narrative to be resonant.[11] Imagine Congress considering a bill purported to be a "fair compromise" sponsored by a senator with a history of obstruction and inflexibility. To see the bill as a fair compromise, the audience would have to be convinced that the sponsor had indeed genuinely evolved, or their skepticism would likely undermine their support.

Scene

As the iconic Snoopy often wrote, "It was a dark and stormy night." Although he rarely got much further than that, Snoopy understands what any good advocate knows: **scene** contributes substantially to a narrative. Depictions of the scene (which may be more familiar as *setting*, which means essentially the same thing in this use) help to create and convey the tone, feeling, and emotional content of the narrative.[12] In some cases, it exerts influence over the conduct of the main characters, often explaining their actions.

The scene can be physical, temporal, or both. In some cases, it is the place or space that is important, while in others the audience must understand the place in history to fully grasp the narrative. In short, actions are influenced by the physical dynamics surrounding their performance and the situation or circumstances in which they take place. Importantly, the scene must be rendered in terms that the audience can imagine as plausible.

The look and feel of a place can be critical to the narrative. For example, depictions of the scene were vital to the success of Senator Edward Kennedy's address to his constituents in 1969 regarding the car crash in which his passenger, Mary Jo Kopechne, was killed. Kennedy focused on it to absolve himself of guilt for the accident:

> Little over one mile away, the car that I was driving *on an unlit road* went off *a narrow bridge which had no guard rails and was built on a left angle to the road*. The car overturned in *a deep pond* and immediately filled with water. . . . I made immediate and repeated efforts to save Mary Jo by diving into *the strong and murky current*, but succeeded only in increasing my state of utter exhaustion and alarm. . . . I suffered a cerebral concussion, as well as shock. . . . [emphasis in original][13]

Kennedy used the scene as the key factor in his own defense, making both he and Kopechne victims of the dark night and winding road on which they had traveled.[14] Advocates in formal as well as informal situations often use arguments based in scene when outside circumstances are good justifications for the claims that they are making. If you've ever justified being late with comments such as "the traffic was terrible today," you've argued based on scenic elements. Decisions about getting a dog or another pet often center on scene. If the reasons include: it would be nice to have another living thing around, I need more exercise, pets in shelters live unnecessarily bleak lives, studies show that people with pets live longer, or a dog is a good security system, you are justifying your new furry friend with scenic elements.

Depictions of the temporal scene—the time period in which the narrative takes place—can similarly be helpful to the advocate. Perhaps you've heard your older friends or relatives say, "But you must understand that things were different then." They are drawing your attention to the temporal scene and suggesting that in order to understand particular actions, one must understand the context provided by the historical moment in which they occurred. In short, argumentative narratives are more potent when the audience can see actions as reasonable responses to the scene.

Narrator

If you are acting as an advocate, you are a **narrator**—the person telling the story. It is in the telling of the story that we structure the reality of the experience for the audience, so it is critical to consider the choices that we make as narrators.[15] Advocates for each side of an issue tend to tell the story a bit differently, so it is important to attend carefully to the choices made by other narrators as well. Advocates often portray different people as heroes, for example, or construct the setting in a way that best suits their perspective. Their interpretations of how the events unfold (the plot) may even conflict.

To be persuasive, the narrator must be perceived as reliable and credible by the audience. As you are aware from Chapter 2, the credibility of the advocate is paramount regardless of the field or type of dispute. The elements of credibility that we discussed in that chapter come into play for the narrator, especially that of trustworthiness. An advocate who is a trustworthy, reliable narrator has met the minimum requirement for persuasion.

There are almost always competing narrators in a dispute. Narrators with different perspectives (and sometimes even other narrators who represent the same perspective) will offer differing narratives. If a couple with whom you are friends goes through a breakup, you doubtlessly know the importance of narrator in argument construction. The couple likely will have dramatically different perspectives as they try to convince you of their need to call it quits. Plots may be laden with the transgressions of the other as the narrator portrays himself or herself as the long-suffering victim who tolerated all manner of slights (from the villainous partner) while valiantly trying to hold the couple together (a heroic effort), only to finally succumb to the inevitable and break up to get out of a toxic relationship (scene). The other partner might well have a completely different interpretation of the events leading to the relationship's demise. As a listener, you must constantly remind yourself that a narrator represents only one perspective, possibly rendered suspect by his or her personal bias. Advocates have differing values, experiences, or motives that influence their interpretations and presentations. Consequently, understanding the assumptions of narrators is often essential to decoding the narratives that they offer. For example, patients hospitalized with a complicated illness frequently express frustration with the different diagnoses or recommendations from the assorted attending specialists. The stories are often incomplete as each doctor discusses the patient's condition from his or her own area of experience (neurologic, oncologic, coronary, infectious disease, etc.). It is for this reason that many cases are assigned a case supervisor as more of a "big picture" person to help patients navigate the well-intentioned but often confusing pronouncements of their doctors.

When identifying the narrators, it is helpful to consider our previous discussion concerning fields of argument. If you and the other narrators are basically speaking from the same background or discipline, you will probably speak and interact with terms and arguments that are familiar to both of you. If your fields differ, however, the knowledge, assumptions, and priorities that you bring to the controversy will as well. For example, if the narrator is speaking as a scientist, that advocacy is going to reflect the traditions and sensibilities of the scientific community. An artist's approach might be different. Likewise, the norms that prevail in particular forums constrain our rhetorical narratives. All of this is to say that we need to identify and prepare to engage productively with those who come from areas of expertise very different from our own if we want to help our communities to make good decisions.

Beware of narrators who make themselves the center of the story, and think carefully before doing this yourself. Regardless of one's motives, this diversion risks being perceived as opportunistic and egotistical. Consider the stance of Reverend Al Sharpton. A veteran civil rights activist, Sharpton uses his talent for drawing media attention to publicize instances of injustice in African-American communities. As his supporters remind us, his flamboyant methods and personality certainly serve an important purpose, but others point out that he sometimes overshadows the causes he champions, leaving the impression that he uses them primarily to enhance his own image. In short, according to his critics, the issues he moves in to support become about Al Sharpton more than anything else. In such cases, the narrator has become the story and his or her motives are called into question. It is notable and interesting that Sharpton played a much lower-key role in the unrest that came to Ferguson, Missouri, in 2014 when African American teenager Michael Brown was shot and killed by a white police officer and the city erupted in rage. Initially, a number of civil rights advocates and celebrities made pilgrimages to Ferguson, including Sharpton, Jesse Jackson, and Oprah Winfrey Network star Iyanla Vanzant. Protesters generally rejected them, reportedly concerned that (among other things) their celebrity would overshadow issues of police brutality and civil rights that the shooting had brought to the fore.[16] The protesters were aware that narrators matter and were willing to sacrifice the profile to be gained by civil rights celebrity spokespeople to maintain focus on the plot.

When a controversy gains the attention of the news media, the media take on a role as narrator as well, and encourage the understanding of controversies in narrative terms. Indeed, we call them news *stories*. In such cases, the advocates who are serving as narrators are treated as *characters* in the media's narrative, and the controversy serves as the plot. This is especially apparent during political campaigns. The candidates are treated as characters, not narrators. The "horse race" becomes the story, not the issues upon which the candidates are campaigning.[17]

The credibility of the narrator is critical. We need to evaluate stories that are filtered. For example, when the media report on a controversy, are they impartial to the point that they simply observe events and let the actors tell their own stories? Has the media's need to select items that constitute an interesting narrative altered the narrative itself? Has an ideological bias turned the media into narrators strategically reporting information that simply supports their own position on an issue (in which case they are making their own argument rather than reporting on one)?

As we construct arguments, it is helpful to add yet another level of analysis to our assessment by asking "who is the narrator" of the evidence or testimony included in the case under discussion. Testimony often constitutes a story within a story. The advocate is ultimately responsible for the veracity of the testimony used, so they should subject the author of the evidence being introduced to careful scrutiny. As will be evident in a later chapter, one of the most important tests of evidence of any kind is source reliability.

Understanding that audiences largely think in narrative terms and considering those narrative elements available to you can help you be a more effective advocate. The following guide summarizes the narrative elements likely present in your own and others' advocacy.

TABLE 5.1

Identifying Narrative Elements

- Plot—story line
- Characters—key players in the story line
  - Heroes
  - Villains
  - Victims
- Setting—the place/circumstances in which the plot takes place
- Narrator—who is telling the story

EVALUATING NARRATIVES

Audiences evaluate competing stories to determine which one they find to be the most plausible and influential. In evaluating the narrative, the audience applies what communication scholar Walter Fisher called a "logic of **good reasons**" to determine what to believe.[18] Audiences are persuaded when they find the account or argument to be coherent and plausible (have **narrative probability**), and aligned with their understanding of the world (have **narrative fidelity**). Narratives that have both narrative probability and narrative fidelity are said to have **narrative rationality**.

Discourse need not be in traditional narrative form to be evaluated in a narrative manner. Indeed, *all* forms of discourse are naturally evaluated from a narrative perspective.[19] That is not to say that discourse is not evaluated in other ways as well; what we think of as traditional rationality is not necessarily negated by processing discourse in narrative terms, especially in specialized fields. Let's look at these particular ways audiences judge competing narratives.

Narrative Probability

Narratives have *probability* when they hang together as a coherent whole. When a narrative is clearly understandable, contradiction free, and consistent with other credible narratives on the same subject, and features characters that behave according to their ascribed roles, the audience finds the story to be logical and therefore probable.[20] For advocates, this means that their arguments are organized and presented in a way that the audience understands. That is, they are free of contradictory claims, they contain evidence that is consistent with claims offered, and the actions of the people/characters are consistent with the motives that the advocate has attributed to them. In short, advocates ask the audience to believe that the narrative is within the realm of plausibility. Recall the defense narrative in the Simpson case that claimed an inappropriate "rush to judgment." Police incompetence and racism became central themes, and arguments about mishandling or planting key evidence clearly fed that theme. Ultimately, jurors believed that key characters (officers and lab technicians) behaved according to the roles assigned to them in the defense's narrative.

Narrative Fidelity

Narratives have *fidelity* when the narrative/account/argument aligns with that audience's general perspective on the world.[21] Fidelity is concerned with the *apparent* truthfulness and reliability of a story, and invites the audience to consider whether the narrative is consistent with what they know to be true from accepted, related narratives, as well as their own experiences and observations.[22] When a narrative is consistent with listeners' beliefs and experiences, they are likely to find it compelling.

Fidelity is not inherent in a narrative. Like credibility, fidelity is ascribed to a narrative by the audience. The complete story must resonate as true with the audience; if only parts of it are believable, the narrative's fidelity will not hold up and the persuasive effect is minimized. However, narratives can continue to gain power over time when advocates cast contemporary events as new facts that confirm their narrative. For example, Second Amendment advocates often view criminal activity as affirmation of the need to be armed for self-defense. New reports of gun violence "fit" the narrative to which they adhere. It goes without saying that successful advocates engage in thorough analysis of their audiences in an effort to see what stories will ring true given the listeners' disposition. Likewise, in the Simpson case, a jury that had heard about or experienced firsthand the abuse of power by the Los Angeles Police Department had no trouble believing the defense's account of what happened to Simpson.

Some view narrative fidelity and common sense as synonymous. That seems to be a useful comparison since, at a practical level, a listener is asking, "Does this seem consistent with what I believe/know to be true?" We are skeptical about arguments that run contrary to our understanding (common sense). Obviously, arguers must appreciate the tendency and adapt to other perspectives. Additionally, as critical listeners we must remain open-minded and acknowledge that our experience is not necessarily the final word on any given subject.

A key advantage to a narrative perspective on argument is that it values the perspective of the audience as they seek to make decisions. We trust juries of our peers to make good decisions about the guilt of defendants, for example, so it follows that citizens can make reasonable decisions in other community matters as well. While there is a time and place for expert judgment, the narrative paradigm reminds us that we need not completely defer to experts in all situations. This does not mean that we should silence the experts and their technical knowledge, but instead that we should take them into account as a part of the decision-making process and avoid automatically substituting their judgment for our own. The narrative paradigm insists that commonsense judgments are based on good reasons—on valid ways of making decisions.[23]

TABLE 5.2

Dimensions of Narrative Rationality

- Narrative probability
  - Coherent
  - Contradiction free
  - Characters behave according to type
- Narrative fidelity
  - Aligns with common sense
  - Consistent with related narratives
  - Accounts for new facts

CONCLUSION

A narrative perspective on argument can greatly expand the advocate's critical analysis. Most arguments "tell stories" and include the central dramatic elements of plot, characters, scene, and narrator. Considering these elements allows the observer to examine the merit of competing arguments (narratives) by looking at the interplay and influence of the argument's dramatic features—a process that mirrors the way audiences choose from competing points of view.

The narrative approach is both liberating and useful because it deemphasizes (but does not ignore) formal logic in favor of a rhetorical logic that determines the persuasive potential of arguments in light of audience-derived standards of judgment. Ultimately, arguments are evaluated in terms of whether an audience finds them coherent (narrative probability) or consistent with what they know to be true (narrative fidelity).

QUESTIONS FOR CONSIDERATION

1. There have been a significant number of mass shootings in recent years. Consider the dominant narratives that emerge when a mass shooting occurs. Who are the dominant narrators (who "gets" to speak and be heard)? Who are the heroes? The villains? The victims presented by the competing narrators? What is the scene?

2. Like the O. J. Simpson trial, the grand jury's notification that it would not indict police officer Darren Wilson for shooting Michael Brown was greeted by angry incredulity and hearty affirmation. How might this be explained using the tools of narrative probability and fidelity?

3. Many attempts to rehabilitate a person or corporation's image are actually a struggle to turn a "villain" into the "hero." Locate some

examples of this and discuss what persuasive appeals went into that change.

4. Consider the competing narratives concerning Donald Trump's viability as a candidate once he became the Republicans' presumptive nominee. What was Trump's narrative? What competing narratives were offered by the Republican establishment, his opponents, and the Democratic contenders?

5. Whether the federal government should be more or less generous in providing aid to America's needy has long been a source of disagreement. Identify the narratives employed by each side. Who are the key characters, and are they heroes, villains, or victims? What are the competing plots? How is setting used in the competing narratives?

KEY TERMS

Characters 66
Good Reasons 72
Narrative Fidelity 72

Narrative Probability 72
Narrative Rationality 72
Narrator 69

Plot 64
Rhetorical Narratives 64
Scene 68

Discovering Arguments: Stock Issue Approaches

"**W**hat remains a mystery to pro-gun advocates is why a college campus should be thought of as somehow separate or different from any other place that people live and work when it comes to issues of self-defense," wrote B. Gil Horman in *Guns & Ammo*.[1] Campus public safety officers, administrators, and faculty, however, suggest a number of reasons that campuses are "separate and distinct" places,[2] making Horman's contention a central issue in the "concealed carry on campus" debates being held across the nation. Mass shootings and other forms of gun violence on college campuses have become all too familiar occurrences, prompting legislatures in a number of states to debate the merit of allowing the concealed carry of firearms at state universities. Do more armed people make campus environments safer? Is concealed carry a deterrent to mass shooters? Should a citizen's Second Amendment right to bear arms trump a university's concerns about the safety of its community? Do the benefits of concealed carry outweigh the risks of increased firearm availability in an environment that houses occasionally drunk, depressed, and/or suicidal students? Does the possibility of concealed firearms in the classroom change the learning climate for better or for worse? These questions form the core of the dispute.

Eight states currently have provisions for carrying concealed weapons at postsecondary institutions, though each state has its own exceptions.[3] In Missouri, the spring 2016 legislative session featured no fewer than four separate bills that would allow concealed carry on campus for the explicit purpose of self-protection.[4] The sheer number of bills being proposed indicates the political currency to be gained by legislators eager to put their names to the cause and prove their pro-gun credentials. The controversy provides a particularly useful lens through which to more closely examine ways of discovering and addressing useful arguments. In the concealed-carry debate, as with all controversies, advocates need to know how to productively navigate the tricky argumentative terrain.

Advocates need means of identifying key issues within a controversy. Audiences bring with them particular expectations that the effective advocate needs to anticipate and address. This is a central tenet of the narrative paradigm discussed in the previous chapter. An understanding of **stock issues**—issues that are central to a topic under dispute—is also an effective way to focus attention on critical matters.[5] Unlike the listener-centered narrative approach, the stock issue approach assumes that certain topics *will* resonate with listeners. The stock issue approach is a bit more formulaic than the narrative perspective but equally valuable. You should select the perspective that works best for you while bearing in mind it need not be an either/or choice since the two approaches share many points in common.

Audience expectations tend to align with stock issues that need to be addressed if the advocate's argument is to be accepted. Different types of disputes (fact, value, policy) ask us to make different types of judgments, and the stock issue approach is especially useful in its focus on topics appropriate to the nature of the controversy. In the sections that follow, we discuss the types of disputes, their associated stock issues, and also how the narrative elements introduced earlier in this text can inform your choice of arguments.

QUESTIONS OF FACT

When advocates attempt to evaluate (or ask an audience to evaluate) the existence of something that is empirically verifiable, they are dealing with **questions of fact**. Please note that a claim does not have to be factually *accurate* to be a claim of fact—it needs to be something that *can be verified empirically* (although it probably has not been verified to everyone's satisfaction or you wouldn't be arguing about it). Why argue about things that are factual? Why not just "Google it"? Because we often argue about factual matters that have not yet been settled. Even facts that seem to represent common knowledge can be wrong. It was considered to be a fact that the earth was flat and that the sun revolved around the earth until scientific advances rendered such truths suspect and ultimately proved them wrong. In other circumstances, conclusive, verifiable evidence is not available and we are making the best decisions we can based on what we know or take to be factual at a given point in time. For instance, either concealed carry on campus *does* or *does not* increase the risk that students will become victims of gun violence, but at this point there is not indisputable evidence that convinces everyone. The province of argument is the reasonable and the probable, not undeniable, unequivocal Truth. So we argue about the evidence that we have until we can come to an agreement about what the evidence supports to a reasonable degree of certainty. To further complicate matters, different fields take different types of evidence as compelling, so even when the question has been settled in one arena, people in other fields or with different expectations about the nature and merit of various types of evidence may still disagree. For example, the gun community may be satisfied with notions that being armed is a deterrent to gun violence, while others will argue that the unique environment of a college campus renders such notions questionable. In such instances, considerable argument takes place over what counts as a fact. That is, the argument may center on the appropriate standards that should be used to determine whether something qualifies as a fact or not.

There are three types of factual claims conveniently associated with time: (1) something is/is not a fact (a *present* fact), (2) something did/did not happen a particular way (a *past* fact), or (3) something will/will not happen (a *future* fact).[6] Questions of fact include the level of risk of mass shootings currently on college campuses—a present fact. There are also some who argue that past campus shootings would have been shortened or avoided if someone on campus had been armed (a question of past fact).[7] Finally, some argue about what will or will not happen in the future when they predict that mass shootings on campus will continue (or cease) to occur. Some claims of a more tenuous nature may also be considered factual, as illustrated in the claim that a proliferation of guns on campuses will lead to an increase in assaults with a deadly weapon on those campuses. Whether they will or will not constitute an increased risk is a factual matter, but since we cannot be sure ahead of time, advocates bring their best arguments to convince others of what we believe will be a future fact. All three of these claims and counterclaims are factual in that they enable a judgment through empirical validation.

Advocates in factual controversies usually are advised to support their claims with the best testimony possible as well as well-documented factual examples. This is especially true with contestable claims of fact. There will be more on this in the next chapter, but in short, weaving testimony and facts into a coherent, believable narrative is usually the way that advocates build compelling cases about issues of fact.

There are two stock issues for questions of fact: (1) What are the appropriate criteria for evaluation? and (2) Does the particular instance under consideration meet the agreed-upon criteria?

You may be certain that you have good reasons for your beliefs, yet there are others who disagree with your reasoning. To avoid the "did not/did too" arguments of our youth, there needs to be a means of evaluating competing facts (standards or **criteria**). In other words, *on what basis should this argument be fairly decided?* Sometimes, the criteria need to be made explicit. At other times, the advocates have an implicit understanding of what it will take to carry the day.

There are many criteria available to help an audience determine who has the strongest argument. The most obvious standard is an empirical one. A police officer who pulls you over for speeding, for example, has used an empirical standard to establish that fact. If the speed limit is 65 miles per hour (the empirical and posted standard used to determine what is acceptable and what is speeding) and the radar gun clocked you at 70 miles per hour, you have exceeded the speed limit. We make determinations like this all of the time, though the criteria are not always stated as clearly as the speed limit signs that line the highway. Saying John is 5 feet 11 inches tall is a rather clear-cut factual statement. However, the claim that John is tall is less concrete. Note how the established claim that John is 5 feet 11 inches tall can be evidence for a related argument.

Advocate Webb:	John is tall! (claim)
Advocate James:	He doesn't look tall to me.
Advocate Webb:	He is 5 feet 11 inches! (evidence)
Advocate James:	So what? That's not tall.
Advocate Webb:	The average height for an American male is just over 5 feet 7 inches.[8] (evidence)
Advocate James:	OK.
Advocate Webb:	Anyone who exceeds the national average would be, by definition, considered tall. (criterion)
Advocate James:	That makes sense, if that's how you define tall.

There are other standards, of course. Civil courts use the standard of *a preponderance of evidence.* That is, they weigh the amount and/or quality of the evidence presented by both sides and determine which evidence is the most compelling in order to reach a conclusion of guilt or innocence. The number of people wrongly incarcerated indicates that judges and juries do not always get it right. In practical terms, one might argue, "My evidence is newer/more relevant/of higher quality than my opponent's, and if you think that I have presented better evidence, you should believe me." In lower stakes decision making, a preponderance of evidence, or put another way, "more likely than not," is a common way that people judge arguments and seems to serve almost as a default criterion. Often, notions of what is a fact are more rigorous when the standard is "beyond a reasonable doubt." When a jury, for example, needs to be as sure as is possible that the decision it reaches is just, "beyond a reasonable doubt" is a useful standard to set. A surprising number of everyday arguments are factual in nature and hinge on disagreements over criteria. For example, one's spouse might argue the other spends too much of the household income on nonessential items. The argument stems from a basic disagreement over the criteria that would define *nonessential.* Argument should support the criteria that advocates explicitly or implicitly suggest to their audience. In other words, live up to your own standards. Don't set up criteria that your evidence can't meet. Also, don't insist on criteria that *no* evidence could reasonably meet.

No matter what criteria you ask your listeners to use, they likely will invoke narrative rationality to process it. It can be best to address the issue directly. Just suggest that your audience listen to all sides of the argument and determine which set of evidence they find the most consistent and plausible (which is essentially the same as a preponderance of the evidence).[9]

The rendering of the plot is instrumental to convincing an audience that the fact(s) in question are or are not true. Plots are based in facts—*what* happened and *how* it happened. In other words, *how* you describe *what happened*—what you include or exclude; in what way you choose to order the events; or the descriptions of the events, characters, and/or setting—will make your argument/narrative either more or less plausible. It is important that an audience believe that the plot has narrative probability (that events *could possibly* have happened in the way that the narrator describes). If plots are too outlandish, the timeline does not hold up, the characters act contrary to type, or the story has other irreconcilable contradictions, the audience is unlikely to be persuaded. Issues of narrative fidelity also play a role. As we discussed earlier, audiences ultimately ask themselves, "Do I believe that the world works this way?" It is important, then, that the plot and characters also align with the audience's view of the world, or at least one that they can imagine.

When arguing about issues of fact, rhetorical narratives should employ support that is accurate, relevant, and organized to move the audience toward desired conclusions. Double-check your supporting material if you need to. Responsible advocates don't mislead their audiences about the facts.

Besides being accurate, arguments/reasons need to be relevant. Choosing relevant arguments can be a bit trickier because it requires determining which arguments are the most critical to the decision being made. Often, advocates see everything as relevant and err on the side of offering every argument they can think of. More is not always better. The audience might be impressed with the number of things you have to say, but they also might stop listening or not be able to select (or remember) the most important arguments or details. In other words, don't offer excessive detail that clouds rather than clarifies. Determine what the audience really needs to know to fully understand your position.

Finally, your arguments need to be organized. Advocates cannot present plot points in a random order and expect the audience to connect the dots. Organization is a tool of persuasion. Figure out how arguments can best be arranged. If you have written down the reasons that you have identified as support for your argument, you will see that they probably fall into the predictable organizational styles that you learned in public speaking class.[10]

TABLE 6.1

Stock Issues in Factual Disputes

- What are appropriate criteria for evaluation?
- Does this particular case meet the agreed-upon criteria?

QUESTIONS OF VALUE

Questions of value involve evaluation of the relative worth or importance of something.[11] Unlike the issues of fact described previously, questions of value invite rendering a *judgment of merit*, not an assessment of fact. Disputes that center on values can be especially difficult because people tend to hold on to their values tightly and often are reluctant to consider the values of others as being as worthy or important as their own. In particular, value disputes tend to involve (1) a qualitative evaluation (for example, *good, bad, appropriate, inappropriate*) or (2) a comparison (for example, that something or someone is *better than/ more important* than someone or something else).

This seems to be a good place to note that people often mistakenly think that value judgments are "just opinion," making competing claims equal in nature and therefore irresolvable. We freely admit that evaluative arguments are often the most difficult to resolve to the satisfaction of all parties. However, they can be more easily resolved when advocates can come to some agreement about the standards by which the object under discussion is to be judged. For example, students have long argued about what constitutes a "good" professor. Some say that good professors are the ones who most readily give high grades, while others maintain that good professors are ones who seem to care, and still others will maintain that good professors are those whose classes are the most rigorous. Unless the students agree on the elements constituting a good professor, they will have difficulty getting others to share their assessment of their instructors. If students would agree that the most important element of good teaching is, for example, *fairness*, they could consider the teachers that they deemed to be fair as good teachers, and those who were less fair in their opinion as not good teachers. The process of reaching that agreement over acceptable criteria for judgment is a difficult but important part of the process. Disputes over questions of value are too important to argue from the point of uninformed opinion, nor should we dismiss well-reasoned arguments as "just your opinion." A discussion of the stock issues in value disputes should help to find a way forward in these difficult encounters.

The stock issues that follow should look very familiar. They are similar to the stock issues that guide questions of fact and are employed similarly as well, differing primarily in the *types* of criteria for evaluation that are used to resolve the question. The stock issues in a value dispute are: (1) What are the appropriate criteria for evaluation? and (2) Does this particular case meet the agreed-upon criteria? The opening example about concealed carry on campus will help us work through the stock issues for questions of value.

The first stock issue asks the advocate and audience to determine the appropriate standard for judgment. Again, sometimes arguments for a particular criterion are made explicitly, and sometimes they are embedded or implied within the argument. Look to the values that people are supporting through their arguments to discover the criteria they are implicitly using. Examples of values include safety, individual freedom, efficiency, financial gain, liberty, compliance, community, health, and a nearly infinite number of others. The criteria in the campus concealed-carry conflict often center on values like safety and freedom, and debate sometimes centers on which of those values should be considered paramount.

The second stock issue applies the specific instance under consideration to the criteria. It asks the audience to apply the criteria to assess the merit of the advocate's position. Again, an example will make these stock issues more clear. For advocates of concealed carry on campus, one of the most important criteria/values is freedom. They indicate that freedom is undermined when laws are created that remove citizens' abilities to fully enjoy their constitutional rights. For them, that which protects constitutional rights (like freedom) is to be valued above all. Specifically, they argue that we should consider how our basic freedom is enhanced or hindered by laws preventing law-abiding citizens from lawfully carrying firearms in a concealed manner. They maintain that this right, guaranteed by the Second Amendment of the Constitution, is profoundly eroded by banning concealed carry on campus. In such disputes, they argue that it is unreasonable to remove constitutional freedoms at institutions supported by the state, especially from those persons who do not have a violent history. Even if nobody perceives a risk to their own safety on a college campus, the advocates maintain that the freedom to be able to enact one's Second Amendment rights must be preserved. The two-step stock issues process would look like this:

Advocate Smith: It is important that we be allowed to carry concealed weapons on campus!

Advocate Wesson: Why do you say that?

Advocate Smith: It all comes down to protecting rights and freedom.

Advocate Wesson: Huh?

Advocate Smith: It is my constitutional right to bear arms. (evidence) Any action that protects rights is good. (criterion)

In this instance, issues of safety are not important in evaluating the argument. Such concerns are no doubt vital, but the claim was formulated in a manner that focused the argument on another issue. The criterion used will constrain available relevant arguments.

The narrative elements in this argument become clear quickly. There are compelling characters: law-abiding citizens concerned with self-protection versus anti-freedom zealots who would crush the Constitution with their naive gun-banning policies. The situation centers on a political climate characterized as hostile to individual rights. The narrators are protectors of the Constitution. These are interwoven as they support the larger narrative: to disallow concealed carry on campus would undermine one of America's most basic freedoms.

Opponents to concealed carry on campuses often argue that freedom is *not* the most important value—safety is. They suggest that the safety of people on campus is the best way to judge whether or not we should allow concealed carry there, arguing that the safety of the community is put in jeopardy when there are more guns on campus. Dismissing the assertions that concealed carry is a deterrent to campus shooters or possibly an antidote to them, opponents point to the responsibility of the university to keep students as safe as possible—something that is much more difficult to do with a proliferation of firearms on campus. The two-step stock issues process looks like this for opponents:

Advocate Wesson: I disagree with your belief that protecting Second Amendment rights is the most important issue.

Advocate Smith: What do you mean?

Advocate Wesson: Protecting the safety of members of the campus community must be our most important concern (criterion).

Advocate Smith: Yes, but guns in the hands of law-abiding citizens offer needed protection and security.

Advocate Wesson: I don't think that is true on college campuses, where guns may fall into the hands of people who are depressed, drunk, or suicidal, and that could be disastrous.

Narrative elements in this argument are clearly present as well. The characters are vulnerable college students, prone to drunkenness and mental illness. The situation is one unique to college campuses in its density of these characters and special status as a designated place of learning and safety, set apart from outside forces. The narrators are only interested in the safety of those in their charge.

As we noted earlier, value disputes are especially difficult to resolve because people value different things. Determining which value is the most appropriate value on which to base a decision is often the most difficult component of resolving a question of value. It shouldn't surprise us that pro- and anticampus concealed-carry advocates have diverging values. It is easier when we can agree on a primary value, as disputants in the concealed-carry campus debate sometimes do. When not arguing that concealed carry protects constitutional freedoms, concealed-carry advocates may co-opt the criterion of safety, noting the greater protection brought to a campus by legions of responsible gun owners. While the anticarry contingent argues that more guns decrease safety due to the increases in suicide and deadly assault associated with a higher density of gun ownership, proponents insist that a well-armed campus deters potential shooters and provides on-the-scene response, which could very well cut a shooter down before he or she has done the maximum damage. If both sides agree that the audience should judge it based on one criterion—in this case, safety—we can argue about which position brings about the greatest amount of (or greatest quality of) safety.

Often, it is productive to argue based on the values proposed by another, or to recognize the values held by the audience in general—the ones that you know concern them the most—and show them how your position supports their goals as well.

Issues of value can masquerade (or are depicted by other advocates) as issues of fact. By now you can see the difference, but perhaps also you will notice how easy it is to claim that it is a "fact" that something "is good," for example. An advocate who can recognize that the controversy turns on a value-based term is better prepared to refute such claims and to bring more nuance and accuracy to the engagement.

TABLE 6.2
Stock Issues in Value Disputes

- What are appropriate criteria for evaluation?
- Does this particular case meet the agreed-upon criteria?

QUESTIONS OF POLICY

If you've ever said, "Someone should *do* something about that!" or offered your own suggestion for solving a problem, you have entered the realm of policy argument.[12] The bills in state legislatures to change the laws around concealed carry on campuses fall into this category. By definition, the questions taken up by decision-making bodies concern what course of action (if any) should be taken. Federal and state legislatures make policy, but so do school boards, city councils, neighborhood associations, and even families. In both formal and informal situations, people argue vigorously about the necessity of doing something, what to do, and the benefits and the drawbacks of particular courses of action. We consider **questions of policy** every day.

Stock Issues in Policy Disputes

It is helpful to think about policy issues through a stock issues model: (1) Is there a significant **problem** that should be addressed? (problem); (2) Will this problem go away on its own without a change in the current system, or is the system itself flawed in ways that prevent correction of the problem? Will this problem persist because people's beliefs/attitudes prevent them from acting in ways to resolve it? (inherency); (3) What would correct the problem? (plan); and (4) What negative consequences does the proposed action have, and do those consequences outweigh the benefits we gain by solving the problem? (disadvantages).

Traditionally, advocates use the stock issues model to support and oppose a course of action. Those stock issues highlight the types of questions most often addressed in controversies over policy. Stock issues draw attention to elements that can constitute a plausible narrative by highlighting concerns that determine the wisdom of acting and mirror the concerns most listeners expect to have addressed.

To illustrate, let's return to our concealed carry on campus example. The bills proposed in legislatures across the country are centered on enacting policy that would mandate that state-funded universities allow students, faculty, and staff with the appropriate permits to carry concealed weapons on campuses, though, as in the one recently passed in Georgia, there sometimes are restrictions as to *where* on campuses (residence halls constitute one exception). As we work our way through the stock issues associated with policy argument, you will see how the arguments for the policy center on the stock issues of problem, inherency, plan, and disadvantages.

Problem

Is there a significant problem that requires action? There must be a significant problem to justify a change in policy. We do not change policies on a whim—it is too disruptive and expensive. There needs to be a compelling reason to go about the difficult work of changing how something is done. The work of Richard Whatley on presumption and burden of proof referenced earlier in the text provides a useful theoretical grounding here. According to Whatley, presumption rests with the current system (status quo), and those who would argue for change must meet a burden of proof as they attempt to overcome presumption against change.[13] The first burden for advocates offering a new policy is proving that there is a very real and compelling need to change the way that things are done. Sometimes, such problems can be proven quantitatively—as in many people are being injured. Proponents of concealed carry on campus will note that there were 23 campus shootings in 2015 alone, with 19 people killed and even more injured.[14] If the numbers are not sufficiently startling or compelling, the need for a policy can also be justified by the *quality of harm*. College students/faculty/staff with bright futures ahead of them were killed in the halls of learning, without a means to protect themselves. Compared to the number of people who populate university campuses, the number is few—but the quality of the injury is significant. In the current example, the problem also may be tied to the damage a ban has on the inherent right people have to protect themselves, some concealed-carry proponents argue, demonstrating the threat against the constitutional right to bear arms as the problem.[15]

Proof of a significant problem is often realized in the way that the argumentative narrative is constructed. Often, the plot is constructed to demonstrate the problem, and the scene and characters rendered, to dramatically support the case that a condition desperately needs to be addressed. In the campus concealed-carry controversy, these elements are not difficult to envision. On one side, the concealed-carry proponents weave a narrative depicting a world in which an alarming number of horrific campus shootings have made the occurrences nearly routine news, always with the same story line—a disgruntled individual shows up on campus, armed with an arsenal and a plan to kill. The killer moves methodically around campus, shooting random helpless students in the prime of their lives and faculty members whose only concern has been teaching, and possibly, protecting their students. Victims are sitting ducks who are unable to protect themselves and must wait on a response from police who do what they can but are inevitably too late to limit the body count. Gun advocates suggest that this has happened repeatedly and will continue to happen—perhaps at a campus near you—until something is done. The accounts often are supported with startling statistics and first-person testimony. The dramatic rendering of the problem makes a case to act to protect our communities of learning. How the problem is rendered is critical to the rest of the argument.

Inherency

Sometimes, problems correct themselves without intervention. Often, however, there are laws or attitudes that prevent self-correction. This facet of policy analysis is known as **inherency** and considers what conditions in the current system prevent the problem from being corrected. If the system will correct the problem on its own, there may not be a need to institute a new policy. Flaws in the system that prevent self-correction are termed **structural inherency**. That is, there is a fatal flaw—usually in existing laws—that prevents action.

Let's consider the structural inherency in the campus concealed-carry debate. Remember, because concealed carry on campus is not the current state of affairs (the **status quo**), it is the burden of those proposing change to demonstrate that there is a reason to act. Part of that burden is proving that the problem cannot be solved without intervention. The structural inherency in this case centers on the laws that either restrict concealed carry or, more accurately, leave the decision to university administrators. In short, structural inherency is one reason why people are unlikely to suddenly begin to carry concealed weapons on campus, since university regulations prevent them from doing so.

There are times, however, when the structure is not a barrier—but the attitudes, beliefs, or behaviors of the people in the system prevent it from working to correct the problem. This is **attitudinal inherency**. Attitudes are often as much of a barrier to changing the way things are done as are structures. Changing attitudes is more difficult than structural change and sometimes a required precursor to workable social change.

There are several easily identified attitudinal elements that have kept concealed carry from being embraced by campuses. Attitudinal barriers to concealed carry include beliefs that (1) campuses are generally safe places (the risk of these types of events is low), (2) increased numbers of guns on campus make campuses less safe, and (3) limits to the Second Amendment are appropriate.

The issue of inherency finds its way into everyday arguments with surprising frequency. For example, "we must stage an intervention because Mary won't acknowledge her substance abuse problem" or "we should buy Grandma a new coat because she would never spend the money on herself" both acknowledge the importance of attitudinal barriers.

Even if the structural barriers are eliminated, attitudinal barriers can remain, which can seriously undermine a new policy's success. Believing in these notions is a common justification offered for university-created prohibitions on weapons. The Eighteenth Amendment passed in 1920 to prohibit the drinking of alcohol is an apt example. The structure (law) had been changed but attitudes had not. The law was circumvented by many and eventually repealed by passage of the Twenty-First Amendment in 1933, ending Prohibition. In short, advocates must not only address the structural issues at play but should also pay close attention to the "hearts and minds" of their audience to increase the likelihood that their policy will enjoy success.

Characters and *scene* are often central narrative elements in constructing compelling arguments around issues of inherency. Inherency is based in systemic elements (rules made by people) and attitudes (dispositions of people). Consider, in particular, the villains and heroes. Who won't let the system change? Why won't they let the system change? Who is trying to help? Answering these questions will help you select and present arguments that assist in demonstrating inherency. Then, determine the best way to depict the major players in your narrative. Are the obstructers "evil" or "uninformed"? Will the audience initially identify with them or with you? Similarly, scene can be very important in establishing inherency and provides an opportunity to offer context to the entire rhetorical narrative by explaining why things are stuck where they are. Consider how the various types of scenic elements, be they place-based, social environment-based, or time-based, can provide the type of context that reveals justification and motive. For example, these "violent times we live in" with "gun violence on the rise," when "police are out-gunned by criminals" are all elements of scene that are woven into the rhetorical narratives of campus concealed-carry advocates. In this case, the scene provides justification quite directly and also clearly indicates motives of key characters. Scene can contribute significantly to a compelling discussion of the structural or attitudinal reasons the problem will not be solved without intervention.

Plan

Even those who have been convinced that there is a significant problem that persists absent corrective action (inherency) will need to be convinced that a viable solution is available (plan). Consider, for example, how the rush by some to repeal "Obamacare" slowed considerably when the discussion shifted to "What do we replace it with?" When advocates have a specific way of changing things that will correct the problems to which they have drawn attention, they offer a **plan**. People usually want to know the details of a plan before they decide to support it, so make sure that you've considered it thoroughly and offer sufficient detail to convince your listener. For example, what exactly will be done? Who/what will be responsible for the plan? How will the plan be paid for? How will the plan overcome the obvious obstacles in its way? Does the plan address the causes of the problems? The agonizing decision by a family to put an elderly loved one in an extended care facility illustrates all of the questions we have just posed.

In 2016, House Bill 859, a concealed-carry-on-campus bill, passed both houses of the Georgia legislature and moved to the governor's desk.[16] The official summary of the bill was:

> A BILL to be entitled an Act to amend Part 3 of Article 4 of Chapter 11 of Title 16 of the Official Code of Georgia Annotated, relating to carrying and possession of firearms, so as to authorize the carrying and possession of certain weapons by weapons carry license holders in or on certain buildings or real property owned by or leased to public institutions of postsecondary education; to provide for related matters; to repeal conflicting laws; and for other purposes.[17]

This plan is fairly straightforward, though the summary's language is admittedly a bit obtuse. In short, the legislation allows anyone 21 years or older with a proper permit to carry a gun anywhere on a state-supported (public) college or university, with the exceptions of the living areas (i.e., residence halls, fraternity and sorority houses) and athletic events.[18] The summary makes some very important details clear: (1) It indicates *what* should happen—conflicting laws will be repealed so that those authorized to possess and carry weapons on campus can lawfully do so, in certain buildings, on property owned by or leased to public institutions; (2) it specifies *who* can carry—"weapons carry license holders"; and (3) it indicates and limits *where*—"certain buildings or real property." Those buildings or property are clearly stated in the original bill,[19] though only generally stated in the summary. In short, the synopsis lays out what the legislature was voting on and what the policy would be if the bill was passed. As a side note, did you notice the part about repealing conflicting laws? That is the bill's authors addressing the issue of structural inherency.

Disadvantages

Advocates often argue against a course of action by suggesting that the proposal is unclear, vague, or impractical, or it fails to address the causes of the problem it was designed to cure. In narrative terms, they are arguing the equivalent of "this will never work" because either the structure of the plan is not sound—the pieces haven't been well thought out (narrative probability)—or because even though the structure of the plan *might* be sound, the listeners' experience tells them that such solutions have not worked in the past (narrative fidelity). These are the types of ideas that get hashed out when advocates try to sell the actual plan as the best way forward to potentially skeptical listeners. In some circles, scholars would include issues of practicality, workability, or feasibility as separate stock concerns (or an issue discussed under the stock issue of plan). We include them under the issue of disadvantages based on the assumption that devoting time, money, and energy to a proposal that doesn't work is, in essence, a **disadvantage** (a costly waste of time).

If we are to convince people to implement a new policy, it is important that the solution offered corrects the problems that demand attention. The policy may have other advantages as well, so telling an audience about those added benefits can be quite helpful to the argument. In the debates regarding concealed carry on campus, proponents of the plan have argued that it will help to solve the problem of mass campus shootings and therein make people safer.[20] The injury and death tolls would decrease, proponents argue, or the events avoided altogether if only responsible gun owners were allowed to carry concealed weapons. If shootings do happen, at least individuals are able to protect themselves. In this way, the plan solves the problem and also further supports and protects the Second Amendment. Notice that although the proposal is a policy question, it contains elements of factual and value disputes. It is not uncommon for arguments to represent chains of reasoning, where claims—once accepted—become the grounds (support) for other claims.

Finally, it is important to consider the drawbacks of implementing the proposed plan. The listeners certainly will. Discovering and presenting the undesirable consequences of the plan will better prepare listeners to make an educated judgment. Moreover, listeners may be entertaining reservations about your proposal, and it is wise to find a way to diffuse them. At the very least, a discussion of the drawbacks enhances the advocate's credibility by demonstrating the scope of the advocate's preparation and may immunize listeners to counterarguments that they may face in the future. In the campus concealed-carry case, listeners will weigh the advantages of secured liberty and increased safety (if they have been convinced that your plan will provide them) against the drawbacks of the policy.

Those who are skeptical about concealed carry on campus will likely consider the disadvantages that might result from implementation. They might argue that the proposal would *not*, in fact, solve the problem of increasing gun violence on campus, bringing evidence that centers on the psychological state of the person who commits this crime. They might also productively imagine a world in which the particular policy was implemented and all of the terrible things that might likely result. Concealed-carry-on-campus opponents often cite the increased danger on campuses posed by an increase in guns in general. They point out that the rate of death by suicide increases when people own or have easy access to guns,[21] and that guns and alcohol are often a deadly combination. They suggest that the financial expenditures required in the form of additional security at meetings and events is cost prohibitive, and that even campus security officials oppose concealed carry on campus.[22]

Those opposed to campus concealed carry often render their disadvantages in vivid narrative terms. In their plot, frightened faculty members teach class each day to armed students who are just waiting for a professor to espouse an opinion with which they disagree or give them a poor grade so that they can shoot the place up. Professors will avoid controversial ideas which, in turn, limits learning opportunities. Residence halls are transformed into Wild West saloons, where a combination of alcohol and guns results in injuries and death on a regular basis. Although guns are banned in residence halls, "Where do you think they will be stored?" they ask. Furthermore, the increasing number of students with mental health issues have easy access to firearms and may use the deadly weapons as a way out of their temporary crises.[23]

Thoughtful people make complicated mental calculations when it comes to policy decisions. They begin with, "Do I believe there is a problem—one that won't correct itself (inherency)?" and if they think there is, move to, "Does this plan sound like a reasonable way to solve the problem? Will the plan work? Are the risks or disadvantages of the proposal too great to warrant trying it?" In the final analysis, policy decisions involve the audience's calculation of the advantages (solving a significant problem) versus the disadvantages created by the policy. But those calculations are not made in a vacuum nor are they capricious. *How* the audience comes to understand the problem, inherency, plan, advantages, and disadvantages rests on how skillfully the rhetorical narrative is developed and communicated.

TABLE 6.3

Stock Issues in Policy Disputes

- Is there significant harm that must be addressed (problem)?
- Will the problem persist absent corrective action (inherency)?
  - Do current laws/structures ensure the continuation of the problem?
  - Do current attitudes ensure continuation of the problem?
- Will the proposed solution solve the problem (plan)?
- Do the benefits of the policy outweigh its drawbacks (disadvantages)?

Considering Narrative Elements in Questions of Policy

Thinking about policy issues through the stock issues lens also helps us consider issues of narrative probability and fidelity. Some issues of problem and inherency are issues of narrative probability. Concerned with the realm of the plausible, narratives that have narrative probability are classified as such because the argumentative narrative is consistent with other reliable narratives, is free from internal contradiction, and has characters that act according to their ascribed motives. That isn't to say that issues of fidelity are not important as well. The description of the problem and the reasons that it will not go away on its own also need to align with the audience members' understanding of the world if they are to believe that the situation needs to be changed. In short, audiences expect stock issues to be addressed before they consider a narrative to be complete and logical. People will often admit that an idea is a good one that would work in theory but deny that it would work in the real world because they do not believe that the world works in a way that would support the plan. Convincing a skeptical audience of the fidelity of an argument (that it could work) is often more difficult than convincing the audience of its probability (that it is technically possible). Those seemingly endless and irresolvable arguments about the government's economic policies are clear illustrations of how an audience's narrative vision influences their willingness to accept particular courses of action. Extending welfare and unemployment benefits is consistently opposed by those who believe that a substantial number of people, given the opportunity, would cheat the system or choose handouts over hard work. On the other hand, proposals based on the assumption that unrestrained free-market capitalism will benefit the country are consistently opposed by those who believe that corporate greed always trumps corporate responsibility. Notice how in each of the preceding examples the audience is responding in predictable ways given the narrative paradigm—on one hand, a belief that particular characters (welfare recipients and corporations) behave according to type illustrates narrative probability; on the other hand, the fact that these arguers could doubtless point to numerous examples or counternarratives is a measure of the potency of narrative fidelity. Ultimately, the narrative elements need to be woven in ways that carefully introduce and support a worldview with which the audience can identify and that simultaneously opens them to seeing the merit of your proposal.

When arguing about regulating Wall Street or reforming the tax code, the conflicting narratives routinely cast the same characters in different roles. Whether Wall Street and big business are the gluttonous villains that take advantage of the people to feed an insatiable appetite for profit, the heroes that generate jobs and keep America prosperous, or the victims of overzealous regulation and petty jealousy all depend on which interest is narrating the story. Scenic elements also depend on the perspective and goals of the advocate; some suggest an environment in which the public is highly dissatisfied that the very rich seem to play by different rules, with the opposing narrative's scene set as one in which governmental overregulation and overreach have made business so difficult to conduct that it has ground the economy to a halt and threatens the future of the nation.[24]

Policy analysis and discussion are mistakenly viewed as issues important only to politicians and to the policy wonks who populate think tanks. Even they know, however, that good analysis is unlikely to be persuasive unless a general audience finds a reason to care about and identify with the issues. The public can and does care about crafting good policy at all levels. Presenting arguments that acknowledge the ways in which people reason narratively, not just formally, is important in policy argument as well. In fact, arguing about policies provides incredibly rich material for constructing compelling rhetorical narratives. Those advocates who recognize this are significantly advantaged over those who consider policy work as sterile, logical exercises devoid of real-world experiences and applications.

After all of this talk of grand policy deliberation, it is worthy of reminder that formal deliberative bodies are not the only ones that do the hard work of policy making. When your significant other says, "I'm bored (problem), there is nothing to do around the house (inherency) so we should go to dinner and a movie (plan) since it would be fun, and we can afford it because I got paid today (advantages/disadvantages)," you are about to have a policy dispute, especially if you would rather stay home.

CONCLUSION

We ignore the narrative assumptions that underpin our advocacy and that of others at our own peril. Failing to understand and consider differing perspectives leaves the basis of our arguments unexamined. That becomes more problematic when we encounter circumstances or co-arguers whose advocacy is based on a different point of view entirely. At their heart, we believe that most disputes are about what people value and the perspective from which they argue. As we stressed in the opening chapter, understanding what assumptions are critical to your own advocacy and appreciating the views of your co-arguers will help you more effectively resolve the issues at hand. That knowledge allows understanding and insight, even though it might not bring agreement. With that insight, a thoughtful advocate can understand the paths available for advocacy. It might be to hold firm to "their" value, insisting on its supremacy, or it might be to step into the values of the audience or co-arguer to determine how you can achieve your overarching

goals by translating your needs into their narrative and values. Perhaps a final example will make this clearer.

In one of the first argumentation classes taught by one of the authors, there was a student who regularly came to class only minimally prepared, rarely participated, and generally acted as though the whole endeavor was a giant bore. Perhaps it was. Regardless, I was very surprised the day she came to me after class and said, "You're right—you have to figure out what they value." She proceeded to tell me that besides being a full-time college student and holding down a part-time job, she was the full-time caregiver for both of her bedridden parents. She had been fighting with Medicare for months, trying to get relief in the form of overnight care. If she could just get someone to help her overnight, she thought, she could do the rest of it—including graduating from college, supporting herself, and maintaining some modicum of sanity. Medicare kept telling her that money for overnight help was not available and did not seem to care that she was wholly overwhelmed and beginning to flounder. Finally at her breaking point, she sat down to consider the values that were in conflict. Medicare, she decided, valued the bottom line. It didn't value her quality of life. Not her sanity. Not her ability to finish college. Not her ability to support herself with a part-time job. Not the quality of care that she wanted to provide for her parents. Not keeping her parents together in the family home. It valued money. So she made her next appeal based on *that* value instead of trying to get Medicare to accept *her* value as paramount. Knowing that she had no legal responsibility for her parents, she told Medicare that she was going to stop taking care of her parents and place them in a care facility for which Medicare would legally be required to pay. She researched the cost of full-time care for two adults and compared it to the cost of overnight care. The difference was immense. She presented her findings to the caseworker, and with that information in hand, Medicare granted the request immediately. Her parents had overnight care one week later. She had determined what was important to Medicare and decided to argue on those terms. She may have lost the satisfaction of Medicare valuing her point of view, but she achieved her goal of quality care for her parents and relief for herself. Sometimes, translating your needs into others' values can make all the difference.

In this dispute, a compelling narrative stressed policy stock issues. With all disputes, it can be productive to consider stock arguments the audience might reasonably expect you to address. With fact or value controversies, arguers must agree on a criterion and apply it to the issue at hand. In policy disputes, the decisions often center on the advantages versus disadvantages of a course of action. Problem, inherency, plan, and disadvantages are key components of a well-rounded policy discussion.

QUESTIONS FOR CONSIDERATION

1. Find an example of how a supposedly settled factual issue later became contested. (Conflicting research over nutrition and new medical research would be a productive area of discussion.)

2. How does the debate over increased surveillance as a means of combating terrorism reflect a clash over values?

3. View or read Barbara Jordan's "Statement on the Articles of Impeachment of Richard Nixon." What standard/criterion does Jordan put forth? How does she argue for her point using that criterion?

4. Imagine you are about to purchase a new automobile. What criteria would influence your decision? Are there other criteria that you did not consider that would have resulted in a different decision? Why did you decide not to consider these contrary criteria?

5. Those who support an unrestricted right to bear arms often use the commonplace "when guns are outlawed, only outlaws will have guns." How is this narrative constructed?

6. In the competing narratives over causes and consequences of climate change, some have argued that climate change is not caused by people. How does this influence their narrative against regulation of pollution as a means of combating global warming?

7. Looking at the issue of attitudinal inherency, consider why *Roe v. Wade* failed to settle the issue of a woman's right to choose an abortion.

KEY TERMS

7 Supporting Arguments

During a failed bid for the Republican presidential nomination in 2012, former Pennsylvania Senator Rick Santorum took issue with President Obama's comment that a college education should be within everyone's reach by proclaiming, "President Obama once said he wants everyone in America to go to college. What a snob."[1] Calling Santorum's claim that Obama is a snob a reasoned argument would be a charitable description. What Santorum offers is an **assertion**—"something declared or stated positively, often with no support or attempt at proof."[2]

We have suggested that there is a difference between **opinion** and **informed opinion**. The latter is a judgment justified by pointing to the evidence upon which the opinion is based; the former is often arbitrary or based on incomplete data. We cannot know with certainty whether or not Santorum is offering an informed opinion. Therein lies the problem, since he does not clearly share his reasons with the audience. It is perhaps more helpful to differentiate between *assertion* and *argument*. Santorum shares his opinion; however, what makes his assertion suspect is the lack of outside support to sustain his claim. Santorum explains himself but does so with even more assertions that seem to be a bit of a stretch. Why is Obama a "snob"? Because he wants everyone to go to college. Even if we give Santorum the benefit of the doubt and classify his statements as an argument (claim plus reasons), it is a claim that goes well beyond what his evidence will allow, since Obama's original statement was that everyone should have the *opportunity* to attend college, which is a bit different from saying everyone *should* attend.

Around the same time that Santorum made his remarks, *The Baltimore Sun* ran a series of articles (as did a number of popular press outlets) suggesting that for some would-be students, attending college may not be a wise choice given the high costs, student debt, and discouraging prospects for employment. Considerable economic data supported their claim. Santorum's assertion, however, presents no outside data in support.[3]

The use of **outside support** (that is, evidence that does not originate with the advocate) is the subject of this chapter. We will consider the difference between opinion and informed opinion, suggesting that support is a key ingredient in the formulation—and ultimately the persuasiveness—of argumentative claims.

WHEN DO I NEED TO USE OUTSIDE SUPPORT?

It is difficult to imagine an argument that is not improved with the addition of outside support. However, the amount and type of evidence necessary varies according to the reputation of the advocate, the disposition of the audience being addressed, the contestability of the claim being offered, or the forum and field in which the argument is made. When we assign research reports or require that students use outside support in their speeches, we are immediately asked, "How much do I need?" Students express frustration when we begin our answer with, "Well, it depends . . ." We do elaborate but constantly stress the speaker's role in making an appropriate decision.

Advocates who possess high initial credibility owing to their knowledge of and experience with the topic being discussed, reputation for accuracy, ability to keep their own biases from interfering with their judgment, and goodwill toward the audience are often given the benefit of the doubt. They are, in narrative terms, considered reliable narrators. On the other hand, speakers who lack credibility with their audience are held to a more rigorous standard reserved for unreliable narrators. Put simply, speakers who embody the healthy argumentative perspective outlined in this book have a distinct advantage in that the evidentiary demands they are expected to meet may be less than those required of a less informed speaker. We hasten to add that it is irresponsible to exploit that advantage at the expense of a reasoned, well-supported argument.

An audience's disposition toward the speaker and subject can range from sympathetic to indifferent to hostile. The greater the gap between the speaker's position and the opinion of the audience, the more essential evidence becomes. Outside support is more potent when it allows advocates to align their opinions with the opinions of sources that are likely to be respected by the audience. Returning to the Santorum example, it is worth noting that he was addressing a forum populated with activists from the conservative Americans for Prosperity Foundation and enjoyed a degree of credibility with that group. The audience shared his beliefs about an elitist president and was not at all skeptical of his subsequent praise for ". . . good decent men and women . . . that aren't taught by some liberal college professor trying to indoctrinate them," and accepted the conclusion, "Oh I understand why he [Obama] wants you to go to college. He wants to remake you in his image."[4] Why the scarcity of quality evidence and reasoning from Santorum? The audience was predisposed to Santorum's position and shared his hostility toward the president, so he likely felt little need to provide outside support. He was effective in that particular situation (though he did not seriously contend for his party's nomination). The problem with his stance is that it turns the audience into an **echo chamber** rather than reflective participants in an argument exchange. It is difficult to imagine Santorum's proclamation gaining significant traction with a more critical audience.

Initially, you may have questioned the comparability of the Santorum/*Baltimore Sun* examples. You would be right, since forum and field strongly influenced the content of the arguments. Santorum was making a political speech in the midst of a contested Republican primary in which he was attempting to exploit his opponent's (Mitt Romney) inability to connect with blue-collar voters. Unfortunately, hyperbole is not uncommon in political contests. On the other hand, despite what many think about the ideological leanings of the media, most outlets follow a journalistic code that demands that claims are based on solid evidence that has received some verification. Additionally, *The Baltimore Sun* article was not an editorial and as a consequence was reporting on a condition. The *Sun's* intent was to inform, while Santorum's intent was to motivate. Both arguments were constrained by the expectations of field and forum in which they took place. Different circumstances tend to elicit different arguments, and awareness of those constraints helps advocates better use situation-specific standards for evaluation and construction of arguments. Nonetheless, we don't want to provide a convenient rationalization for advocates who offer ill-considered ideas. Support of some kind is appropriate in most circumstances even though it appears that standards for what constitutes responsible advocacy seem to have deteriorated. Although the amount of outside support the advocate should use is influenced by speaker, audience, forum, and field, this does not give advocates license to limit their research because they believe they will be speaking in a circumstance where the evidentiary demands are modest. Responsible advocates are expected to be knowledgeable about their subject. Ethical advocates are expected to be confident in the truth of their claims and willing to explain them when asked.

The advocate's most valuable commodity is his or her ability to offer listeners an informed opinion rather than merely a gut reaction. Careful research characterizes ethically responsible argumentation. Even when addressing true believers, it is suspect to pander to an audience by offering clichés and commonplaces that have become so ingrained that people are no longer willing or able to reflect on their reasonableness. Even in rhetorically safe environments, advocates should be confident that they can coherently explain the basis of their claims. If the audience does not demand good reasons of the speaker, advocates should demand them of themselves.

WHY DO I NEED TO USE OUTSIDE SUPPORT?

Think of outside support in terms of its impact on speaker credibility. Knowledge or competence is one standard by which an audience assesses the advocate's credibility, so it follows that when advocates demonstrate their knowledge, the audience is likely to be impressed. It is not enough that the speaker has outside support; the audience must be aware that the advocate possesses it. Giving credit to outside sources of information that the audience will find credible requires that sources be cited orally if the argument is spoken instead of written; the audience cannot *see* quotation marks or a written bibliography. Successful advocates also make their experience and level of knowledge apparent to the audience without appearing arrogant.

Outside Support Checks Potential Speaker Bias

Generally, we argue about matters that are important to us and about which we have strong opinions. Passion productively drives the advocate's preparation and presentation. On the other hand, advocates must realize that their strongly held opinions can prove to be a liability if they create blind spots to competing points of view or distort the interpretation of available information. For the open-minded advocate, the research process provides a needed reality check against the potentially corrosive influence of his or her own preconceived notions.

It is not enough to have an opinion, conduct a quick Google search to confirm it, and then call it quits. Those who do so are conducting research in a quest for endorsements rather than conducting an investigation. Lazy advocates live in fear that they will encounter contrary information that will force them to reflect on their opinions, and in the interest of expediency may make the ethically suspect decision to ignore inconvenient facts. Responsible advocates embrace competing ideas and think through ambiguities to arrive at an informed judgment. There is plenty of information out there, but research need not be endless. We propose ideas when we are *reasonably* confident in their accuracy. When research reaches a point where we encounter redundant accounts, assuming we have not intentionally avoided sources of information that may express judgments at odds with our own, we can feel confident that we have made a good-faith effort at investigation. Of course, the research process is ongoing for advocates who are willing to modify opinions in light of the new ideas that they encounter.

Outside Support Builds Audience Trust

Being well prepared signals the speaker's goodwill toward the audience by taking them seriously. We have probably all been subjected to speakers who disappoint us because of the seemingly unprepared nature of their comments. Maybe you have worked with a group that asked its members to come to the next meeting prepared to discuss a particular point only to have subsequent deliberations derailed by members who have not done their homework. Such encounters often result in feelings of anger and resentment. We may wonder to ourselves, "Do they think so little of us that they willingly disrespect us by wasting our time?"

If an audience's initial reaction to the speaker and his or her ideas is one of indifference or hostility, the use of outside support is essential. The audience may not be predisposed to believe the speaker but will be more receptive to ideas that align the speaker with outside sources that the audience will find compelling. At the very least, novel ideas are more difficult for an audience to dismiss if they are endorsed by respected others.

Outside Support Makes Your Presentation More Interesting

Just as audiences are impressed by speakers who are dynamic, they are also more likely to be moved by evidence that is dynamic. Statistics that border on the surprising, testimony that is fresh and elegant, or examples that are engaging carry greater persuasive impact. They also carry greater risk. Statistics or examples that are so surprising that they strain credulity (lack narrative rationality) might be dismissed. Dramatic testimony grabs attention, but statements that are too dramatic may come across as exaggeration. Advocates who believe that they are somehow insulated from the backlash from audiences that react with disbelief to counterintuitive statistics or incendiary testimony because, after all, "someone else said it" are sadly mistaken.

Outside Support Provides Reasons to Question Existing Beliefs and Narratives

Finally, the use of outside support is valuable in that it can provide reasons for an audience to question the vision of the world that dominates their thinking. As we discussed earlier in the text, people consider both the plausibility (narrative probability) of an argument/narrative as well as how well it matches what they believe to be true in the world. Sometimes, the argument we are trying to make is decidedly incongruent with the way that the audience understands the world. Take, for example, an advocate who is trying to persuade parents who come from generations who believed the adage "spare the rod, spoil the child" that alternative forms of behavior management would be more effective and appropriate. In such cases, clear, compelling, and undeniable support is the astute advocate's primary tool for inducing a willingness of reluctant audience members to question their own predispositions. One criticism often leveled at narrative paradigm centers on the concept of narrative fidelity. If an audience's understanding and experiences in the world are limited or otherwise flawed, critics point out, how could they be persuaded to believe a good or even objectively true argument that did not conform to their beliefs about the world? The answer, we think, is to introduce the audience to such compelling support or examples that they cannot help but reconsider the basis on which they are judging the narrative.

Having established that advocates should research thoroughly and utilize the fruits of that research in their arguments, it is now appropriate to consider the options available to the speaker in selecting support.

TABLE 7.1

The Rationale for Outside Support

- Encourages fair and comprehensive treatment of subject
  - Exposes areas where advocates' personal bias constrains fairness
  - Encourages consideration of alternate viewpoints
  - Allows greater probability that the speaker has been thorough in his or her research
- Enhances the audience's trust in the advocate
  - Shows the advocate took the audience seriously enough to prepare
  - Aligns advocates' ideas with those of trusted others
- Adds interest to presentation
  - Provides evidence that is dynamic/elegant
  - Provides evidence that is fresh/unique/surprising
- Provides reasons to question existing beliefs and narratives
  - Points out flaws in existing narratives
  - Provides new information to counter existing narratives

GENERAL EVALUATION OF OUTSIDE SUPPORT

Roman philosopher Cicero is credited with codifying the **canons of rhetoric**.[5] Just as the term *literary canon* refers to those significant and influential works with which the "well-educated" literary scholar should be familiar, the rhetorical canon designates those areas that should be mastered by those who want to become effective speakers. The canon includes invention, arrangement, style, delivery, and memory, and provides the basic framework for most contemporary texts on public speaking and argumentation and debate. The topic of **invention**—finding things to say—is especially relevant here. You may recall our earlier reference to Aristotle, who equates the art of rhetoric with discovering the available means of persuasion. In a word, invention. According to Aristotle, the foundation of persuasion is proof, which he characterized as **artistic** (originating with the speaker) and **inartistic** (proof not originating with the speaker such as witnesses, written contracts, admissions secured through coercion, etc.).[6] The distinction between the two is significant in its insistence that persuasive argument is not simply an uninspired recitation of data (inartistic proof) but an artistic endeavor that requires the advocate to extract logical claims from available information. Outside support is important, but the skill and imagination of the advocate are critical. Remember that evidence supplements but does not replace the advocate's need to offer clear, logical, well-reasoned arguments. In the following section, we consider lines of investigation that could profitably be used regardless of the type of outside support the advocate is employing.

Does the Evidence Support the Conclusion?

Evidence should clearly support the conclusion drawn from it by the advocate. Too often, speakers offer dramatic claims that go well beyond the scope of the evidence upon which they are based. Such was clearly the case in the Santorum claim that begins this chapter. Unless we listen carefully, we are easily misled. Perhaps listeners are simply wowed by the invocation of evidence and don't listen critically to its content. Perhaps advocates' desire to offer dramatic claims leads them to unintentionally overstate their evidence. Much to our embarrassment, critical listeners will call us on it, but even if they didn't, responsible advocates try to avoid misleading overstatement. Remember that the purpose of argument is, in collaboration with others, to reach sound decisions. The "garbage in, garbage out" cliché is appropriate here. The next chapter details criteria by which examples, statistics, and testimony should be evaluated as we demonstrate the various ways support offered by the advocate can fall short of supporting the conclusion the advocate wishes listeners to reach.

Is the Author of the Outside Support Credible?

The author of the evidence should be credible. Outside support should enhance the reputation of the advocate. We have previously discussed the dimensions of credibility important to the audience's assessment of the advocate, and we should bear in mind that those same dimensions factor into an audience's evaluation of the outside support used by the speaker. Outside support should be drawn from people whom the audience will consider knowledgeable, who have a reputation for accuracy, and who are relatively free from biases that would render their conclusions suspect. It is not out of the question that advocates we initially respect can be diminished by sources that they rely on to support their arguments. Our disappointment not only calls into question the supposed knowledge of the advocate but may even cause us to reevaluate our stance on the ideas the speaker expresses, even if we were initially willing to embrace those claims. If our reaction to the advocate is to wonder, "Is that the best you can do?" it shakes our confidence in ideas with which we used to be comfortable. More frequently, we look with disbelief on the rogue's gallery of sources utilized and conclude that we would just as soon not have our ideas or opinions associated with sources we find to be uninformed and unreliable.

Is the Publication From Which the Information is Drawn Reliable?

Primary and Secondary Sources

The distinction between primary and secondary sources is critical to the advocate. When locating outside support, **primary sources** are a much safer bet. For example, data and conclusions taken from experimental or survey research are best drawn from the published reports from those who actually conducted the research (primary source). When using remarks someone made in a speech or formal hearing, look first to the speech text, or court or hearing transcripts (primary source). The alternative is use of **secondary sources** that feature someone else's account of what the author of the evidence said. Newspapers, books, or magazines are commonly used secondary sources where the reader must trust the judgment of a third party—the author of the article—to report the information faithfully. Consider whether the information was taken out of context or misquoted by the author of the story. Do the conclusions or statements reported represent the true intent of the primary source? Advocates have substituted someone else's judgment for their own when they rely on secondary sources. Since advocates are ultimately responsible for what they say, secondary sources are a risky venture. For the speaker who presents inaccurate or misleading information to an audience, statements like "oops, I guess the article I read got it wrong" are not an acceptable excuse but rather an admission that the speaker is irresponsible.

We recall taking a college debate team to a tournament where the topic for debate concerned the separation of church and state. The tournament was in November, so the annual debate about "the war on Christmas" was heating up again. Our team was stunned when our opponents offered numerous court cases in which they were able to quote judges' rulings that revealed assaults on religious freedom so extreme they challenged the imagination. Our team lost. Had our team been a bit more versed in the concept of narrative fidelity, we might well have thought "that just can't be right" rather than "whoa, we're toast." Teams from other universities had similar experiences, and debaters began to look up the cited cases only to find that the actual rulings bore little resemblance to the incendiary testimony being offered during the debate. It turned out that the team using the evidence had obtained it from a website that was notorious for twisting facts or engaging in exaggeration to serve the sponsoring organization's ideological agenda. The site contained a list of court cases with quotes that unfairly characterized the actual rulings. That these interpretations originated from a secondary source was never mentioned. The offending team later modified their position, but their credibility was severely undermined. They never escaped the reputation they had earned, which caused teams they would debate against in the future to continually challenge their information and left critics who would adjudicate their future performances predisposed to view with favor challenges to the team's integrity when it came to their use of outside support. This example not only points to the perils of not adequately checking your facts but also indicates how an advocate's behavior can create an unfavorable climate that limits opportunity for future productive dialogue.

Nonetheless, advocates use secondary sources frequently, and if they are suitably vigilant, it is not a problem. Remember that when secondary sources are utilized, the advocate is trusting someone else to faithfully report and interpret the words (or statistical data) of another; thus, he or she must have confidence in the person reporting the information and the publication in which it appears.

Publication's Reputation for Accuracy

There is a hierarchy of source credibility, and responsible advocates ask, "Does the publication have a reputation for accuracy?"[7] In most cases, we can trust publications that utilize a **peer review** system, meaning that recognized experts review, critique, and/or suggest modifications before an item is accepted for publication (assuming it is not an ideologically driven publication whose review board consists largely of zealots). Academic and scientific publications generally meet the test of peer review. The academic/scientific publishing enterprise prints articles with the assumption that new ideas, via their publication, are subjected to expert scrutiny as others are then free to embrace or challenge them as they submit their own findings for publication. The notion that ideas are tested in this way constitutes an example of the argumentative perspective with which you are now familiar. The appearance of rigorous editorial review does not always assure quality, as was evidenced in a minor scandal in the field of psychology when the pharmaceutical industry retained "experts" and funded studies, which were presented at professional gatherings and often published, that extolled the benefits of their products in treating depression and related conditions, and arguably resulted in a trend toward overmedication.[8]

Generally, as the rigor of editorial review declines, so does the reliability of the publication. There is, for example, a dramatic difference between what appears in print after being filtered through the editorial process and what gets reported on the web, where there is often no quality control at all. Even if the information is reliable, its credibility can be tarnished as a result of the publication in which it appears. For example, the testimony of a NASA scientist quoted in a reputable magazine or newspaper is likely to be reliable given the journalistic code of ethics that governs the content of most mainstream media. We become a bit more skeptical of the same NASA scientist when his or her testimony appears in a science fiction magazine, and will probably dismiss the testimony altogether if we find it sandwiched between stories about alien abductions and reports of Elvis sightings in a supermarket tabloid.

Is the Outside Support Dated?

Recent evidence generally is considered superior, especially when it is possible that circumstances have changed since the information was published. For example, when the United States began its military involvement in Iraq shortly after tragic terrorist attacks on September 11, 2001, there was "expert" testimony indicating that our military intervention was urgent because Saddam Hussein was developing weapons

TABLE 7.2

General Assessment of Outside Support

- Does the evidence support the conclusion it supposedly substantiates?
- Is the author of the outside support credible?
- Is the publication from which the evidence is taken reliable?
  - Is it a primary or a secondary source?
  - Does the publication have a reputation for accuracy?
- Is the outside support dated?

of mass destruction. Relying on that speculation became impossible once it was determined that Iraq did not have a significant program of nuclear weapons production. Now, an advocate arguing for renewed military presence would look foolish and uninformed if they based an argument for continued or renewed military involvement in Iraq on dated and discredited evidence and opinion.

We have stressed throughout this text that it is difficult to generate inflexible rules about argument since context, subject, and a host of factors make it impossible to slavishly adhere to absolutes. Such is the case with recency of evidence. In a debate about the original intent of the Constitution, for example, liberal use of testimony from the authors of the document would seem quite appropriate. One can also imagine situations where advocates must weigh the persuasive implications of their choices: Does the credibility of the source cited justify its use when there is more recent but less credible evidence available? Is the information so clear and compellingly worded that its persuasive stylistic elements trump the potential drawbacks of lack of recency? Is it wise to use evidence—no matter how sound—when it is clear that the audience will be repelled by the source of the information? The preceding list of dilemmas is certainly not exhaustive but should indicate that a number of variables need to be considered by the advocate in gathering and using outside support.

CONCLUSION

Very few of us possess the credibility to influence the attitude or behavior of another by simply telling them to "trust me" or "take my word for it." Consequently, outside support is critical for responsible and persuasive advocacy. Sometimes, outside support is presented directly to substantiate our claims. At other times, the existence of outside support is strongly implied and we are able to provide it when asked.

Outside support enhances the credibility of the speaker by showing that his or her opinions are not arbitrary but rather the product of thorough investigation. As long as we keep an open mind as part of our process of inquiry, our exposure to contrary opinion serves to check our own potential bias. The inclusion of interesting and compelling outside support can make us seem more dynamic by adding interest to our presentations. Since the information upon which we rely for outside support is derived from what we read or hear from others, the credibility of the source should be carefully evaluated.

QUESTIONS FOR CONSIDERATION

1. Are there any individuals whose opinions you are generally likely to respect/embrace? What is it about the advocate that makes you give him or her the benefit of the doubt?

2. Are there individuals whose opinions you greet with skepticism or disbelief? What is it about those individuals that causes you to doubt them?

3. Terry Watkins reported on the web that heavy-metal music was inspired by the devil and harmful to listeners. His conclusion was reportedly based on "scientific" research suggesting that plants exposed to metal music died.[9] The research received a stinging criticism by Linda Chalker-Scott.[10] Review these sources (see endnotes) and determine how secondary sources often report outside support in a way that is misleading.

4. How do the conclusions offered in the above-cited research illustrate the tendency by some advocates to offer claims that go well beyond what is reasonably permissible given the outside sources upon which the claims are based?

5. What makes a mainstream press publication more credible than a supermarket tabloid?

6. Politicians often argue that the mainstream press reflects a liberal or conservative bias that renders its reporting (especially reports unfavorable to the politician) suspect. Is this a fair criticism?

KEY TERMS

Artistic Proof 99

Assertion 94

Canons of Rhetoric 99

Echo Chamber 95

Inartistic Proof 99

Informed Opinion 94

Invention 99

Opinion 94

Outside Support 94

Peer Review 102

Primary Source 100

Secondary Source 101

Types and Tests of Evidence

Now that you have an idea of the reasons for using outside support and a basic understanding of some of the factors influencing evidence quality, it is time to turn our attention to the most frequently utilized sources of support: examples, statistics, and testimony. Keep in mind that there is no single type of evidence that is inherently superior to the others. The type of support you choose should suit you, the audience, forum, subject, and situation. It is often helpful to utilize a variety of support types when making your case.

EXAMPLES

Examples may be thought of as specific instances that are used by the speaker to support a claim. For instance, to clarify what constitutes a horror novel, we might suggest that "Stephen King's work is illustrative." Examples are often succinct stories that have the benefit of interesting the audience. They can improve speaker credibility by demonstrating the speaker's experience and background, such as, "Let me tell you what happened to my fishing business after the BP oil spill."

Examples that recount a true story or experience are called **actual examples**. Personal examples tell the audience something about the speaker and have the benefit of highlighting the speaker's experience with the topic under discussion. Cancer survivors recounting their personal experience with the illness are able to establish credibility because they have firsthand knowledge of the topic, and the act of sharing this personal experience with listeners creates empathy. The late First Lady Nancy Reagan became a proponent of stem cell research and was able to obtain a sympathetic hearing given that stem cell research offered promising prospects for the treatment of Alzheimer's disease, which had afflicted her husband, President Ronald Reagan. She spoke from experience, and people listened.

Beyond personal examples, advocates also use stories of another, **historical examples**, or **comparative examples** to illustrate a point. In such instances, the speaker is not necessarily claiming direct personal experience but is still able to enhance his or her credibility by demonstrating indirect knowledge, reasoning prowess, and a capacity for creative thought. For example, advocates for the decriminalization or legalization of marijuana frequently reference this country's failed policy with the prohibition of alcohol, suggesting through historical parallel that current laws against marijuana use result in similar problems (i.e., crime, loss of revenue, excessive punishment of people for their personal habits or for minor infractions). Advocates of legalization point to other countries that have legalized or decriminalized marijuana, producing benefits without significant adverse consequences, and suggest that the results of legalization in the United States would produce similar benefits. They are reasoning by analogy: "If X works in situation A, it should also work in situation B." Use of examples to help the audience envision the consequences of a proposed action is a favorite of policy makers in deliberative forums. In the marijuana example, it is worth noting that efforts at legalization (with few exceptions) have been frequently rejected by politicians and the public, indicating that reasoning by analogy only works when the examples, ideas, or actions compared are perceived by listeners to be generally alike (though public attitudes are shifting, the majority simply doesn't buy, at this point in time, the notion that drugs and alcohol are comparable). As states like Colorado legalize marijuana use, however, the basis was provided for a new analogy to justify legalization and opposition to it. "It worked/didn't work in Colorado" is becoming the new popular analogy.

Advocates also make use of **hypothetical examples** (imaginary events or scenarios), which can be effective in encouraging audience engagement. An advocate might ask, "What would you do if you were attempting to board a plane to visit family over the holidays only to be informed by the armed guards who escort you from your seat that your name appears on their no-fly list and you will be detained for questioning?" In this hypothetical example, the audience is invited to imagine an experience. The requirement for this type of example is that it represents a sufficiently plausible (though imaginary) situation and thus is more effectively evaluated in terms of criteria of typicality and relevancy discussed later in this section.

Examples merit critical scrutiny when they are used to support claims. Remember that an example is only a single instance that leads to a more comprehensive generalization. With that in mind, we turn to items to consider when employing or judging examples.

Is the Example True?

The example must be *true*. This requirement applies to actual, not hypothetical, examples. The criteria of truth seem obvious, but you might be surprised how often examples are misused. Sometimes, it is simply an innocent mistake as the advocate recounts a personal experience and forgets key details. On other occasions, we enter a gray area where faulty recollection or a desire to embellish undermines the accuracy of the example and the credibility of the user, as Brian Williams did in the example in Chapter 2. During his presidential bid, Vice President Al Gore discussed his role in the Senate as an early and enthusiastic supporter of the information superhighway during a 1999 interview on CNN, saying, "During my service in the United States Congress, I took the initiative in creating the internet."[1] His critics and political opponents recast his words and made an issue of the arrogance of a man who would claim he "invented" the Internet. While he really made no such claim, the story fed a larger narrative about Al Gore as a person prone to self-serving exaggeration, which severely damaged his credibility. Both Gore and his critics were guilty of exaggeration. Similarly, Vice President Joe Biden contributed to the unraveling of his presidential bid when in 1987 he offered a stirring account of how he was the first in his family to attend a university, peppered with references of his ancestors' hard work in the coal mines only to emerge after a 12-hour shift to play football together. Strong stuff. The problem was that what the audience took to be his life story was drawn almost verbatim from a speech delivered by Welsh Labour Party leader Neil Kinnock in which he discussed his humble beginnings (the story was also used by Kinnock in his campaign advertisements). Biden claimed he had used the story a number of times in past speeches and simply "forgot" to give proper attribution.[2] The impact was devastating at the time and provided a catalyst for further investigation of charges of plagiarism by Biden. We recall a student presentation where the speaker spoke with passion about his work in low-income communities as indicative of his selfless commitment to volunteerism and compassion for the less fortunate. The speaker failed to mention that his "volunteer" work was the result of court-ordered community service for a criminal infraction. The example was arguably true in a literal sense, but the truth about his community-mindedness was certainly suspect.

Is the Example Typical?

The example must be *typical*. An occurrence that is rare or unusual is suspect as an example when it is used to represent a more general trend or condition. Perhaps you have heard stories about how "my grandfather, the chain smoker, lived to be 97" or "my sister was thrown from her car in a horrible collision and the paramedic said she would have been killed if she was wearing a seat belt." These are examples that may be compelling to those who have experienced them, but they represent exceptions, not the rule. This illustrates how an advocate's personal experiences may act as blinders that prevent him or her from fairly considering an issue. Upon hearing examples that strain credulity, the audience falls back on notions of narrative fidelity—easily rejecting examples that are inconsistent with what they have heard or experienced previously. Worse yet, audiences may not recognize the examples as atypical and erroneously believe that the exceptions are indeed the rule. Advocates may choose to use unusual examples for their shock value in getting an audience's attention but must weigh the risks associated with their invocation.

Is the Example Relevant?

Examples must be *relevant*. Avoid telling a story just for the sake of telling a story; the examples should clearly relate to the argument. Americans often respond to rags-to-riches stories where individuals achieve success through their own hard work and perseverance. These accounts are often stirring and inspirational. Now imagine an average audience listening to a speaker born to privilege telling them, "I became a success . . . so can you." For a person born to more humble circumstances, it is a stretch to say that they have the same prospects as someone who inherited a fortune and has benefitted from the political, social, and economic opportunities readily available to one born to wealth. Such audiences would not only see the example as atypical but also irrelevant in that it suggests a riches-to-riches rather than rags-to-riches example. Football coach Barry Switzer's famous line that "some people are born on third and go through life thinking they hit a triple" has been repeated in forums ranging from rock-and-roll songs to political conventions as a way of stressing that, in some instances, such examples are completely irrelevant in proving claims about hard work and equal opportunity.[3]

Like most things, when used to excess, examples can become a liability. An advocate whose primary source of support for an argument is personal example can come across as self-absorbed. In addition, unless the audience has a compelling reason to view examples used by advocates as the typical and representative offerings of a highly credible source, they may wonder if they simply represent the ramblings of speakers who haven't bothered to do any research on their argument beyond talking to a few friends or recalling stories about themselves.

In conclusion, examples, used responsibly, can be a potent form of support. It is helpful when the advocate realizes that examples, while useful for adding clarity and color and cultivating audience identification, do have inherent limitations. It is unwise to depend on examples to the exclusion of other forms of support that do a better job of showing the scope and significance of a condition.

TABLE 8.1

Evaluating Examples

• Is the example true?
• Is the example typical?
• Is the example relevant?

STATISTICS

In April 2011, there was one of several congressional debates over defunding Planned Parenthood because the funds received by the organization may be used for abortion services. Senator Jon Kyl proclaimed, "If you want an abortion, you go to Planned Parenthood. And that's well over 90% of what Planned Parenthood does." Kyl was supporting his argument for defunding by using **statistics**—a numerical representation. Unfortunately, his use of the statistic was breathtakingly irresponsible. It appears he made it up, and when reminded that the actual amount of money used by Planned Parenthood for abortion services is actually only 3%, his office explained that his "remark was not intended to be a factual statement."[4] That rationalization is wrong on so many levels, and we suspect the speaker fully expected his supporters to view that "statistic" as factual.

Listeners are often impressed with statistical evidence, but like any form of support, one needs to listen critically and to consider the source of the information. Hopefully, the next time Senator Kyl uses statistics, his listeners will be a bit more skeptical.

We led this section with the Kyl example because it illustrates one of the key problems with statistical evidence: We are often not as critical of statistics as we should be. Although statistics are highly effective in identifying the scope of a problem or condition and are compelling ways of illustrating trends, the quality of statistical support must be evaluated, as with all forms of support, in terms of its relevance, reliability, and recency. In other words, we must avoid a tendency to assume that statistical information, given its quantitative nature, is somehow more valid than other forms of support.

You can no doubt think of a number of statistical claims: "x% of Americans are obese" indicates the scope of a problem or condition, and "violent crime has increased x% since 2010" illustrates the use of statistics to suggest a trend. The statement that "those who live in poverty are x% more likely to commit a violent crime" hints at a cause-and-effect relationship, as does the claim that "those with a college education earn x% more than those who lack a college degree." Because we are so readily persuaded by claims that are quantified, we must be particularly vigilant in our assessment of statistical support. Avoid assuming that simply because the support is numerical in nature, it is inherently more potent.

TABLE 8.2

Common Uses of Statistics

• To show the scope or significance of a condition
• To show a trend
• To show cause and effect or correlation

Is the Conclusion Supported by the Statistic?

It is essential that the statistics relate directly to the claim they are used to advance. For example, during and after the passage of the Affordable Care Act (commonly referred to as Obamacare), the argument that the policy represented an unpopular and intrusive overreach by the federal government was a common criticism. The statistic most commonly used in support noted that the majority of Americans opposed the measure. Unfortunately, the statistic about opposition to Obamacare only partially relates to the claim that the health care policy constituted federal overreach. Granted, many did see the expansion of federal authority as problematic; however, it was also possible that some respondents opposed the policy because it *did not go far enough*. In fact, either side might well have used the statistic to bolster its point of view. The problematic nature of the support becomes evident when one asks the question: Does the statistic really support the claim being offered?

Does the Sample Represent a Reliable Cross Section?

When we derive general claims from statistics, particular attention should be paid to **sample size** and representativeness. Consider public opinion polls. Given the current level of sophistication in selecting individuals to be surveyed, polling organizations are able to offer broad conclusions based on a numerically limited sample. Sample selection is not an arbitrary act but rather is based on selecting a demographically **representative sample** (age, gender, income, etc.) that will permit the pollster to generalize the findings to the entire population. During the 2012 presidential contest between Republican Mitt Romney and Democrat Barack Obama, both sides were confident they would be victorious. Both sides had polling data to support their optimism. The Romney camp was convinced that Obama's pollsters had made fundamental errors in their sampling process. Republicans pointed to an "enthusiasm gap," which they assumed would mean lower turnout among Democrats. They concluded that models (and sampling) that were based on the voting patterns resulting in Obama's election in 2008 were suspect and adjusted their own polling to reflect their assumption that key Democratic-leaning groups would be less likely to vote in the upcoming contest. Democrats, on the other hand, sampled based on patterns observed in 2008. Obama won the election, and the anticipated enthusiasm gap never materialized as voter turnout among traditionally Democratic-leaning constituencies (particularly the young, African American, and Latino voters) was higher than it was in 2008. Pollsters who predicted that in 2016 Hillary Clinton would handily defeat Donald Trump for the presidency provide a cautionary tale to those who would believe poll data without question. While reputable polling organizations get it right a majority of the time, there are still notable exceptions.

Often, surveys may be conducted by groups who want to gauge the opinion of a particular target audience. A politician may seek information from constituents, charities may seek input from donors, educational institutions will reach out to alumni and interest groups, or you may informally poll your friends as you prepare to purchase a new cell phone. Such research can be valuable but can also be misused. For example, liberal MSNBC commentator Ed Schultz invites his viewers to "tell us what you think" in response to a current-events question. The results are reported at the end of his television broadcast. The responses invariably mirror the preferences of Schultz since those who disagree with him are unlikely to be viewers. It would be irresponsible of him to equate the attitudes of his viewers with the mood of the nation as a whole, and he seldom does. On the other hand, Schultz comes dangerously close to doing so when he is on the lecture circuit, claiming he can "gauge the mood of the people" by picking up recurring narratives. Of course, these stories are derived largely from the more liberal-leaning individuals that attend his speeches. Schultz is not alone; many ideologically driven commentators and politicians get feedback from the like-minded and sometimes, intentionally or not, assume that what they are hearing represents a larger, more inclusive public. Critics refer to this as an *echo chamber*, and it illustrates one of the reasons we have consistently counseled readers to seek out diverse perspectives before making a judgment. In short, consider the organization or individual gathering data and contemplate whether bias or vested interest may undermine the credibility of results.

Do Contextual Variables Undermine the Reliability of the Statistic?

Context influences statistical reliability. A corporation attempting to measure employee attitudes during a time of corporate prosperity would probably notice a high degree of employee satisfaction, while the same survey, if conducted during the anxiety-inducing climate of cost cutting and increased efficiency, would yield different results. In short, timing and historical context are important and should be considered when evaluating statistical data.

Words matter. In Chapter 9, we discuss the importance of language use in framing arguments. The mere labeling of post-9/11 security measures as the *Patriot Act* carried with it the implication that it might be somehow unpatriotic to resist enhanced security precautions during a time of national crisis. The same can be said for surveys. The way questions are phrased influences the reaction of respondents. Few would respond in the affirmative to a survey that asks, "Do you support the murder of innocent children?" but the public debate over abortion is complex, and survey responses are different when rape, incest, or protecting the life of the mother are introduced and references to "murdering innocent children" are revised. We consistently encounter surveys where the questions are structured to ensure a particular response from those surveyed. Political pollsters, special-interest groups, and a host of others can strategically phrase questions to get a desired response.[5] As an advocate, don't simply react to the numerical representations statistics provide, but look to see if the questions that elicited a particular response are fair.

Often, surveys offer fixed-choice questions, meaning that the respondent picks from a narrow list of possible responses. A question like, "What do you believe should be this nation's greatest priority?" might list options such as national security, immigration reform, economic growth, or protecting the environment. The fact that response options have been listed serves to limit the utility of answers since the answer will only indicate which one of the *offered* options is viewed as more important to the respondent. If the pollster exercises care, the information can be valuable in indicating national preferences. However, for those who may be concerned about other issues, like reforming entitlement programs, AIDS research, a more productive working relationship between the president and Congress, and a host of other alternatives, there is no opportunity to express preferences (unless it gets filed in the vague category called *other*). Listing options inflates their attractiveness as a response and often forces respondents to pick an answer that does not truly reflect their attitudes. A further complication is that the inherent ambiguity in the possible answers allows differing interpretations by respondents. People who pick a particular response may have radically different notions about the meaning of the category. If respondents list "environmental protection" as an important national priority, do they mean that we need more government regulation to protect the planet, or do they believe regulations are already excessive and constitute an unacceptable barrier to economic growth and, if the latter reflects an individual's attitudes, should they pick "environmental protection" or "economic growth" as their answer in our fixed-choice scenario?

Do the Statistics Reflect Current Reality?

Finally, the issue of recency is important in evaluating statistics. A public opinion survey reflecting past public dissatisfaction with raising taxes or a relatively conservative stance on controversial social issues (i.e., abortion, gay rights, legalization of

TABLE 8.3

Evaluating Statistical Support

- Relevance
  - Is the conclusion clearly supported by the statistic?
- Representativeness/Reliability
  - Does the sample represent a reliable cross section of the relevant population?
  - Do contextual variables undermine the reliability of the statistics?
  - Do leading or ambiguous questions render the statistics suspect?
- Recency
  - Do the statistics reflect current reality?

marijuana, etc.) might now be viewed with suspicion given the presidential election of 2012 where the successful candidate pledged to raise some taxes and offered a decidedly progressive social agenda. The reversal of that trend in the 2016 election further clouds the issue. Public opinion surveys are a snapshot in time, and their value often resides in their recency.

The preceding discussion is not meant to suggest that statistics are an unreliable means of support but rather to suggest that they should not be accepted without scrutiny. Fair-minded, highly trained, and conscientious social scientists work hard to avoid the types of problems that we have been discussing and generally do a good job. On the other hand, not all pollsters and consultants are fair, well trained, and conscientious. Some may manipulate data to direct rather than record public opinion, and an awareness of the ways in which they do so is important to the advocate. Even the best-intentioned researcher is capable of unwittingly generating misleading or ambiguous questions.

TESTIMONY

When advocates use the words of another to express or support their claim, they are using **testimony**. A courtroom analogy is illuminating. During a trial, lawyers often build their case or attempt to undermine the case presented by opposing council through the use of witness testimony. If you have watched courtroom dramas on television, you are no doubt aware of the basic moves lawyers make in assessing testimony: Is the testimony responsive to the question or issue at hand (relevancy)? Is the witness' testimony credible, free from bias, consistent with the facts as well as other statements the witness has made, and based on direct observation or knowledge rather than hearsay (reliability)? If expert witnesses are introduced, are they knowledgeable and do they have sufficient experience and training to offer reliable opinions on the matter under discussion (reliability)? When we make arguments and support our opinions by quoting others, we consider similar issues in assessing the strength of our claims, which are based on lay or expert testimony.

Lay testimony comes from individuals who have no specialized knowledge concerning the subject about which they are testifying. If you have watched a news broadcast, you likely have seen reporters talk to the "person on the street" to get his or her reaction to a news item. The responses reflect reactions or opinions from the respondents indicating how they feel about a particular topic. The testimony is often colorful and interesting, and while it may reflect direct personal experience in that it is a first-person account of an event, it may not constitute informed or well-reasoned analysis of a situation. The power of lay testimony rests with the degree to which viewers identify with the respondent. Often, viewers generalize that these single bits of testimony reflect the more generalized opinion of "real people" responding to an event. Making that assumption can be ill conceived, and we encourage you to use the tests for evaluating examples (particularly representativeness) when assessing lay testimony.

Navigating the Internet (where anybody can post an opinion) exposes us to the limitations of lay testimony. There, we confront a wealth of uninformed opinions, misrepresentations, and polemic that compete for space with more informed judgments. We often make arguments in informal settings where we use lay testimony usually preceded by "I heard that . . ." or "I have a friend who said that . . ." However, on matters of consequence or in more formal settings, lay testimony is often insufficient as audiences prefer testimony from experts possessing a special level of knowledge about the subject under discussion. For example, a medical examiner's statements about cause of death would be considered **expert testimony**. Expert testimony is often held to a higher critical standard than lay testimony, but the basic areas for evaluation are the same. We will now examine expert testimony more thoroughly but remind you that the criteria, with modification, apply to lay testimony as well.

Does the Evidence Support the Conclusion?

It is critical that the testimony clearly supports the conclusion we draw from it. Advocates often offer dramatic or strident conclusions, yet the testimony upon which they rest is more modest. In addition, testimony may be loaded with reservations and qualifiers (i.e., "in most cases," "probably," etc.) that undermine its potency. For example, in the ongoing debate over the quality of online instruction relative to traditional classroom models, the claim that online instruction is superior is often supported with testimony that "today's students learn differently." While the testimony is likely accurate, it falls short of proving the more general conclusion when it equates the term *different* with the notion of superiority contained in the claim. On the other hand, testimony that students do not like online classes as well as traditional classes does not support an indictment of online instruction—it may simply mean that teachers who struggle with the technology, not the technology itself, are to blame. In essence, it is important to consider the claim offered by the advocate to ensure that it faithfully represents the judgment offered in the testimony.

Is the Basis for the Conclusion Offered in the Testimony Clear?

All too often, testimony expresses a source's conclusions absent an adequate accounting of how those conclusions were reached. When this is the case, we initially explore dimensions of source credibility. Asking ourselves whether a source is honest, trustworthy, or free of apparent bias indicates to us whether it seems safe to take the leap of faith required to accept **conclusionary evidence**. Sources with a high degree of credibility that we know to be contentious and who have a reputation for honesty usually receive the benefit of the doubt.

The advocate who is able to tie his or her conclusions to the judgments of respected others enjoys an advantage. Nonetheless, testimony that is conclusionary in nature can be frustrating for those trying to evaluate the basis for an advocate's claim. Imagine that you have submitted a research paper that you believe is quality work only to have it returned with a grade of C- and no explanation from your professor. Even if you have respect for your instructor (he or she enjoys credibility with you), your reaction will probably be negative as you struggle to understand why the paper merited only a grade of C-. Listeners may have a similar reaction to brief conclusionary evidence, wondering how the author reached that conclusion.

When crafting arguments based on testimony, it is advisable to use testimony that offers some rationale for the conclusions it expresses. At the very least, the advocate should provide sufficient background to explain the basis of the testimony.

Does the Source Have Relevant Knowledge or Direct Experience?

Check the credentials of your sources of testimony. Does the author of the testimony have adequate training to render a credible opinion on the subject under discussion? Explore the individual's academic credentials or other relevant training. A distinguished career in law enforcement may make one an expert on criminal behavior or the justice system. Likewise, a successful business career may make an individual's ideas concerning economic policy more believable. Remember that expertise is a field-specific concept. Enjoying the status of expert in one area does not confer expertise in others. Dr. Benjamin Spock was one of the nation's most influential pediatricians. His advice on child care was revolutionary, and his book *Baby and Child Care* first published in 1946 was second only to the Bible in sales. In the 1960s, Spock became a political activist who was vigorous in his opposition to nuclear proliferation and American involvement in the Vietnam War. Spock's high profile gained him public attention and a healthy degree of influence, but the shift from pediatrics to politics placed him in a field where his perceived expertise was limited. He remains far better known for his perspective on child care than his contribution to U.S. foreign policy.

When evaluating expert testimony, it is important to determine if it is really from an expert. All too often we confuse having a high profile with credibility. Consider the number of actors or musicians who comment on a variety of social and political issues. Admittedly, some of them may indeed be experts, but familiarity and easy access to the public forum does not equate with knowledge.

Is the Testimony Consistent With the Source's Past Statements?

Politicians occasionally note that their positions on a particular issue have "evolved." There is nothing wrong with modifying one's own opinion; after all, a basic premise of this text is that one should be open to new information. However, when someone suddenly takes a stand that is contrary to positions he or she publicly held in the past, listeners become suspicious. Why the sudden change? Is the shift the product of thoughtful consideration or political expediency? The audience may suspect that such shifts of opinion are self-serving.

In June 2013, the public became aware of the federal government's massive surveillance capacity and its apparent willingness to pry into the private e-mail and phone conversations of its citizens. Politicians of both parties expressed concerns about the breadth of the intelligence-gathering operation, characterizing it as a violation of citizen freedom and privacy or an instance of government overreach. Surprisingly, much of this criticism came from congresspersons who years earlier had ignored cautions from civil libertarians and enthusiastically endorsed the Patriot Act—the very legislation that enabled the government's increased surveillance activities. Why the sudden shift in opinion? Perhaps some did indeed carefully consider the facts and their opinion evolved. On the other hand, one might be suspicious of the motives in play since some politicians could use it as further ammunition to attack a president already reeling from charges of allowing the IRS to target conservative opponents and suspected of dishonesty in explaining the attack on the U.S. embassy in Benghazi just prior to the presidential election of 2012. It is also possible that congresspersons who were being criticized by their more liberal constituents could use the issue to solidify their position with left-leaning supporters prior to the 2014 midterm elections. Observers are left to wonder if this shift of opinion is a product of principle or politics. At the very least, the departure from past positions raises questions about the sincerity of the source.

Is the Source Free From Apparent Bias?

Reputation is an important dimension of reliability. Do you trust the source? Does the source have a reputation for honesty? Simple questions about how often the source has been wrong in the past or how often the source has been less than honest are appropriate. Official warnings about Iran's developing nuclear capacity have led to a number of crippling economic sanctions against Iran, yet the public has remained skeptical about the need for a more overt military response. It is reasonable to conclude that public resistance is not the result of insufficient information about Iran's nuclear initiatives but rather public memory about similar claims made by the White House about Iraq's weapons of mass destruction, which precipitated America's lengthy military involvement. Later, claims about the presence of nuclear and chemical weapons proved to be greatly exaggerated at best and demonstrably false at worst.

In selecting support, it is wise for the advocate to consider the potential bias of the source of information. Is the source offering claims that are self-serving or rendered suspect by the source's own vested interest? Arguably, no one is completely free from bias, but when the testimony appears self-serving it is suspect. On September 11, 2012 (the anniversary of the 9/11 attacks on the World Trade Center and Pentagon), the U.S. Consulate in Benghazi, Libya, was attacked, resulting in the killing of four Americans. Election year politics seemed to influence early accounts about the nature of the attack. Initially, the incident was tied to Muslim disgust with the release of the incendiary film *Innocence of Muslims*, which led to anti-American protests in numerous countries. There was a perception that the administration was happy for the public to embrace the cause-and-effect relationship and was resistant to acknowledge a terrorist attack in the days following the raid. With President Obama standing for reelection in under 2 months, critics noted the self-serving nature of the accounts and realized heeding his caution to wait for a thorough investigation meant the president would not have to answer for a terrorist attack in the final days of his reelection campaign. Obama's opponent, Mitt Romney, was joined by a chorus of critics who felt that the arrival of armed personnel who launched the attack on the U.S. facility indicated premeditation, not reaction to a film. Critics attempted to use the incident to make Obama's "weakness" in foreign policy a campaign issue. Clearly, bias was present on both sides of the controversy. The administration's stance seemed especially self-serving since waiting for a "thorough investigation," coupled with claims that the attack was not a terrorist attack (though Obama used the ambiguous term *act of terror* in an early reaction to the incident), would remove the issue from the president's reelection bid. Years after the incident, critics remain unsure of White House accounts of the event. Bias or vested interest does not always mean that one is lying, but it does alert the listener to the possible motive to do so.

Are the Source's Conclusions Contrary to What We Know to Be True?

There have been a number of occasions where we have heard or read something and our immediate reaction is "that doesn't sound right to me." In those instances, our natural skepticism kicks in. This healthy skepticism is an example of expectations for narrative fidelity. Of course, information that is novel or at odds with conventional wisdom is not necessarily inaccurate, but such utterances do merit a heightened degree of scrutiny (recall our earlier discussion of burden of proof). In such circumstances, we should apply the tests of evidence outlined in this chapter to evaluate the information with which we are confronted.

Billionaire real estate tycoon and winner of the 2016 presidential contest, Donald Trump, provides an illustrative example of a disconnect between his opinion and what many others believe to be true. Trump, an outspoken critic of President Obama, would often support claims about the president's shortcomings as a leader by proclaiming "nobody respects us" or "the rest of the world thinks we are a joke." The exaggerated nature of his statements made them suspect, but more telling was that such an appraisal seemed at odds with the fact that Obama, winner of the Nobel Peace Prize as president, was given rock star treatment in his early travels abroad. The critical listener would be motivated to question the disparity. Closer inspection revealed that Trump would often justify his claim by noting "all my friends say" or "everybody I talk to says," which indicates that his conclusions were probably based on his private communications with a select group of like-minded individuals—hardly a reliable sample. In short, noticing an apparent discrepancy between Trump's statements and other relevant facts led to the type of critical appraisal that more realistically reflects the accuracy of Trump's proclamation. This does not necessarily mean that Trump's criticism has no merit, only that there are significant indications to the contrary that help us evaluate the veracity of his remarks.

Are the Source's Conclusions Confirmed by Other Experts?

When evaluating testimony, ask whether other experts share the opinion. In daily interactions as well as in more formal argumentative settings, we encounter a wide range of opinions. Sometimes, a consensus of opinion develops and we can be relatively confident in the testimony. On other occasions, we determine the merit of an opinion based on the reputation (credibility) of the person offering the testimony. It is helpful to think of opinions offered in testimony in the same way we think of examples as we question their representativeness and reliability.

Does the Testimony Reflect Contemporary Thought on the Issue under Discussion?

Recency is an appropriate test of the value of outside support. For example, a discussion of the direction of U.S. defense policy based on testimony of experts from the Cold War era would certainly be suspect since the Soviet Union (now defunct) hardly constitutes our most significant security concern given the global terrorism threat.

The issue of recency is worth revisiting at this juncture because it gets at the credibility of testimony by suggesting that testimony from individuals aware of contemporary thought on a given issue is of higher value than opinion that reflects outdated thinking. On the other hand, it would be a mistake to assume (as the title of this section seems to suggest) that *correct* and *contemporary* are synonymous. It also can be a mistake to dismiss ideas simply because they are dated.

Recall the previous example concerning the debate over the value of online instruction viewing it from the perspective of recency. Supporters argue that today's students learn differently from their predecessors and that online learning is of equal or greater value than traditional lecture-oriented instruction. From this perspective, contrary opinions may be easily dismissed as desperate and dated objections that simply fail

TABLE 8.4

Evaluating Expert Testimony

- Relevance
  - Does the testimony clearly support the claim being offered?
- Reliability
  - Is the testimony credible?
  - Does the source of the testimony have relevant experience or knowledge?
  - Is the reputation of the source suspect?
    - Does the source have a reputation for thoughtfulness/honesty?
    - Is the testimony consistent with sources' past statements?
  - Is the source free from apparent bias?
  - Are the sources' conclusions contrary to what we know to be true?
  - Are the sources' conclusions confirmed by other experts in the field?
- Recency
  - Does the testimony reflect contemporary thought on the issue under discussion?

to grasp the new educational landscape. On the other hand, such critics often dismiss the accumulated wisdom on instruction and learning that dates back to the days of Socrates. This debate will doubtlessly continue into the foreseeable future but centers in large measure on whether one sees tradition as relevant to contemporary discussions of teaching and learning.[6]

CONCLUSION

This chapter extends the previous discussion about the need for and general use of outside support by examining the most commonly utilized forms of support: examples, statistics, and testimony. Examples are specific instances used to support a more general claim. Frequently, examples have the added benefit of enhancing a speaker's credibility because the advocate is able to stress his or her own experience when personal examples are used. Additionally, when nonpersonal examples are utilized, the depth of the advocate's exposure to (knowledge of) a topic is implied. The evidentiary value of examples

is generally a function of their truth, typicality, and relevance.

Like examples, statistics should also be true, typical, and relevant. Audiences seem to be impressed with statistical support, yet statistics must be examined with care to ensure that they faithfully support the conclusions advocates and listeners draw from them. Numbers do not "speak for themselves" but are often influenced heavily by the context and condition under which they were gathered.

When advocates use the words of another to support their claims, they are using testimony.

Source credibility is critical in evaluating testimony, and a variety of questions centering on source bias, knowledge, and consistency with previous statements help us evaluate quality. Understanding the most commonly used types of support and ways of evaluating them is critical to advocates who want to make a strong case. Audiences want to know not only *what* our conclusions are, but also *how* and *why* we came to them. We can then select the types of support most likely to resonate with the particular audiences we are addressing. A solid understanding of support also allows us to critically evaluate the arguments of others, and therein can serve as the basis for critique of their arguments as we hold each other to standards that provide for the audience the best examples of reasoned discourse and the best basis on which to make informed decisions.

QUESTIONS FOR CONSIDERATION

1. On November 3, 1948, the front-page headline of the *Chicago Tribune* proclaimed, "Dewey Defeats Truman." The paper had gone to press before election results showed that Harry Truman had been victorious. What factors led to this errant claim?

2. Proponents of a single-payer health care system note that the United States should move in that direction since it is one of the few industrialized countries that does not guarantee free health care for its citizens. Does the comparison support their conclusion?

3. Is the conclusion that "Obama wants to take away your guns" supported by credible evidence?

4. A blog titled "Electronic Cigarette Dangers— New Research" (http://www.skepticalraptor .com/skepticalraptorblog.php/dangers-e- cigarette-vapors-updated-research/) argues that e-cigarettes are dangerous. In what ways do the authors' conclusions exceed what is proven by the evidence used?

5. Consider the number of times your friends have introduced support for their claims with the statement "I heard that ..." or "I read that ..." What factors influence whether or not you find their support compelling?

KEY TERMS

Actual Example 105
Comparative Example 105
Conclusionary Evidence 114
Examples 105

Expert Testimony 114
Historical Example 105
Hypothetical Example 106
Lay Testimony 113

Representative Sample 110
Sample Size 110
Statistics 109
Testimony 113

Effectively Presenting Arguments

Language and Style in Argument

The 24-hour news cycle, popularity of talk radio, and nearly universal access to the Internet have contributed to a coarsening of our collective style of engagement. Hot-button issues are created and maintained by those who know that combativeness and stridency translate into donations and ratings.[1] Political deliberation has not been much better. Politicians engage in brinkmanship, use language to polarize, and often shun compromise by deriding those who work with the opposition to reach agreement.[2] Unfortunately, many mirror the combative style observed in the media, which in turn undermines the productivity of their own argumentative exchanges.

Style impacts persuasiveness. Audiences take advocates more seriously when their style—that is, the way that people express themselves, from their demeanor to their word choices—is engaging and fitting to the advocate, the audience, and the occasion. By understanding and attending to elements of style, advocates (even reluctant communicators) can develop the skills to effectively present arguments and engage audiences in thoughtful decision making.

It is difficult to consider argument style without discussing the politician with the most dramatic and deeply polarizing style in recent memory. Donald Trump, the Republican presidential victor in 2016, parlayed his tough businessman persona into the popular reality television show *The Apprentice* featuring his outrageous and often mean-spirited remarks culminating in his signature line: "You're fired!" Buoyed by the popularity of his television show, Trump toyed with the media about the possibility of a run for the presidency in 2012, but ultimately did not enter the race. When the 2016 election cycle started and he did enter the fray, his campaign celebrated his dramatic, combative style. He was "an outsider who is telling it like it is," his followers cheered. He made bold, headline-grabbing proclamations and hurled what many viewed as sexist and racist insults at his opponents (or anyone who got in his way). His calls for policies such as building a wall between the United States and Mexico to keep anyone from crossing the border and banning all Muslims from entering the country lest they be terrorists won him accolades from the Right, particularly that subset of Americans who were angry about the direction the country had been heading under President Barack Obama. The tough, take-no-prisoners approach was also appealing to those who thought Obama had weakened America's position in the world, opening the administration to attack on many fronts. Trump rallies became events where dissenting voices were not only dissuaded, but thwarted. As the primaries rolled on, Trump supporters seemed to relish identifying dissenters in their midst and pointing them out so that Trump could proclaim from the stage "Get 'em out of here!" In the end, he won the presidency, so people must like his style, right? In fact, his occasional attempts to soften his positions for the general election were perhaps a disappointment to hard-core followers nostalgic for what his general election opponent Hillary Clinton called "the real Donald Trump." Pundits watched with interest when after the election Trump seemed to moderate some of his campaign stands (for example, indicating he was not particularly interested in prosecuting and jailing Hillary Clinton or completely eliminating all elements of Obamacare), yet the old Trump emerged with angry tweets aimed at the *Saturday Night Live* comedy show as well as the cast of the popular Broadway show *Hamilton*, coupled with his consideration of some highly divisive selections to serve in his administration. Immediately after the election, it became difficult to predict what direction he would take the country. While he maintained the steadfast loyalty of his committed followers, there were unprecedented levels of fear and public protest by citizens unsure of his philosophical stand. Green Party candidate Jill Stein filed for recounts in key states. Ultimately, Trump signed a host of executive orders which enacted many of his most divisive campaign pledges. As this book was being written, it was unclear whether or not cooperation to reach common goals was imminent. At any rate, it is clear the incendiary rhetoric that characterized his campaign had a corrosive effect on postelection unity, leaving the country deeply divided.

We believe that antagonistic engagements exemplified by Trump and others are *not* typical of the experience advocates generally have when working within communities.[3] To be sure, there are many advocates who get what they want through bullying, bombast, flattery, or cajoling, but we do not consider "doing anything to win" to be a useful or ethical definition of *effective*. People go to meetings every day with their coworkers and decide things like how to best grow their company or what the newest web analytic reports mean without calling each other names or threatening to build a wall around their section of the office. Parents decide whether or not to vaccinate their children without brinkmanship. Classmates working on a group assignment find a way to decide who should do what and the best way to get the assignment completed on time without exchanging insults.[4] Trump's candidacy capitalized on the public's deep level of anger and frustration with the government. The divisions exposed by the election do not seem to bode well for the necessary calm compromise of governing. Advocates have an obligation to argue vigorously in a manner that also creates a climate where productive decision making can flourish. That, we believe, is essential to an effective argumentation style.

THE VARIETY OF PERSONAL STYLES

Advocates' personality and disposition influence their presentation style and shape their ability to adapt to the forum in which they speak. The styles that advocates use can be categorized into three basic types, described first by Roman rhetorician Marcus Tullius Cicero as grand, plain, and middle styles.[5] Some people speak very naturally in the **grand style**, approaching most situations in a formal manner and using language that is elevated and full of imagery as well as complex, yet elegant, sentence structure.[6] Dr. Martin Luther King Jr. spoke in the grand style, and more recently, President Barack Obama has often employed the grand style when the occasion required. Notably, Obama was also able to employ a more informal personal style when necessary. The presidency is a formal office, so presidents face more situations that require that they speak in a more elevated style than most of us. You might be able to identify people around you who are more formal than others in their way of speaking—a boss, important community member, or local politician might use the grand style.

Others present their arguments in a **plain style**. President George W. Bush prided himself on speaking plainly without pretense, as have many advocates who are more populist in nature. Their approach is less formal, word choices are more basic, and sentence structure relatively uncomplicated.[7] The plain style is well suited to interpersonal communication and our conversation with friends.

Of course, many speakers fall somewhere in between the grand and plain style in the aptly named **middle style**. The middle style balances the formality usually associated with public forums with the personalization often present in the plain style. As a result, the speakers—in either public or more interpersonal situations—can be authoritative yet project personal warmth. First Lady Michelle Obama has often used the middle style. Her style is clear yet eloquent, appropriately formal but also personalized. Her style is also impassioned and forceful without being overly aggressive. Her address at the 2016 Democratic National Convention is an extraordinary example of the power of the middle style.[8] Professors in the classroom often use the middle style, as do those providing information to the general public.

Each style can be effective, and astute advocates consider which manner of delivery fits their own communication style most naturally (they play to their strengths), what the situation and subject demand, and what is most likely to appeal to their particular audience. We discussed the influence of the occasion and audience more specifically earlier in the text, so we won't go into detail here. In short, one should take into consideration the requirements of the forum as well as the characteristics of the audience when determining the most effective style to use. In the next section, we explore some factors to consider in determining the most effective presentational style for your particular argument opportunities.

STYLE SHOULD REFLECT A CONSTRUCTIVE VIEW OF ARGUMENT

Sometimes, the more people argue, the more they become convinced that their position is the only correct one. The process can calcify our existing ideas instead of allowing us to be flexible and responsive.[9] This inflexibility is due primarily to the view of arguments as something to be won and opponents and audiences as enemies to be vanquished. Only when advocates redefine *winning* as engaging an audience to make the best decision possible can they move away from viewing others solely as adversaries and approach them as decision-making partners. HelpGuide, a nonprofit organization that collaborates with the Harvard Medical School, reinforces our point, noting that:

> If you view conflict as dangerous, it tends to become a self-fulfilling prophecy. When you go into a conflict situation already feeling extremely threatened, it's tough to deal with the problem at hand in a healthy way. Instead you are more likely to shut down or blow up in anger.[10]

One's style reflects his or her attitude about the process and can range from combative to compassionately conversational.

The advocate's verbal style should be inviting rather than incendiary. Think of the number of occasions you have decided *not* to participate in arguments because of the strident and abrasive demeanor of the other person. In social media terms, people who start and participate in "flame wars" might be a good example, though it happens in face-to-face interactions as well. When the goal is to genuinely engage others in an effort to facilitate responsible decision making, parties with different perspectives and interests need to feel encouraged to come to the table.

Respecting the intelligence, experience, and goodwill of listeners invites productive dialogue. Although we are sometimes loathe to admit it, it is arrogant and counterproductive to assume that listeners are incapable of raising valid points or unable to come to reasonable decisions. Admitting that those with whom we engage have considered the issue in dispute carefully and come to a different decision is difficult. Nonetheless, most issues are complicated and knowledge, experiences, and values often differ. Taking others seriously, and signaling that acceptance by hearing and trying to understand their point of view, provides the advocate with a better understanding of the complexity of an issue. This may not alter their position, but it may change the tenor of the interaction, resulting in an easier exchange for everyone involved.

Some of the most compelling advocates embody a healthy **argument posture**, approaching their audience with a generosity of spirit and practices of kindness. Understanding and valuing diverse opinions, even if they are not shared, speaking kindly instead of in a rude or a patronizing manner, and making arguments while allowing others to save face all go a long way toward an interaction that is productive and a foundation for future engagement. According to HelpGuide, "When conflict is mismanaged, it can cause great harm to a relationship, but when handled in a respectful, positive way, conflict provides an opportunity to strengthen the bond between two people."[11]

Interactants can leave happy with the process and convinced that their opinions have been taken seriously even though the disagreement remains. We don't necessarily need to like those with whom we engage in argument to afford them respect and kindness. There will be times when we do not initially like or respect those with whom we argue. Even then, treating them with respect costs us little and can usually improve the quality of dialogue and decision making, so it is worth the effort.

STYLE AND CREDIBILITY

Delivery style influences credibility. At the very least, arguments should be presented clearly and without significant verbal or nonverbal distractions. Arguments are more persuasive when delivered with **competence**, **confidence**, and **conviction**; a bit of flair rarely hurts. We will not belabor those concepts taught in public speaking class, but if you are participating in a public forum, the following practices are worth considering as a means of building and maintaining an effective persuasive style.[12] We also believe that less formal interpersonal discussions are improved with credibility-enhancing delivery (although we are less overt about it in intimate exchanges).

Demonstrate Competence

Advanced preparation usually manifests itself in a more fluent and forceful presentation. Understand the issues and how those who disagree with you perceive them. Display command of the subject through presentation style and thoughtful responses to the opposing viewpoints (reading, research, and personal experiences help your credibility). Be organized, remembering that formal presentations generally involve a clear opening, a few main points, and a short conclusion. Use words correctly. Signal nonverbally that you understand the forum by dressing in a way that will earn you respect from the audience (or at least do not let your appearance be a distraction). If writing a response, use the conventions of the medium and consider being even a bit more formal if it would be useful. Listeners make inferences of competence from argument and presentation style, so a dose of humility is often appropriate. Work to demonstrate your knowledge without coming across as a know-it-all who deserves to be taken down a peg.

Demonstrate Confidence

Often (and surprisingly) the only way that audiences know of a speaker's nervousness or lack of confidence is if they are told. Even when we are confident in our positions, most of us are nervous when we are speaking in public—especially if we don't quite know what to expect. Close friends or those with whom you have a relationship are generally familiar with your style and read you pretty accurately. In more formal circumstances, the task is a bit more difficult. As we have noted previously, preparing so that you understand the issue, the audience, and the demands of the occasion can reduce anxiety.

There are some standard practices that provide a baseline. It is important to speak loudly enough to be heard, but not so loud that you're shouting. Making appropriate eye contact reassures the audience that you are present and interested in them, and also allows you to gauge their response. Enunciating words (speaking clearly without mumbling) will help your audience understand you and will reduce the fatigue they will experience from prolonged listening to someone difficult to understand. Maintaining a conversational pace is difficult for some but is vital. Adrenaline increases speaking rate, so you might need to monitor your speed to be sure that your audience is able to adequately process your arguments. Remove physical distractions (like jewelry) with which you might fidget. Planning and using gestures for emphasis will (ironically) make you look more relaxed or even spontaneous, and has the added benefit of helping to dissipate nervous energy. Assuming a body posture that invites instead of rejects interaction also signals your confidence and willingness to engage. To do this, face your audience if possible, keep your hands and arms loose at your sides or on the table (except on those frequent occasions when you should gesture), sit or stand comfortably tall, and affect a neutral or friendly facial expression. Confidence will develop as you gain experience, but until it does, do not call attention to your nervousness or uncertainty with apologies or excuses that will only lead the audience to doubt your credibility because they attribute your nervousness to potential uncertainty on your part.

Demonstrate Conviction

Convincing advocates speak with conviction, exhibiting appropriate levels of confidence and emotion to humanize themselves while conveying their passion. We have previously noted that dynamism is a useful attribute, provided that it is not interpreted as condescending, arrogant, or uncontrolled. Using facial expressions that match your message so that you are sending consistent verbal and nonverbal cues also contributes to the demonstration of conviction. A speaker who smiles pleasantly through a tough discussion on the need for support of domestic abuse shelters, for example, would not appear to be taking the cause very seriously. Don't hesitate to show your passion, but also recognize that being overly emotional in some situations—be it sad, frustrated, or angry—can make it easier for others to be dismissive of your ideas. There are occasions when showing displeasure or anger when speaking on behalf of an issue is appropriate. However, speaking only in angry or frustrated tones can make you look petty, peevish, or like a raving lunatic. Effective advocates are not bullies, and their communication styles should not reflect such a demeanor.

TABLE 9.1

Your Communication Style

- Level of formality should match subject and forum
  - Grand—elegant, complex, florid (important formal or ceremonial events)
  - Middle—modest formality (class lecture)
  - Plain—informational, conversational, direct (friendly interpersonal exchanges)
- Style enhances credibility
  - Demonstrate competence
  - Demonstrate confidence
  - Demonstrate conviction

LANGUAGE AS A COMPONENT OF STYLE

Choose words carefully. Audience judgments are influenced by the advocate's word choice. Consider those people that you have known who habitually use aggressive, strident, or insensitive language. We are sure that at least one comes to mind. They can be fun to listen to if the stakes aren't too high, but they also get tiresome quickly. They sometimes gain a following—right-wing talk show king Rush Limbaugh and Sean Hannity of Fox News are prime examples. To be sure, the Left has its own antagonists. Many radio talk show hosts (most notably Howard Stern) and pundits on MSNBC have made a career of it. Some people admire those with strident styles because they believe that the speakers are saying what other people are afraid to say, even though sensitivity and common courtesy would indicate that there are some things better left unsaid. Indiscretion might occasionally pass for entertainment, but when it comes to facilitating honest dialogue about the serious issues that we are working to resolve, we are not enthusiastic about the tactic. Audiences rarely learn anything from these so-called discussions that generally serve to echo and validate existing prejudices and inoculate listeners from diverging opinions. As we turn to a discussion of language in argument, we will consider the nature of language, then its role in argument.

The Nature of Language

Meaning is negotiated, generated as we communicate and come to an agreement on what words mean. We find these agreed-upon meanings in traditional dictionaries and refer to them as **denotative meaning**. For example, there is no essential "tableness" to a table, but we have decided that tables are "a piece of furniture that has a flat top and one or more legs."[13]

To further complicate matters, many terms have a field-specific meaning. That is, what words mean in one situation is not what they mean in another. For example, when Illinois governors were charged in a court of law and the court of public opinion with being corrupt (there have been several), the meaning was different from what the computer technician has in mind when proclaiming that your computer's hard drive is corrupt. As you can imagine, terms that seem very clear to one advocate may end up being problematic for others.

More specifically, fields and communities have their own jargon—that is, any term that is specific to a particular community or context. Those outside of that community would not likely understand jargon without some explanation. If you have ever left a conversation with a medical doctor with the uneasy feeling that you did not completely understand the diagnosis, it might be because the medical jargon that was used was unfamiliar. Concern over a diagnosis of rhinitis would lessen once you understood that the term generally means a runny nose. Obviously, jargon-laden presentations are fine with specialized audiences but out of place when addressed to a more general audience. It is important to learn the appropriate jargon to effectively communicate with your audience in specialized contexts. It is equally important to explain any jargon to an uninitiated listener or, better yet, avoid it altogether if it better suits the audience.

Meaning can change over time as words come to signify or include new meanings. Slang is a good example of this and likely encountered when speaking with people from a different generation or even someone from a different region. Consider the various meanings of *hot*. It has meant angry (1920s), fast (1920s), electrically charged (1920s), stolen (1930s), and sexy (1950s).[14] The Urban Dictionary serves as a particularly entertaining place for hashing out definitions, letting users submit their own and others giving them an up or down vote. One (unedited) definition of hot: "1. someone thats EXTREMEMLY good looking but not like cute, more like sexy. when they walk by u turn ure head and wish u had a pausse button or something. 2. something that is in some way attractive, 1. *omg that guy on the skate board wa so hot! 2. as paris hilton says 'thats hot.'*"[15] The definitions provided on Urban Dictionary may or may not be widely agreed upon but reflect the various ways in which they are being deployed at the moment, and presumably will serve as a record that demonstrates the way that their usage changes over time.

This is a good time to reiterate the necessity of defining terms that may be unfamiliar to listeners or that are used in unfamiliar ways. Clarity helps advocates avoid unnecessary misunderstandings or having arguments that miss the point. For example, if arguing with your friends about whether or not to eat at a fast-food restaurant, it might be helpful to everyone to determine exactly what that term means. Do you consider Chipotle, Panera, or other "fast casual" eateries to be in the same category as McDonald's, Burger King, and Taco Bell? What defines a fast-food restaurant? Carrying your own tray and/or bussing your own table, or something else? Being clear about your own meaning and asking questions when you are unclear about how others are using important terms can go a very long way toward facilitating productive conversation.

Understanding a word's denotative meaning does not give access to meaning tied up in the experiences and emotions others associate with a word—its **connotative meaning**. Meaning comes from what words connote as well as what they denote. It can be easy to forget that other people sometimes have very different associations with particular terms. Consider the word *family*. The *American Heritage Dictionary* defines family as "two or more people who share goals and values, have long term commitments to one another, and reside usually in the same dwelling place," or "a group of persons of common ancestry."[16] Yet those definitions may not fully encompass your own understanding of family or take into consideration the feelings that many experience when they hear the word. How you understand and respond to the term is dictated not only by your own understanding of the culture's conception of family but also by your experience in your own family. The Charles Manson family certainly conjures our recollections of the group's murderous rampage, which is at odds with notions of a typical family. Both are different from the Corleone family. Basically, references to family can be positive or negative based on one's history with his or her own family.

Sometimes, people have such strong emotional reactions to words that they have difficulty paying attention to the thought the speaker intends to convey. These "trigger words" may induce anger, sadness, or even elation depending on the hearer's cognitive and emotional associations. Naturally, these words are different for each individual, but some common trigger words are slurs or polarizing terms used in hot-button social issues. The term *paternalistic* may be seen by some as indicative of loving concern, while others use the same term to imply the inappropriate treatment of mature individuals as children incapable of independent thought and action.

Understanding the place of connotation in meaning making is especially important. Often, advocates offer ideas that generate significant emotion. The terms that they choose to use are then vital if listeners are to attend to arguments carefully and critically instead of reacting on a purely visceral level. Steering away from trigger words is an appropriate strategy. At the very least, advocates should recognize that their meaning might be more easily shared with those who share their experiences and that they must work carefully with those who do not.

The Functions of Language in Argument

Choosing words can be a complicated endeavor. With a handle on some of the basic elements of the nature of language, we turn our attention to what words do, with particular attention to how they function in the context of argument.

Our word choices demonstrate both what we think and also how we want others to think.[17] Language structures thought and our persuasive efforts. For example, when in discussions about immigration issues, advocates choose between many labels but primarily *illegal* or *undocumented* to signify those people who have entered the country without going through proper channels for immigration. In doing so, they make a choice that not only signifies particular understandings and beliefs about the issue but also encourages others to understand the issues in the same way. In this case, those labels carry with them a set of understandings and assumptions about the legal status of immigrants without papers that document them as legally being allowed to reside in the United States. Referring to individuals as *illegal* highlights their status relative to law and judges their adherence to the rules of the system, while referring to the same individuals as *undocumented* highlights their lack of proper documentation instead of their legal status. The labels orient us differently. The label of *illegal* (bad) indicates that others are *legal* (good). The label of *undocumented* is contrasted with those who are *documented*, which we could see as a good/bad dichotomy, but the term is somewhat less judgmental. Each label implies a response option—we respond to lawbreakers (illegal) differently from those with paperwork problems (undocumented). As you can guess, the labels used by advocates on differing sides of immigration issues choose their labels to support their understanding of the policy that they want to advance. It's easier to lock up or deport illegals than those who are simply undocumented. It's easier to argue for paths to citizenship for the undocumented without the sting of the legal designation of illegals. Not incidentally, *people* are not illegal, so the label itself is problematic. Examples like this abound. Consider the varying labels of the same categories in your own life. When we choose to describe people as *homeless* or, alternatively, *bums*; when we label something a *peacekeeping mission* or an *invasion*; or when we choose the term *freedom fighter* over *rebel*, we reveal our own preferences or biases and invite an audience to join us in that understanding.

As is evident from this example, an advocate's choice of words serves to focus attention on some aspects of a situation and downplay others. Like those cell phone pictures that we take at angles that most flatter our best features, and crop and filter to obscure others, language choice can make some attributes more salient and others less so. Let's consider another example. As terrorism sponsored by the Islamic State of Iraq and Syria (commonly referred to as ISIS or ISOL) heated up in 2015, so did a controversy about the Obama administration's refusal to use the term *radical Islamic terrorism*.[18] Ted Cruz was particularly vociferous in his attacks on the president during his run for the Republican nomination for president: "The broader solution is a commander-in-chief willing to speak the truth, willing to name the enemy—radical Islamic terrorism—and willing to do whatever it takes to defeat radical Islamic terrorism."[19]

In essence, Cruz accuses Obama of using the administration's preferred term of *ISOL* or *ISIS* or simply *terrorists* to deflect the reality that Cruz thought was paramount—the group's Islamic faith. The Obama administration agreed that it was deflecting focus strategically: "That's why ISOL presumes to declare itself the 'Islamic State.' And they propagate the notion that America—and the West, generally—is at war with Islam," Obama explained.[20] For Obama, *Islam* was not the issue, political *terrorism* was, so his word choices reflected his effort to frame the controversy in ways that made room for his preferred response.[21]

Word choice not only reflects what we think (and want others to think); it high-lights our similarities and differences. Words signal to others who we are. If, for example, people tell you to "have a blessed day," they are revealing something different about who they want you to think *they* are, and who they think *you* might be, than if they tell you to "party on."[22] As we discussed earlier, audiences are persuaded more by people with whom they identify in some salient way. One way to signal like-mindedness is to use language and make stylistic choices that recognize and perhaps reflect the worldview of the audience. Speaking more like our conversational/argument partners in rate, tone, word choice, and/or topic is called **convergence** and tends to bring parties together by highlighting their similarities.[23] For example, if when talking you match your usual conversational style (tone, energy, level of formality, use of slang) and select topics in which both of you are interested, you have converged. When advo-cates want to demonstrate their similarities with an audience, reflecting their commu-nication style can be a way to signal a desire to bridge the divide. If the identification is genuine (as opposed to being employed purely for manipulation), the audience may be inclined to give advocates a more receptive hearing.

Convergence can be problematic with those who are hostile or use particularly aggressive communication styles. It is often not useful to match those communica-tion styles, and **divergence**—assuming a style clearly distinct from the other—can sometimes both deescalate the situation and reinforce the reasonableness of one's own judgments. Divergence can also be useful when attempting to draw clear distinctions between your ideas and those of others, even if the exchange is not particularly hostile. As we indicated previously, word choice reflects one's understanding of people, situa-tions, and issues. So, for example, when a university faculty member insists on talking about those they teach as *students*, not as *customers* or *the headcount*, and their work as *teaching*, not as the university's *product*, they are very intentionally diverging—setting themselves apart through their use of language—from an existing conversation that views higher education as transactional in nature.

Convergence and divergence can have a significant impact on credibility, so it is especially important to consider their merit in the situations in which we argue. Several movies feature a big-shot (like Michael J. Fox in *Doc Hollywood*) who gets "trapped" in a "backward" small town but maintains a big-city style. He is initially reviled for the way he communicates with the locals, who see him as pretentious and arrogant. Inevitably, he is taught a lesson about the wisdom of the folks around him and how much of a jerk he has been. He then either leaves or stays (depending on who he has fallen for) but either way has gained a new respect for his neighbors. His change of heart (and style) earns him the affection of the townspeople. The lesson here is about choosing the appropriate style for your audience. You do not want to converge in a way that is awkward to you or makes you seem to be mocking your audience, but if you are going to boldly stake your claim as distinct, there are risks to be considered.

All language choices create meaning, so it is imperative that advocates are alert to those times when language is being used purposefully to obscure instead of clarify. Teenagers are often masters of the use of strategic ambiguity. They are going "out" and will be "with friends" who will "hang out" at "someone's house" where there will, of course, be "an adult" present. Most of us have been there, and also have been pressed for more specific information by parents who knew that we were attempting to avoid answering their questions directly because we assumed that they would not approve. Unfortunately, it is not only teenagers who use the suspect strategy of strategic ambiguity to avoid conflict, shirk responsibility, or secure an ultimately meaningless agreement. We cannot always be as specific as our audience would like; sometimes, we just do not know enough to commit to a particular course of action. The problem occurs when advocates use **ambiguity** to obscure their real agenda or their lack of information. Advocates should be as specific as reasonably possible and not require the audience to continually press them for details. Politicians are particularly bad about this. Campaign themes or agendas are frequently expressed as catchy but vague slogans. A famous example of strategic ambiguity was President Bill Clinton's assertion that he "did not have sexual relations with that woman" and his later claim that an incomplete understanding of what constitutes "sexual relations" was the basis for that statement when it came to light that oral sex had been a part of their relationship.[24] This was easily recognizable as a legal dodge to cover up his affair with White House intern Monica Lewinsky and clearly meant to deceive. We hope you can see the need to clarify ambiguous terms when engaging someone in argument. A question like "could you tell me a bit more about what you mean by x?" is a good way to aid mutual understanding.

Language should accurately represent, clarify, and support arguments. We wrote extensively in earlier chapters about the ways that we understand arguments in narrative terms and how paying attention to that form of understanding benefits us as advocates. Word choice goes a long way toward making narratives clear and interesting. To frame an analogy, the best novels are not those that are strictly outlines of the plot. Instead, they offer glimpses of the characters and scenes in ways that can be vividly pictured in our minds. They use colorful and specific language, rendering ideas richly with descriptions that appeal to several senses. Arguments need not be dedicated to elaborate character or scene development, but the descriptions of each and the labels selected will help others understand our perspective and arguments better than they otherwise might. In short, language can help audiences visualize ideas, empathize with

TABLE 9.2

Language Use

The Nature of Language

- Meaning is not inherent in words
- Words can have field-specific meanings
- Different fields and communities have their own jargon
- Meaning of words can change over time
- Defining terms that you use is often helpful
- Part of a word's meaning resides in its connotative element

Functions of Language in Argument

- Language reflects and shapes our thoughts
- Word choice orients us toward some aspects of a person/situation and away from others
- Word choice highlights both our similarities and our differences
- Language can be used to obscure meaning

certain actions and characterizations while reviling others, and relate to narratives on a deeper level. Ultimately, careful attention to language will improve the listener's understanding instead of clouding the issue and should increase arguments' effectiveness.

CONCLUSION

Assuming a posture of openness and genuine engagement is not always easy. In fact, when one cares passionately about an issue, it can be downright painful to be civil to those who oppose us. But such civility enhances cooperation. The orientations offered in this chapter facilitate productive argumentation and can work to guard against the types of argumentation that so easily undermine productive civic and personal relationships.

We believe that good decision making is most likely when an advocate's style and use of language invite rather than discourage others to engage and maintain or increase the advocate's credibility instead of compromising it. Playing the role of tough and uncompromising advocate disregards the potential wisdom to be provided by others and reflects a lack of concern about the relationships with those with whom we engage.

QUESTIONS FOR CONSIDERATION

1. Does your natural personal style fall into the plain, middle, or grand style? In what situations that you have encountered or likely will encounter might you need to alter that style?

2. Why do you think it is often so difficult to disagree with someone but not get angry and defensive?

3. Locate a word that has had a clear change in denotative meaning and discuss how the meaning changed over time.

4. In what interpersonal situations have you found yourself most likely to converge with others? To diverge? Why? Does it seem to happen naturally, or do you need to work at it?

5. Is the strategic use of ambiguity ever appropriate for an advocate? If so, in what circumstances?

6. Watch a video clip of Hillary Clinton's keynote address commemorating Bloody Sunday at First Baptist Church in Selma, Alabama, in 2007 as an example of an attempt at stylistic convergence. What does she risk? What could she gain? Is it an effective rhetorical choice? Why or why not?

KEY TERMS

Ambiguity 133
Argument Posture 125
Competence 126
Confidence 126

Connotative Meaning 130
Convergence 132
Conviction 126
Denotative Meaning 128

Divergence 132
Grand Style 124
Middle Style 124
Plain Style 124

10 Responding to Arguments

To this point, our attention has focused significant consideration on how one might productively argue. The process begins with a proper mind-set, requires honest self-appraisal (credibility and potential bias) by the advocate, attends to audience disposition, offers reasonable arguments that are logically and emotionally compelling, utilizes quality outside support, and ends with a presentation that is stylistically sound. At first glance, it may appear that we take the perspective that the reader is always the advocate, preparing to initiate an argumentative exchange. We are really co-advocates, involved in give-and-take, so we alternate roles between advocate and audience (receiver) in the process. The material in this text is equally valuable in both roles. This chapter assumes command of the previous material and expands on it by highlighting some of the unique features involved in listening and responding to arguments made by others.

LISTENING EFFECTIVELY

Imagine viewing an object through a highly distorted lens. You would miss many of the details. The object itself will be ill defined, and you will try your best to identify the image by filling in the gaps. You will try to recall objects that resemble what you are viewing to aid in your identification. Days later, when you attempt to recall what you have seen, you will remember your potentially suspect reconstruction and forget those areas of ambiguity that challenged your initial identification. This process is analogous to the way we listen to arguments and indicates the necessity for focused listening. We do not want to miss important details or allow personal experiences and beliefs to distort the argument as we attempt to make it "fit" within our cognitive structure. With the passage of time, we will recall our initial (and potentially flawed) understanding of the topic and conveniently forget details that do not confirm our initial appraisal.

Paying attention is a prerequisite to argument. It is only possible to understand an argument if one is intentionally listening and focused on the message. Focus is often difficult. Arguments, by definition, challenge ideas and values, making it difficult to give them a fair hearing. Psychologists use the term **selective defense mechanisms** to describe how people manage information that is inconsistent with their beliefs. We use **selective exposure**, gravitating toward information that supports our preexisting point of view and often paying insufficient attention to competing ideas. Our **selective perception** of arguments refers to distortion caused by our tendency to reinterpret—often inaccurately—statements to make them fit our preconceived notions. Finally, we use **selective recall**, often forgetting "inconvenient" ideas.[1] Selectivity is a natural psychological response that can create problems if we are not sufficiently attentive.

The hard work of listening demands complete concentration. There are countless distractions that vie for attention. Many of us have encountered a listener's blank expression, indicating that we are not being heard. On other occasions, our listeners are distracted, perhaps riveted on something seen through a window or by a new message on their mobile device. In such circumstances, it is easy to wonder if it is worthwhile to continue the exchange. Common courtesy dictates that we listen when someone is talking, so if you are tempted as a listener to engage in some activity in addition to listening, please bear in mind that research indicates that people are not nearly as good at multitasking as they think they are.[2] On the other hand, if you have friends that you consider good listeners, you already know the positive effect good listening has on a speaker.

Good listening goes beyond paying attention, however. Keeping an open mind is critical. It is tempting (and at times acceptable) to immediately judge what we hear, but it is often better to suspend judgment until the argument is clear and the other advocate has had sufficient opportunity to make his or her point. Withholding judgment also provides an opportunity to more appropriately form a persuasive response. If you have ever immediately responded to a text message or e-mail only to discover upon reflection that your response was in error or phrased in a way that angered the receiver, you've learned that lesson. Unfortunately, there are many occasions where a terse response derails a discussion by creating a negative communication environment. These hazards are present in both online and face-to-face exchanges.[3]

LISTENING FOR RELATIONSHIP AND CONTENT

Once tuned in to an advocate's message, it is advisable to initially listen for specific types of information. Careful **listening** can help form preliminary impressions that provide a basis for more directed listening for specific argument content. Put another way, an argument often contains hints that the alert listener can use as a first step in preparing to respond.

Listening for Relational Cues

Listening with an open mind can reveal important relational elements woven into the argument. Listen with care because three relationships are on display and playing a substantial role in any argument situation. These are: (1) the other advocate's relationship with the topic, (2) your relationship with the topic, and (3) the relationship between you and the other advocate. If the other advocate has personal experience with or is passionate about the topic, expect your burden of proof to be increased should you offer a contrary view. Additionally, keep in mind that discounting someone's personal experiences as unrepresentative or unimportant will likely undermine the chances for a civil exchange. Your relationship to the subject being discussed is also important, especially if it means that personal biases will prevent you from giving others a fair hearing. Finally, the relationship between the advocates is critical. People will respond differently depending on their relationships with each other (as friend, spouse, boss, employee, etc.). When engaging someone with whom you are familiar, you probably have a good idea of their response patterns as well as their interests, which allows you to maximize identification and common ground. When addressing unfamiliar listeners, you probably fall back on generalizations gleaned from a demographic profile. Listen carefully for **relational cues in argument**, as in "listen for what is felt as well as said." Conflict resolution experts believe that "when we listen we connect more deeply to our own needs and emotions and to those of other people."[4] If one is able to identify cues as to how the other advocate views the relationships involved, it is easier to make appropriate choices about demeanor and meeting the expectations inherent in the exchange.

Listening for Central Arguments

A listener must determine what (if any) argument is being made. "What's the real issue here?" and "What does the speaker wish me to do or believe?" are useful questions to keep in mind. Often, an argument is a complex **chain of reasoning** in which claims, once established, become the basis for other arguments. Listen for the advocate's ultimate destination. Advocates usually put their main argument in one of two places—at the beginning of the presentation or near the end. It is easiest to identify and follow those who clearly state their point at the outset and then explain and back it up with support. Still, some speakers will make their case, building as they go, only revealing their claim as their conclusion. Arguments presented in this way require especially close attention (and perhaps some note taking) and a reconsideration of the evidence and logic after the conclusion has been revealed. Arguments can be disjointed and difficult to follow, so identifying the connections is critical. Finally, arguments that are wholly unclear may require the judicious use of follow-up questions for the purpose of clarification. We can't argue well if we don't all start from the same place.

Sometimes, after hearing an advocate out, it may seem that he or she has made a good point and that further argument is unnecessary. There may be other reasons to disengage. Perhaps the other advocate really just wanted a sounding board and was seeking affirmation, not argument. It is also possible that the argument seems trivial and is not worth pursuing, in which case one might politely change the subject rather than risk potential damage to the relationship or communication environment over an inconsequential matter. Finally, the same reasoning might suggest that there is little chance of a productive exchange or argument resolution, so it is better not to argue.

Listening for the Types of Issues in Dispute

After identifying the central argument, consider whether the claim under discussion is one of fact, value, or policy. The classification, coupled with an understanding of stock issues, will illuminate the central issues in the dispute. For claims of fact and value, it is critical to listen for what particular criteria of judgment are suggested. The search is complicated by the fact that criteria are often only *implied* by the speaker, who has perhaps assumed that listeners share their standards for evaluation. Also, the speaker may not offer or even imply criteria, in which case the arguments offered may appear rambling or confusing. If confusion arises, you may need to judiciously intervene, asking the speaker to clarify the position. If the claim offered is one of policy, expect a problem/solution organization, and pay especially close attention to the significance of the problem being discussed and the advisability of the plan that is offered to solve that problem.

Using a narrative approach to evaluate the reasonability of the rhetorical narrative being offered is an alternative to a strict stock issues approach. Consider the following: Who is the narrator (credibility or potential bias is important to note)? Who are the characters? Are heroes and villains depicted in a believable fashion, and do they behave predictably according to type? Is the plot logical? How does scene influence plot and characters? Basically, attempt to assess whether the narrative is logical and plausible (narrative probability) as well as consistent with what you know to be true from your knowledge of related narratives (narrative fidelity).

Listening for Outside Support

Listen for the types of evidence advocates use to support their claims. Often, arguments will be supported with examples, real or hypothetical, that reflect advocates' own experiences or experiences of others with whom they are familiar. Use of testimony and statistics is common in more formal arguments. At this point, getting a feel for the speaker's own experiences with the topic, the type and scope of research that the speaker has done, and whose opinions the speaker respects is important. Later, the tests of evidence will become critical, but at this point, a general impression about the type and quality of information used by the advocate provides a useful framework to begin crafting a response. Be sure to note if primary or secondary sources are prominent and, if they are secondary sources, determine if they are to be trusted.

Do not feel compelled to follow a checklist. Evaluating narratives and outside support is a complicated endeavor, and the give-and-take of argument does not afford time for unlimited reflection before responding. With continued practice, asking relevant questions becomes second nature. Importantly, not every possible test of support needs to be applied. The nature of the argument and the context in which it occurs suggest relevant questions and indicate when some concerns are irrelevant or diversionary.

A reminder to keep an open mind is worth repeating here. Yes, it is important to evaluate the supporting foundation upon which an argument rests, but it is also critical to fully comprehend the argument. Continual interruptions to dispute details creates the impression that a listener is being overly contrary, may undermine a constructive communication environment, and may risk missing the big picture in a haste to land counterpunches.[5] The goal of initial listening is more to understand than refute. You may hear things that you mentally file away for use at an appropriate time. Remember, people like to be heard. Judicious interruptions to achieve mutual clarity are perfectly permissible, but don't overdo it.

TABLE 10.1

Listening

- Listening well
  - Focus
  - Keep an open mind
- Listen for relevant personal relationships
  - What is the relationship between arguers?
  - What is the speaker's relationship to the topic?
  - What is your relationship to the topic?
- Locate central argument(s)
- The types of issues in dispute
  - Consider stock issues
    - Issues of fact
    - Issues of value
    - Issues of policy
  - Is narrative rationality evident?
    - Narrative probability
    - Narrative fidelity
- How is outside support used?
  - Primary or secondary sources
  - How prominent are various types of support?
    - What do they indicate about level of research?
    - What do they indicate about relationship to the topic?

Offering Appropriate Nonverbal Feedback

Part of being a good listener is providing appropriate nonverbal and verbal feedback. Astute advocates observe such cues and incorporate responses to them into their presentations. Argumentation is an exchange. Strictly speaking, offering feedback is not *listening*, but it is a reliable indication that we are listening, so we attend to it here. Having an argumentative exchange with a wholly unresponsive partner can be as frustrating as it is unproductive. As a listener, providing signals to advocates that we are interested and attentive helps to facilitate a respectful exchange. It is not enough to listen; listeners need to listen actively in ways that convey respect and consideration—and then to expect the same when it is their turn to speak.

The feedback that listeners provide through nonverbal behavior is influential, and mismanagement can derail conversation. Nonverbal communication includes all of those ways that we convey messages with our bodies (eye contact, posture, general demeanor) but do not verbalize. Eye contact is vital to effective communication because it demonstrates interest in what another has to say. If you have ever been in a conversation with someone who is looking around the room or checking their social network, you know how important eye contact can be. We do not recommend an unrelenting stare, of course, as prolonged eye contact can be unnerving to the recipient, but instead suggest eye contact with sufficient frequency and duration to make it obvious that the speaker is the focus of attention. Occasionally, when the speaker has made a particularly interesting point, a listener's gaze may naturally move upward to indicate reflection, which tends to send a positive message. The main target of eye contact is directly into the eyes of the conversant. Looking slightly over the person's head because it makes us more comfortable is not fooling anybody. It is not difficult to tell where another's gaze is directed—especially in close proximity exchanges. Arguments are more productive when the person we are engaging knows we are paying attention.

Posture, movement, and gestures are important for listeners, though they are most often discussed as advice for speakers. They also convey attentiveness and receptivity to the speaker. It is difficult to communicate with those who are slouching in their chairs or shuffling their feet as they stand facing you; engaging in a variety of distracting gestures (twirling a pencil, fixing their hair, or drumming their fingers impatiently); orienting their bodies away from you; or adopting a closed posture. On the other hand, listeners who occasionally provide a nod to indicate agreement or comprehension are easier to talk to.

Facial expression also plays a significant role in interaction. A blank stare or look of boredom is not very helpful. A face that is genuinely expressive provides necessary feedback to the speaker.[6] It is a good idea to know how your facial expressions are perceived by others so that you are able to minimize expressions that are likely to be perceived as negative. As teachers, we frequently gauge student interest and comprehension through facial expressions. We also encounter a few students who, in the interest of a favorable class participation grade, are convinced we can be fooled by eye contact, smiles, and appreciative nods, a tactic that is revealed when we ask them to enter the conversation or comment on what we have just said. The safest route is to actually *be* interested in what others have to say rather than faking it. Nonetheless, you may wish to monitor your expressions. For example, if you constantly find yourself in situations where you elicit angry or defensive responses that seem unrelated to the verbal content of your messages or that occur when you think you are simply listening attentively, then your nonverbal behavior may be responsible. One of your authors mastered what he intended to be a look of nonjudgmental attentiveness when listening to student speeches in class. He noticed that students seemed inordinately worried about their performance (even when it was outstanding) and would often stay after class to ask, "Was that all right?" Unfortunately, it was not until later when a student mentioned, "You looked so angry when I spoke," that the instructor realized his facial expressions sent the wrong message and he modified his behavior.

Offering Appropriate Verbal Feedback

Listening is an active process where audiences are able to provide verbal as well as nonverbal feedback. The key to effective verbal feedback is that it can provide encouragement and perhaps focus for the speaker. Verbal feedback can be as simple as a well-timed "yes," "right," or "uh-huh." Don't overdo it since even affirmations can become distracting if used to excess, but such affirming verbalization lets speakers know they are on the right track and that you are comprehending or agreeing.

Occasionally, more pointed responses are appropriate. To ensure understanding of the argument, listeners may need to ask questions that add clarity to the discussion. Repeating can be particularly effective. Telling the speaker, "What I hear you saying is . . . is that correct?" gives the speaker the chance to address misperceptions. Questions to solicit additional information, such as "I am not sure I follow you here. Could you say a bit more?" are also very effective. These questions should be phrased in ways that are nonthreatening and unlikely to negatively impact the communication environment. Interruptions should be both timely and minimal. You will soon get a chance to respond and can reasonably expect the same courtesy. On rare occasions, it might be necessary to express disagreement if it seems vital that something be cleared up before the discussion can proceed. Still, phrasing questions in such a way as to avoid personal attacks is beneficial. Saying, "I have read an article that takes a different view; they say . . . . What do you think about their point?" is much better than saying, "You have a grossly misinformed opinion . . . . The truth is . . . ." Remember, the primary objective is first to listen to and understand the other's position, not to rebut every idea. Your response will come a bit later as you direct greater scrutiny to the quality of reasoning offered by the advocate.

TABLE 10.2

Promoting a Positive Communication Environment

- Maintain an open and cooperative environment

- Offer appropriate feedback
  - ○ Nonverbal feedback
    - ■ Eye contact reveals your interest
    - ■ Nondistracting posture, movement, and gestures
    - ■ Facial expression is enabling
  - ○ Verbal feedback
    - ■ Audible affirmation
    - ■ Limited timely interruption
      - □ Repeating speaker points
      - □ Questions to clarify
      - □ Seek needed information
      - □ Questions are nonthreatening

- Aim for understanding rather than rebuttal

PREPARING TO RESPOND

Having listened well and grasped the arguments being offered, it is time to respond. It is wise to argue key issues while conceding those points that seem minor or that do not hurt your overall position. The nature of the argument being offered determines what response options are better choices, so don't stick slavishly to a predetermined checklist—choose your points of contention carefully.

Prepare in Advance

Advance preparation is critical to arguing persuasively. Admittedly, some arguments are spontaneous, and the opportunity to brush up on issues in advance is limited. On the other hand, even in what appear to be unplanned encounters there are ways of making accurate assessments about the topics that will emerge. Knowledge of the other advocate's interests, the situational demands that make particular issues salient, and the forum in which we find ourselves can provide important clues to the topics likely to be considered. Thinking through the argumentative possibilities can relieve a listener's stress and help ensure they have something to say at the appropriate time.

In formal contexts, the topics in dispute are often known in advance and advocates can anticipate arguments. Even when topics are not announced beforehand, it is safe to assume when one receives an invitation to speak that there is some reason for the invitation. The advantages of prior preparation are considerable as long as advocates don't let their preconceived positions get in the way of giving the other a fair hearing (in other words, having our minds made up and listening selectively). We strongly recommend prior preparation when the opportunity is available but caution against sticking to a script that prevents the kind of give-and-take or spontaneity that makes argumentative exchanges so invigorating.

Adopt an Appropriate Style

If possible, determine the appropriate tone/style of a response in advance. There is a much better chance of productive interaction if our manner of expression meets the expectations of the audience and matches situational requirements. A respondent's relationship with the advocate will exert a strong influence. As we have noted earlier, there are people (generally high-credibility advocates) that are usually treated with a degree of deference. When addressing someone who seems particularly sensitive or has a deep personal stake in the issue, it is worth taking a bit more care in expressing our reactions. Those with whom we have close personal relationships expect a friendly exchange. Revisit the section on audience analyses in Chapter 4 when considering the expectations that can guide your approach.

The situation or context in which an argument takes place should exert a strong influence on an advocate's approach to the argument. Think of the number of times you wisely decided that a disagreement with a friend or significant other could wait until he or she were in a better mood. Telling a roommate that "I am sorry your grandfather just died, but I think we should address your personal hygiene so I can quit spending a fortune on air fresheners for our apartment" is a statement oblivious to context.

The forum of the argument also should influence an advocate's style. Different forums have different conversational conventions. With close acquaintances, friendly and informal patterns tend to govern our exchanges. In formal forums, it is often expected that we respond in a more formal fashion. A famous example is the Chicago Eight trial where eight leaders of the protests surrounding the 1968 Democratic Convention were tried for conspiring to incite violence. As a means of expressing their contempt for and distrust of the legal system as a vehicle for justice, the defendants continually interrupted the proceedings (Bobby Seale was actually bound to his chair and gagged before the judge ordered a separate trial). In refusing to rise when the judge entered the room, slouching in their chairs with their feet on the table, leaving the table to confront witnesses, yelling at opposing counsel, and a host of other slights, they unnerved presiding judge Julius Hoffman, who gave the defendants and their attorneys contempt citations totaling approximately 9 years of jail time, which was added to the sentences on the original charges. Their convictions were ultimately overturned. This is an exceptional example—and not a suggestion that we would endorse in most circumstances—but does reinforce the basic premise that knowing and conforming to field-specific expectations is important if you desire a fair hearing.[7]

Finally, argument style should meet constraints imposed by the topic. A lofty elegant discourse reflecting a grand style would sound out of place if the topic under discussion is lighthearted or minor. On the other hand, a relaxed, informal treatment of a serious topic would seem insensitive. Failure to respond in a fashion appropriate to the topic makes the advocate appear out of touch.

An amusing example of the relationship between style and constraints imposed by topic, situation, and relationship is found in the 2014 Sprint advertisements featuring James Earl Jones and Malcolm McDowell. The actors, well known for their elegance of expression, played the roles of Lizzy and Kim exchanging brief text messages, which Jones and McDowell delivered orally. A typical conversation has Jones (Lizzy) breathlessly noting that "Ryan is a total Hottie McHotterson," to which an equally impressed McDowell (Kim) replies, "Obvi. He's amazeballs." The comic value of the commercials resides in the clear disconnect between the actors' formal, elegant manner of expression and the informality that characterizes a text message exchange. Indeed, Kelly Kazek, writing for *AL.com*, did a translation of the dialogue since ". . . some of us past the age of 14 may not understand the lingo."[8]

A sense of the appropriate on the part of the respondent is vital. We believe that an inappropriate or unnecessarily aggressive demeanor is the primary reason that arguments escalate into unproductive shouting matches.

Model Courtesy and Fairness

Usually, if exchanges are characterized by mutual respect and common courtesy, the argument will fall into a back-and-forth pattern as the advocates examine their respective positions and attempt to reach a decision. In other words, taking turns speaking is expected. It is important that participants have equal and sufficient time to speak. In formal debates, there are often predetermined time limits that are enforced to ensure fairness. In informal arguments, turn taking is negotiated and usually works out equitably if advocates value each other and respect the process. Do not monopolize the conversation. Such behavior shows a lack of respect for the persons you are engaging and encourages them to give long-winded answers out of fear that they may not get another chance to speak.

Occasional interruptions may be necessary, but advocates should try to minimize the number of intrusions and keep aggression in check. If interruptions seem necessary, they should be done politely (e.g., "Before you continue, would you allow me to comment on what you just said?"). Talking over someone or attempting to outshout a person is rarely advisable. Keeping responses focused on issues will help to avoid many of the behaviors that turn productive argument into personal combat. If things are getting heated, consider trying to deescalate the situation. Often, a kind word ("Your perspective on this is very interesting, I want to explore it more" or "I respect your commitment") will help reestablish a more favorable climate. Another effective tactic is to focus on points of agreement before returning to the contested issue. A simple statement like "It looks like we agree on . . . so we just have to figure out how to get past this one point that is holding us up" can go a long way in furthering the dialogue. It is like pressing the reset button. There will be rare times the gap between positions cannot easily be bridged, in which case you should consider whether or not continued arguing will damage an important relationship or diminish the chance of future productive dialogue. In those cases, ending the discussion is only surrender if one adheres to a view of argument as combat.

Depersonalize Argument Appropriately

People usually have a personal stake in the issues about which they argue. With passionate advocates on both (or many) sides of an issue, the key to productive argument is to maintain a focus on issues rather than the people involved. Consistent with our earlier discussion of the importance of empathy and open-mindedness, be mindful of the fact that you won't get far if the other person sees your responses or questions as personal attacks. For example, we have had discussions about responsible and effective medical treatment. We have inclined toward traditional medical treatment yet frequently engage those who are firm believers in alternative treatments (herbal remedies, aromatherapy, light therapy, etc.). We have managed to have those discussions absent personal animosity. No one has ever hinted that the other would soon face a health crisis because of their "uninformed" or "irresponsible" health care choices. In fact, when we have discussions with a genuine interest in finding new ideas and keeping an open mind, the discussions tend to be both challenging and invigorating as we are forced to think through our own preferences. We are willing to be persuaded and in some cases have altered our medical choices as a result. We understand that alternative

TABLE 10.3

Responding Appropriately

- Preparing to respond
  - Prepare in advance when possible
  - Adopt an appropriate style
    - Appropriate to relationship
    - Appropriate to situation
    - Appropriate to forum
    - Appropriate to topic
- Facilitate a respectful exchange
  - Courtesy and fairness
  - Appropriate depersonalization of argument

perspectives are to be valued and try to honor other points of view. Imagine how these discussions would have gone if laced with statements about how our uninformed pigheaded counterpart was killing a loved one because of his or her reckless behavior. That being said, there are occasions where we truly believe someone is taking an irresponsible position. In such instances, we would try to get someone to just consider another perspective but would not insult them.

MAKING A RESPONSE

Having listened carefully, assessed the situational requirements for tone and style, and made some informed decisions about the types of issues that are important to raise, it is time to craft a response. The specific techniques outlined earlier in this text concerning argument construction will be instructive in this process, and the suggestions in this section provide additional practical guidance as to structure.

Seek Out Common Ground

We have used phrases like *identification, empathy, perspective taking,* and *finding common ground* as traits that characterize the effective advocate. When responding to arguments, these attributes should be reflected in an advocate's discourse. A key to successful argument is the ability to find points of agreement to use as a basis for establishing trust and rapport from which one can move to more thorny issues where points of view differ more dramatically. We tend to respect and agree with those with whom we have much in common. Explore these points of similarity and use them as starting points for arguments. For example, a discussion between spouses about schools for their children might start with points of agreement (e.g., "We both want to get the highest-quality education for our child") and then move to more disputed areas (e.g., "Let me show you why a private school gives the highest-quality education"). This approach highlights similarities as a starting point for argument.

Identify Argument Deficiencies with Tact

When responding, often there is a need to identify deficiencies in the other advocate's position, seek clarification, and/or offer counterarguments. This is called *offering a* **rebuttal**. Take care to identify deficiencies in the other's argument with tact. Disagreeing with someone does not require making that individual look like an idiot. Pointing out weaknesses in arguments without implying that the other advocate is misinformed, unintelligent, or irrational goes a long way toward making a point without provoking a defensive response. The strongest arguments go beyond simply pointing out flaws in the other's position to offer constructive alternatives. In short, when noting weaknesses in someone's position and offering alternatives, do so to understand or resolve the issue, not to simply show them up.

Relevance is a good starting point for counterargument. Consider the claim at the heart of the exchange and then determine whether or not the arguments offered do indeed apply to/support the claim. For example, particular types of claims (fact, value, or policy) imply certain requirements (stock issues). Noting failures to address stock concerns helps to demonstrate that a position being offered falls short of truly proving the claim. Don't be misled by impressive-sounding arguments that actually have nothing to do with the claim under consideration.

As a respondent, explore whether the other advocate's personal stake in the topic prevents them from acknowledging or considering alternative points of view. Is there a bias evident? One's personal experience will color his or her perceptions, and attitudes cause us to selectively attend to, perceive, and recall contrary points of view. Consider if that could be the case in this instance. However, be careful. We are not inviting you to engage in ad hominem attacks but rather opening up the possibility that you may remind other advocates or the audience of issues that they have yet to consider.

Examine the outside support offered (or not) by the advocate. On points of common understanding or in situations where speakers enjoy high credibility, their burden of proof is lessened. Still, don't let someone get away with offering unwarranted assertions. When support is used, refer to the tests of evidence offered in Chapter 8 to point out deficiencies. Of course, it is a good idea to go beyond noting a deficiency by offering counterevidence.

Finally, look for flaws in reasoning and address them. The earlier discussion of narrative rationality, stock issues, and outside support from Section Two will guide your formulation of responses. Occasionally, we hear arguments that seem to be sound but upon closer examination are the product of flawed reasoning. An investigation of claim/evidence relationships will reveal suspect arguments. Some reasoning errors have become so commonplace that scholars have identified them as **logical fallacies**. Consult the partial list of fallacies contained in Appendix B if you prefer to use a set list as a starting point for investigation. Regarding the fallacies, your rebuttal should not be "LIAR!" but an explanation of how the reasoning falls short of proving the speaker's claims. Once again, offer alternative interpretations. In most cases, it is sufficient to explain why reasoning is flawed and to offer counterexamples. Remember, not every fallacy is intentional, and an ethics challenge might be an overreaction.

Stay Organized

After identifying points of response, the next step is to present those arguments in the most clear, organized, and memorable way possible. Listeners may be lost if the rebuttal is disjointed, evasive, or vague. If you have ever been in a discussion and forgot what issue was being debated, or gotten off on a tangent and misplaced your original point, you understand how easily lack of organization on the part of the advocates can derail conversation. The arguments in which we engage run from simple or narrow personal exchanges that are relatively easy to manage, to lengthy formal presentations. The following five-step presentational framework is generally designed for formal arguments, so it may seem a bit out of place in informal exchanges. However, even in those simple exchanges it is wise to remember that listeners must be able to follow your logic. As advocates, we know that an oral argument lacks the organizational aids present in written documents. There are no visible bold headings to direct attention to key issues. There are no visible indented paragraphs to indicate you are moving to a new issue. There are no quotation marks, block quotes, or footnotes to signal that an outside source is being used.[9] Speakers need ways to compensate for these deficits and achieve clarity. The following steps should help structure a clear response.

Locate the Statement

Clearly indicate which point of your co-arguer's positions is being addressed. It is a simple process where you say something to the effect of "I would like to take a look at the claim . . ." This may also involve a brief recap of the position in the interest of clarity. It is generally best to deal with claims in the order they were presented, but certainly there are circumstances where cutting through the clutter and focusing on essential points, even if they occur later in the presentation, is necessary.

State Your Claim

Once listeners have been oriented, it is time to state the claim (your counterargument). Claims should be brief, direct, and memorable. You may have to return to them later as you attempt to point out that the person with whom you are arguing has failed to address your point or has misunderstood your position, or perhaps simply to provide a starting point for subsequent rebuttals where you have to trace the evolution of an argument for your listeners.

Explain Your Claim

Once the claim has been presented, explain as clearly as possible how you reached that conclusion. It is a bit like solving a math problem and showing your work. The audience deserves to understand and appreciate the quality of reasoning that went into the claim. This invites listeners to follow your thought process.

Support Your Claim

Following the explanation, provide outside support for the claim. Return to key points of the explanation by providing evidence as needed with statements like, "Let me return to the point I made about . . . and show how this is not just my opinion but represents the consensus of experts." The advantage of this structure is that the audience has been alerted regarding what they should infer from your evidence, thus focusing their attention. Of course, not every point requires outside support given shared understanding and the nature of the issue under discussion. For example, in an exchange with a friend concerning which movie you should see, it would seem strange to say, "Now, returning to my point about how *Finding Nemo* is playing at the multiplex theater, I quote *The Daily Times*, August 10, 2017, which claims that *Nemo* will be showing at noon, 3 p.m., 5 p.m., and 7 p.m. tonight." We expect that listeners will take our word for it in such situations. In other situations, it is wise to quote outside sources while mentioning the author, his or her qualifications, publication, and date so listeners can assess the credibility of the support offered.

Conclude Your Argument

Once the point has been made, a brief conclusion is in order. The purpose of the conclusion is to remind the audience of the point you have just made while giving them a reason to value the argument. Does your point provide a more reasonable interpretation than that given by your co-arguer? Does your point outweigh the argument to which it is addressed? Should your argument be considered a significant point that merits careful consideration when a decision is made? The conclusion step discusses the relative impact of your claims.

In many formal exchanges, a number of arguments are offered. Use this five-point pattern for each argument. The process may seem awkward at first, but you will discover ways to increase clarity and brevity with practice. The payoff is that your target audience will find your points more memorable. If this process sounds familiar, it should. The cliché "tell them what you are going to say, say it, then tell them what you just said" informs the process. It is a form of stylized redundancy that is critical in oral argument.

Seek Closure

Finally, arguments should result in some sort of decision. Attitudes may be changed or behaviors modified. When engaged in an argument, keep in mind that some form of resolution is the goal. In the end, your point may carry the day, or maybe you will change your position based on the arguments made by others. In most cases, however, some form of accommodation or compromise is an appropriate conclusion. It is critical to enter the fray hoping to reach some decision rather than just planning to score debating points or humiliate others. Recall the noncombative perspective on argument which opened this text and how it alters traditional notions of "winning." This means that even when no decision is made, all participants are "winners" if they have succeeded in getting others to understand their position or have succeeded in creating a relationship where future dialogue is possible. The prospect of future communication is important since arguments often unfold over time. Women's suffrage, national health care, and civil rights legislation took a long time to accomplish but were ultimately embraced when well-intentioned individuals aired their differences and then acted. The formal arguments resulting in landmark legislation were sparked by public

TABLE 10.4

Offering Counterarguments

- Making your response
  - Seek common ground
  - Identify argument deficiencies with tact
    - Lack of relevance
    - Potential bias of advocate
    - Insufficient support
    - Flawed support
- Stay organized
  - Locate the statement
  - State your claim
  - Explain your claim
  - Support your claim
  - Conclude the argument
- Seek closure
- Preserve the prospect for future discussion

interest that in turn pushed the issues forward. On a less formal level, our personal decisions are often based on open dialogue over a long period of time. Couples argue over whether they will have children, where they will live, and how they will spend and save their money or how they will manage their retirement. We also maintain friendships because we have come to respect our friends' opinions or have worked to achieve a history of effective compromise.

Occasionally, we simply decide that there are differences that we will accept and come to unspoken agreement that certain topics are out of bounds. These interpersonal arguments, handled properly, can strengthen rather than destroy relationships. A positive climate that does not discourage argument is critical even when we may not be wholly satisfied with decisions made.

CONCLUSION

Argument is an exchange. When responding to another's claim, creating a climate for productive discussion is essential. It starts with careful listening in which we try to understand another's perspective and listen with an open mind. Initially, listening should be focused on the purpose of clearly understanding an argument, and later with an ear toward responding to deficiencies discovered in the argument. When we do respond, we should do so in a manner that respects the person with whom we disagree and avoids behaviors that would escalate our arguments into full-blown verbal combat. We must also respond in a clear, organized fashion that is appropriate to the relationship, situation, forum, and topic.

Ultimately, we hope to make decisions based on our argumentative exchange, but at the very least, we want to make sure our behavior does not undermine the opportunities for future exchange.

QUESTIONS FOR CONSIDERATION

1. Identify some ways in which you might interrupt to seek clarification or challenge statements made by another without being perceived as antagonistic.

2. Watch the June 10, 2009, MSNBC interview featuring Contessa Brewer and John Ziegler discussing David Letterman's comments about Alaska Governor (and Republican vice presidential nominee) Sarah Palin. Does a combative mind-set prevent effective listening and focused argument? Review some of the web-based reactions to the exchange and try to identify how the personal biases of those observers influence their perceptions of the interview.

3. Identify an instance when you and a friend or significant other seemed to be "talking past each other" during an argument. What factors led to this miscommunication? What, if any, steps could have been taken to make the argument more productive?

4. Is it ever appropriate to question the character of the person making an argument as a part of your response? Why or why not?

5. Revisit the example used at the beginning of Chapter 4 concerning how delegates supporting 2016 Democratic presidential primary runner-up Bernie Sanders reacted to revelations that the Democratic National Committee had attempted to facilitate the selection of Hillary Clinton as the party's presidential nominee. Were these responses justified? Productive?

6. Select a speech or article and construct a rebuttal using the steps outlined in the "Identify Argument Deficiencies With Tact" section of this chapter.

KEY TERMS

Chain of Reasoning 138
Listening 137
Logical Fallacies 148
Rebuttal 147

Relational Cues in
    Argument 138
Selective Defense
    Mechanisms 136

Selective Exposure 137
Selective Perception 137
Selective Recall 137

Additional Resources

The Toulmin Model

An argument is basically an assertion for which support can be provided.[1] According to Stephen Toulmin, an argument involves a *claim* that expresses the "destination" (the belief or action) we are being asked to accept. If your first reaction to an argumentative statement is to wonder "What's the main point here, where is the advocate going with this?" or "What is the advocate asking of me?" you have focused your critical attention on the claim. Clarity and precision result from claims that are not ambiguous, overstated, or understated. It is irresponsible to overstate claims.[2] For example, one could claim that the Carolina Panthers will win the Super Bowl this season, but that is a risky prediction. So the assertion may be stated more tentatively, indicating the degree of confidence we have in the claim. This involves the use of qualifiers often reflected by terms like *probably, most likely, generally, surely,* etc.[3] Advocates may also express circumstances when their claim would not be valid, offering rebuttals that note occasions that would render the claim untrue.[4] The Panthers prediction might look like this: The Carolina Panthers will probably (qualifier) win the Super Bowl this year unless the star quarterback, Cam Newton, suffers a season-ending injury (rebuttal).

Arguments should offer some basis or support for the claim, which is termed *grounds*. Calling a claim "well grounded" expresses confidence in the support offered for an assertion. Support can include common knowledge, other previously established claims, statistics, testimony, examples, or a variety of forms of data. Key questions to ask when investigating grounds include considerations of whether the advocate has sufficiently compelling proof for the claim. It is not out of the question that claims offered with suspect support or no support at all will be dismissed by the listener.[5]

Simply showering an audience with evidence does not always sustain a claim. The evidence must be relevant and must clearly support the conclusion drawn based on that evidence. Sometimes, that connection needs to be made explicit, so a *warrant* (a statement linking grounds to claim) is offered. Often, warrants are implied when they suggest norms of reasoning or generally accepted rules that allow us to see the grounds/claim connection. Other times, warrants suggest statutes or formulas that justify an inferential leap. Questions common to the analysis of warrant include: "Given that starting point (grounds), how do you justify the move from these grounds to that claim? What road do you take to get from this starting point to that destination?"[6] Once a warrant is identified, uncertainty may remain, making it necessary to request *backing* for the warrant by asking, "Is it really a safe move to make? Does this route take us to the required destination securely and reliably? And what other general information do you have to back up your trust in this particular warrant?"[7] The following example illustrates how these elements might be applied:

Democrat:	Hillary Clinton will be the next president of the United States. (claim)
Republican:	What makes you so sure? (request for grounds)
Democrat:	Clinton has strong support from Hispanics, Blacks, and women. (grounds)
Republican:	So what? (request for warrant)
Democrat:	That block of voters is a substantial portion of the electorate that typically votes Democratic, and Clinton is a Democrat. (warrant)
Republican:	Are you sure they will follow past voting patterns? (request for backing)
Democrat:	Sure. They are part of the Obama coalition that propelled him to the presidency. Obama and Clinton are much alike, and Obama has given Clinton his endorsement. (backing)
Republican:	Still, I think you overstate the case. I don't sense a high degree of enthusiasm with those groups, not to mention a hesitancy to vote for what would seem like a third term for Obama. There seems to be a significant distaste for the way things are run in Washington. Many may reject Hillary Clinton, who is seen as the "establishment candidate," and will instead vote for change.
Democrat:	You may be right. Still, I think that Clinton will probably (qualifier) be our next president—unless this election turns into a referendum on the political class (rebuttal) or she fails to energize the Obama constituency. (rebuttal)

Identifying arguments is complicated by the fact that most exchanges offer multiple arguments, whereas claims, once accepted, become grounds for additional arguments. For example, a doctor may diagnose you with appendicitis (claim) based on your symptoms (grounds) and what medical research indicates those symptoms signify (warrant), and then use that claim as grounds for an additional claim that you should have your appendix removed. Similarly, we speak of these arguments as "making a good case" in the same sense that an attorney's closing argument at trial will consist of a variety of individual arguments that must be accepted before we reach the final destination of judging the defendant guilty or innocent.

The components of the Toulmin model are a lot to take in, and the elements are often implied rather than stated in many arguments. In most exchanges, advocates do not have the luxury of calling a time-out to diagram the argument to check it for completeness. Reactions are often a bit more spontaneous as we naturally consider clarity of claim, quality of support, and the connection between the two without throwing around all of the jargon from the Toulmin model.

In most cases, it is sufficient to present arguments in a clear fashion by (1) offering a claim, (2) explaining how we arrived at that conclusion, (3) offering needed support, and (4) concluding with a statement of the importance of the argument. The components of the Toulmin model are easily accommodated in this structure, which we explain in more detail in Chapter 10.

Logical Fallacies

As you listen to the arguments of others, you are attempting to understand and assess their reasoning process. Fallacies are "defects that weaken arguments."[1] Occasionally, advocates commit fallacies with the intent of misleading an audience by making weak arguments appear strong. In other cases, fallacies are innocent occurrences inadvertently committed by an advocate. In either case, you are being asked to accept a suspect conclusion. One who accidentally engages in fallacious reasoning is not necessarily committing an ethical breach unless there is an intent to mislead. Observing a consistent pattern of shoddy reasoning in speakers leads us to be more skeptical of their opinions. A pattern of misbehavior undermines the credibility of an advocate, calling their trustworthiness, honesty, and sincerity into question. There is a great deal of literature about logical fallacies.[2] Some of the lists provided are more extensive than others, and we intend our treatment of common fallacies to be representative rather than exhaustive.

Hasty Generalization

Offering a conclusion based on insufficient data represents a hasty generalization. It is helpful to think about this fallacy in *quantitative* terms: a general conclusion is supported by insufficient or unrepresentative examples. When Bernie Sanders, a contender for the 2016 Democratic presidential nomination, claimed that politicians are all corrupted by the influence of big-money lobbyists or that American businesses are motivated only by greed, he was committing the fallacy of hasty generalization. Examples of politicians voting to protect the interests of their campaign contributors or businesses that consistently allow profit to trump social responsibility no doubt exist and are perhaps common. Still, is the generalization true? You might note a number of counterexamples of politicians who consistently stand up to powerful special interests. You may also be aware of businesses driven by a sense of social responsibility. The point is that to assess the merit of the generalization, we need to know that it is based on sufficient instances. While the Sanders example is arguably a close call, we caution you about advocates who misrepresent the strength of their claims. "All politicians are corrupt" is certainly an overstatement.

Imagine a friend attempting to persuade you to purchase a CD by a particular music group by proclaiming, "I heard their music—they are phenomenal." Your confidence in the claim would depend on what your friend has heard by the group in question (one song or their complete body of work). Your music library may be loaded with artists with a compelling song or two but whose other work fails to measure up to the high expectations you formed based on the limited samples you have heard. Your purchase was based on a faulty generalization about the group. As an additional example, think of the number of times you sat through a boring movie because you thought those action scenes featured in the trailers were representative. The logic that drives the hasty generalization is also apparent in the fallacy of division and the fallacy of composition discussed next. It is helpful to think of them in *qualitative* terms.

Division

In the fallacy of division, one makes a generalization and mistakenly assumes that the generalization is true in *all* cases. As the Republican presidential nominee, Donald Trump was facing a lengthy legal battle over whether his Trump University had defrauded its students (he ultimately settled the case). Trump questioned the objectivity of the Indiana-born judge of Hispanic descent who was hearing the case. Trump noted how he had made immigration a centerpiece of his campaign and proposed a wall between Mexico and the United States to maintain border security. Trump's suggestion of mass deportation of undocumented immigrants from Mexico further eroded his popularity with Hispanics. When Trump then assumed that what was true of Hispanics in general (they disliked him) must also have been true of the judge (a qualitative assessment) and would prevent him from receiving a fair hearing, he committed the fallacy of division. You may recall from the earlier chapter on demographic analysis of your audience our repeated cautions to be careful about how tenaciously you should embrace generalizations you make about your listeners. For example, it may be true that younger audiences are more open minded than their older counterparts, but the elderly certainly don't hold a monopoly on dogmatism or narrow-mindedness. There are frequent exceptions.

Composition

The fallacy of composition is the opposite of the fallacy of division. Compositional fallacies carry the assumption that what is true in a singular case is also true of the whole. We return to Donald Trump for clarification. Candidate Trump had proposed a temporary ban on all Muslim immigration. His mistake was in assuming that what may be true of a limited number of radical Islamic terrorists was perhaps true of the whole of Islam—thus the proposed ban. You have no doubt noted the similarity between the fallacy of hasty generalization and the fallacy of composition. The distinction is subtle, and we believe it is more important to know the logical moves involved rather than the label. In essence, a hasty generalization implies a generalization based on too few examples, while composition assumes that what is characteristic of the individual parts is true of the whole. In any case, the generalization is improper.

Bandwagon Fallacy

Assuming that because a claim is popular it must be true is an example of the bandwagon fallacy. Because we like to fit in, we are often susceptible to the bandwagon effect. We might decide on a certain brand of jeans or tennis shoes because all the cool kids wear that brand. Advertisers are quick to take advantage of our tendency to equate product popularity with product quality. Consider another example: If we were to argue a film was good because it made a lot of money at the box office, we have not really addressed the film's quality. Admittedly, popularity might be an indication of merit since often there must be some reason for the popularity, but the bandwagon fallacy plays on that assumption and invites a superficial analysis.

We have sat through a number of departmental meetings where a colleague will claim that a class they teach is the department's most popular. The frequent, but generally unstated, claim that therefore the class is of high quality or that the instructor must be the department's best goes well beyond what the data will allow. Other factors such as the convenient times at which the class is offered or perhaps the fact that the course is a required class might be critical variables that determine popularity of the class. The bandwagon fallacy assumes popularity equates with merit.

One need only reflect on the most popular ideas that turned out to be dangerous or wrong to appreciate the pitfalls of the appeal to popularity. Pointing out and explaining that popularity and merit are not synonymous is a good way to address the bandwagon fallacy.

False Cause

The candidate who proudly claims that "after I became governor, unemployment in our state dropped by 4%" may be guilty of the false cause fallacy. Since cause-and-effect reasoning is so essential (especially in policy disputes), exploring the strength of suggested cause-and-effect relationships is a useful line of argument. A reduction in unemployment may be attributable to a particular candidate, but as is often the case, there may be multiple contributing causes. Perhaps a general national economic upturn is responsible. Perhaps introduction of a new business or project (which the candidate had nothing to do with) is responsible. Perhaps it was just a coincidence, in which case a correlation is mistaken for a cause-and-effect relationship.

When evaluating cause-and-effect relationships, ask whether the suggested cause is the sole cause or merely a contributing factor. If the cause is a contributing factor, how important is the contribution? How often have we complained that our job would be great if we just had a different boss, only to discover that after our boss resigns (or is inexplicably promoted) we are still miserable? Obviously, our "unreasonable" boss was not the sole cause of our distress.

"Post hoc, ergo propter hoc" is a Latin phrase which can be translated as "after this, therefore because of this." The term *post hoc fallacy* is an example of false cause—a chronological relationship is mistakenly presented as a cause/effect relationship. Saying "I got a good night's sleep last night and did well on my chemistry exam today, so my performance always improves when I am rested" may confuse a temporal relationship with a cause-and-effect relationship. Yes, being well rested might be a key to success, but so is the fact that you read the assigned chapters or that the test covered material with which you were already familiar. We don't recommend turning in early and skipping your study group and assigned reading in the interest of getting a couple extra hours of sleep because you are convinced that sleep is the only key to academic success.

Straw Person

Mario Cuomo attempted to highlight what he saw as President Ronald Reagan's indifference to the poor in a powerful keynote address at the 1984 Democratic National Convention:

> There is despair in the faces you don't see . . . Maybe, Mr. President, if you asked a woman who had been denied the help she needed to feed her children because you said you needed a tax break for a millionaire or for a missile we couldn't afford to use . . .[3]

The speech was an elegant indictment of the administration, loaded with vivid imagery. It also illustrates the straw person fallacy where an exaggerated version of a position is attacked. In this example, Reagan's trickle-down economic philosophy and his spending priorities are painted in sinister terms. Overstatement is not uncommon in the motivational speeches one hears at a nominating convention, but we need to understand that the speaker is taking some liberties. Opposing a tax cut because it means children will starve was an exaggerated depiction of a policy that Cuomo presents purely for the purpose of attacking it.

In essence, the straw person fallacy distorts a claim and then proceeds to attack the weakened version. If you encounter such tactics, it is a good idea to seek some clarification as you attempt to get the discussion back on track by indicating how the claim has been distorted.

Ad Hominem

An advocate's credibility is perhaps his or her greatest asset. The ad hominem fallacy takes direct aim at an advocate's credibility by attacking the person's character rather than his or her argument. We previously discussed the tragic accident in which Senator Ted Kennedy's passenger, Mary Jo Kopechne, drowned when the car he was driving home from a party ran off a bridge. Years later, a group attacking Kennedy's opposition to nuclear power offered a bumper sticker proclaiming, "More people have died in the passenger seat of Ted Kennedy's car than have ever died in a nuclear accident." Now that's an ad hominem! The merits of Kennedy's arguments are not addressed, but his character is called into question as a means of discrediting him.[4]

Ad hominem attacks are particularly damaging in interpersonal arguments when in a moment of indiscretion or anger we make a hurtful personal comment. Imagine a friend attempting to offer some advice on how you might preserve your relationship with a significant other, and rather than consider the merit of the advice you simply say, "I am not taking advice about my relationship from someone who has a history of hopping from one meaningless encounter to another." An ad hominem can be tricky since a person's character does influence how confidently we can embrace his or her claims. One's rocky marital track record may indeed make that person's relationship advice suspect. We believe that considering the character of advocates is appropriate but are convinced that attempts to divert attention away from the merits of their argument through personal insult are irresponsible.

Slippery Slope

If you are from the generation in which the children's story *If You Give a Mouse a Cookie* figured prominently, you are already familiar with the slippery slope and know that if you give that mouse a cookie, soon he is going to want a glass of milk, and then a straw to drink it with, and on and on until he feels so at home that he has drawn and hung a picture on your refrigerator, where he notices he is again thirsty for a glass of milk—and a cookie to go with it. Give him a cookie, this cautionary tale tells us, and we will forever be giving him cookies. Slippery slopes are a common logical fallacy.

On occasion, you will hear an argument that suggests that allowing one thing to happen will inevitably lead to a number of other (and usually worse) consequences in the future. Picture individuals at the top of a steep and slippery hill—if they take the first step off, they will not be able to stop the downward slide until they are at the bottom.[5] In the arguments against the legalization of marijuana, for example, people argue that once we start legalizing drugs, there will be no stopping it—and soon *every* drug will be legalized. It also was fairly commonly used in the debate over the legalization of same-sex marriage. If we redefine marriage as something other than between one man and one woman, opponents of the measure argued, where will it end? That first step could lead to bigamy, polygamy, and people marrying their pets.[6]

Slippery slope arguments are based in fear of what a policy (or action) sets into motion, not necessarily the policy itself. Therein lies the fallacious reasoning. Most of the time, there is *not* inevitability, as action must continue to be taken with decision points along the way that can either continue, discontinue, or reverse a path. Legalizing marijuana does not mean that cocaine is next—at least not without another conversation about it.

When you encounter an argument of a slippery slope, it is sometimes useful to ask about all of the events that would need to occur for the "inevitable" negative consequences to occur. A truthful advocate will admit that the slope might not be as slippery as it first appears. Or that it might not even be a slope at all. What is true, however, is that ideas can sometimes gain momentum and that change can happen incrementally because people see the result, evaluate it, and make decisions differently than they had before. Change, then, is less a result of a slippery slope than of the incorporation of new information into the decision-making process.

False Dichotomy

"You're either with us or against us" is a statement often used by those fighting for change. It feels true—if one is not actively on board, perhaps they could be considered to be against the group. But we could also argue that the statement is a false dichotomy. One might be undecided, or sympathetic, or completely apathetic—in any case, neither for nor against the group in question. The false dichotomy suggests that there are only two mutually exclusive options available. It is sometimes called the *either-or fallacy* for that reason.

As the Black Lives Matter movement emerged in response to the well-publicized deaths of black men at the hands of vigilantes and police in mid-2010, and as police were then also targeted and killed in retaliation, polarizing rhetoric suggested that the people needed to be either on the "side of the police" or the "side of Black Lives Matter," and that the two were mutually exclusive—that someone could not support both at the same time. Many came forward (including the St. Louis chief of police) to expose the dichotomy as false—that it was possible to be sympathetic to the concerns regarding policing as it intersected with race but also to support the police as well.

The false dichotomy is fallacious reasoning because there are often many more than two options available—if one is willing to look for them. Even if there are two primary options available, they are not always mutually exclusive. On a basic level, if you and your roommate are trying to decide what to do for the evening, you might think you could either go out or stay in. That's true in a strict sense, but the choices are much richer than that. You could stay in and go out later. You could go out and come home early. You could have people over. You could go out and get food and bring it back. The options are not exactly endless, but they are more varied than the binary choice we initially considered. When encountering an argument made in either/or terms, we need to consider it carefully. It can be useful to point out additional possibilities or to reject the dichotomous nature of the statement. Perhaps the answer can be "both/and" instead of "either/or."

Appeal to Ignorance

An appeal to ignorance occurs when advocates suggest that something must be true simply because there is no evidence that it is *not* true. In short, they claim that a *lack* of evidence *is* evidence. We are sure that you can see where this common type of fallacy can be troublesome in both interpersonal and more public interactions. As you will recall, the person making a claim has the responsibility to bring the evidence to support that claim. A lack of evidence is not appropriate support. You would be incredulous if a professor, without evidence, accused you of cheating with only the statement "there is no evidence this work is your own" as her explanation. Similarly, accusing romantic partners of cheating on you because they can't prove that they aren't is another form of appeal to ignorance. Of course they can't prove that they are *not* doing something.

When encountering appeals to ignorance, it can be useful to point out the flaw directly. Considering alternative reasons why there may be a lack of evidence can also be helpful in enabling an audience to understand why the lack of evidence is not itself proof. For example, perhaps we *have* been contacted by alien beings but we didn't recognize them as such, or the government knows and has kept it under wraps, or the aliens have a different communication medium that has kept them from contacting us. While you still might not be persuaded that aliens have contacted us, at least you have pushed for evidence beyond an absence of proof.

Weak Analogy

Analogies are useful in argumentation because they help us understand new concepts by comparing them with things with which we are already familiar. Analogies bring clarity in ways that mere description does not. Analogies are strong when the objects of comparison are sufficiently similar and the relationship between them is accurately depicted. Weak analogies are those in which the objects of comparison are not similar enough in important ways.

Weak analogies are problematic because they inaccurately represent the point being made. It is useful to remember that no analogy is perfect, nor does it need to be. The two things only need to be alike enough *in whatever way is important.* One popular analogy used in the debate over gun control is the phrase *blaming guns for violence is like blaming spoons for obesity.* Related analogies for blaming violence on guns included blaming cars for deaths related to drunk drivers and pencils for misspellings. The point intended by these analogies is that a gun is a tool of a person—it does not act on its own. The pro-gun community finds this to be a powerful analogy. The gun control community disputes the analogy's appropriateness by contending that the *nature* of that tool is sufficiently different to undermine the comparison. Spoons, cars, and pencils were not designed to kill, they contend, so such comparisons are weak. Pointing out the weakness in the analogy is an effective tactic. If the two things being compared are fundamentally different, explain how. Be careful to counter the fundamental components of the analogy. Objecting that peripheral elements do not match up will just come off as nitpicking or missing the point.

Red Herring

Red herring arguments are those in which the advocate purposefully misses or ignores the point being made and instead attempts to draw the audience's attention to another issue entirely. The rhetorical equivalent of "hey, look over there!" it is a means of distraction, used when an advocate does not want to address the issue at hand. The fragrant name of this fallacy is drawn from a practice used in training dogs to hunt foxes, wherein smoked herring were dragged across the trail to throw the dog off of the scent—distract it from its goal.[7]

Red herrings are problematic because they are designed to derail direct argument. In most cases, advocates using the herring want to change the subject because they do not want to engage the matter at hand, though in some cases they use it to change the subject in order to pursue their own agenda. This happens in informal and formal interactions. When conversations with our friends or family take a turn toward a subject that we don't want to discuss, we sometimes employ red herrings. Thanksgiving dinner seems to be a prime opportunity to use this fallacy as a strategy. When questions from Uncle Larry turn to such things as, "Have you decided what you are going to do with your life?" "Are you dating anyone?" "How did this semester go at school?" they are sometimes met with comments about the wonderful meal you are enjoying, "Could you pass the potatoes, please?" or a comment about the success of the family's favorite sports team. We wouldn't advocate the use of red herrings in argumentation but can probably forgive them when it comes to family dinners. Unfortunately, red herrings also happen in more formal and high-stakes circumstances as well. In political debates, where candidates try to pursue their talking points regardless of what question is asked, red herrings abound. Somehow, when politicians refer to them as *pivots* and praise their strategic value, their thinly veiled contempt for responsible debate seems less apparent. When a debate moderator asks a candidate to explain an earlier statement, it is not unusual to have him or her refuse to be pinned down and attempt to redirect the conversation by saying something to the effect of "the *real* issue is my opponent's failure to . . ." Faced with a red herring, advocates can point out the nonanswer and change of subject, and attempt to redirect the conversation to the original issue.

TABLE B.1

Logical Fallacies

• Hasty Generalization
   ○ Division
   ○ Composition

• Bandwagon

• False Cause
   ○ Correlation vs. Causation
   ○ Multiple Causality
   ○ Chronological vs. Causal Relationship

• Straw Person
• Ad Hominem
• Slippery Slope
• False Dichotomy
• Appeal to Ignorance
• Weak Analogy
• Red Herring

Glossary

Actual Audience. The people in attendance, or watching/reading a presentation at a later time.

Actual Example. Examples that recount a true story or experience. A form of outside support.

Age. An element of demographic composition involving chronological age.

Ambiguity. Language used purposefully or accidentally in a manner that obscures rather than clarifies.

Argument. The communication process through which the reasons that inform our statements are explored.

Argument Field. The type of argument community in which an argument takes place (e.g., science, religion, art, business, law). Fields have their own norms and expectations that govern argumentative exchanges.

Argument Posture. How advocates situate themselves in an argumentative engagement—refers to relational orientation and mind-set rather than physical comportment.

Argument as Process. A focus on the interactive elements of an argumentative exchange. Example: "They are *having* an argument."

Argument as Product. A focus on the structural aspects (content) of an argumentative statement. Example: "That is a good argument."

Artistic Proof. Forms of support originating with the speaker.

Assertion. A claim offered without support.

Attitudinal Inherency. Dispositions or beliefs. In policy analysis, inherency is a means of explaining why the present system is unable to solve a particular problem.

Background Authority. Credibility afforded based on the status associated with an individual.

Backing. Supporting material for a warrant. A component of the Toulmin model.

Burden of Proof. The burden assumed by an advocate attempting to justify a change in an existing practice/idea/policy. Example: In a court of law, a person is presumed to be innocent until proven guilty.

Canons of Rhetoric. Codified by Roman philosopher Cicero. Areas that should be mastered by those who want to become effective speakers. The canon includes invention, arrangement, style, delivery, and memory, and provides the basic framework for most contemporary texts on public speaking and argumentation and debate.

Chain of Reasoning. An extended and complex argument in which claims, once established, become the basis for other arguments.

Characters. The people or things involved in the narrative plot. Three basic character types are generally presented in argumentative narratives: heroes, villains, and victims.

Claim. The end point (destination) of an argument. The statement we are being asked to accept. A component of the Toulmin model.

Communication Relationship. The disposition of interactants toward each other.

Comparative Example. Examples that serve as a point of reference or comparison to support an argument about a similar situation or issue. For example, "The criminalization of marijuana is like the prohibition of alcohol."

Competence. Displaying command of the subject.

Competitive Mind-Set. A belief that merit or worth is best determined through comparison to others.

Conclusionary Evidence. Testimony that expresses a source's conclusions absent an adequate accounting of how those conclusions were reached.

Confidence. Self-assured. A sense of trust in one's abilities.

Connotative Meaning. That part of a word's meaning derived from the experiences and emotions that one associates with the term. Often a product of past experiences.

Convergence. To come together. Communicating more like your conversational/argument partner in rate, tone, word choice, and/or topic.

Conviction. Conveying belief through the exhibition of appropriate levels of confidence and emotion.

Cooperative Mind-Set. An attitude favoring working together.

Credibility. The image of the advocate held by listeners.

Criteria. Standards used to judge an argument.

Cultural Factors. An element of demographic composition concerned with how culture (primarily race and ethnicity) influence knowledge of and experiences with issues under consideration.

Deference. Accepting a person's opinions because we recognize his or her relative superiority under the circumstances, as in "I will defer to your judgment in the matter."

Deliberative Speaking. Discourse with the purpose of supporting a particular course of action. One of three purposes of speaking described by Aristotle.

Demographic Composition. Characteristics of a target population. Frequently used as a marketing tool. Understanding demographic composition can assist advocates in making appropriate argument choices. Demographic factors include (but are not limited to) age, knowledge and experience, geographic factors, gender, cultural factors, and group affiliation.

Denotative Meaning. Agreed-upon meanings of words, usually found in traditional dictionaries.

Devil's Advocate. Intentionally taking an opposing position whether one believes it or not.

Disadvantages. A stock issue in questions of policy focusing on the drawbacks of a proposed plan.

Divergence. To distance. Assuming a style clearly distinct from the other in rate, tone, word choice, and/or topic.

Dynamism. A compelling presentational style.

Echo Chamber. Ideas and arguments that move only inside a closed system, being amplified and retransmitted without scrutiny from outside the system of understanding. Example: news media that exclusively report information that confirms their predetermined narrative, failing to take differing perspectives into account.

Epideictic Speaking. Discourse with the purpose of celebration (including commemoration). One of three purposes for speaking described by Aristotle.

Examples. Specific instances that are used by the speaker to support a claim.

Expert Testimony. Words from others who possess a special level of knowledge about the subject under discussion. A form of outside support.

External Constraints. Factors outside of the advocate that affect what can or should be said.

Familiar Audiences. Those audiences, including friends, family, and coworkers, with whom the advocate is already acquainted.

Forensic Speaking. Discourse with the purpose of rendering a judgment. One of three purposes for speaking described by Aristotle.

Forum. The physical setting, and accompanying expectations, in which advocacy takes place.

Gender. An element of demographic composition concerned with the genders performed by the audience members and how that may affect their experiences, perceptions, and receptivity to arguments and argument style.

Geographic Factors. An element of demographic composition concerned with the region and/or community in which the audience lives.

Good Reasons. An acceptable rationale. Audiences are persuaded when they find an account or argument to be coherent and plausible (have *narrative probability*) and aligned with their understanding of the world (have *narrative fidelity*). The narrative paradigm insists that commonsense judgments are based on good reasons—on valid ways of making decisions.

Grand Style. Communicating in a formal manner using language that is elevated and full of imagery, and has a complex, yet elegant, sentence structure.

Grounds. Basis or support for a claim. Support, data, evidence. A component of the Toulmin model.

Group Affiliations. An element of demographic composition concerned with the commonalities apparent because of the listener's membership in a particular group or organization (political, occupational, social, educational, etc.). Understanding these affiliations helps the speaker determine areas of interest or preexisting stances on issues that help with argument construction.

Halo Effect. A tendency to assume that because one is credible in one area, he or she must also be credible in others.

Historical Example. Actual examples drawn from history that serve to support or illustrate a claim. A form of outside support.

Hypothetical Example. Examples that involve imaginary events or scenarios. A form of outside support.

Identification. The process of highlighting areas of commonality between speaker and listener.

Inartistic Proof. Forms of proof not originating with the speaker (i.e., outside support).

Informed Opinion. A knowledge-based statement or judgment usually based on research or direct knowledge by the person offering the opinion.

Inherency. A stock issue for questions of policy addressing why a particular problem persists.

Initial Credibility. The image an advocate brings to a communication event.

Intentional Competition. Individual attitudes reflecting one's tendency to judge his or her performance in light of the performance of others.

Invention. Finding things to say. Determining arguments to be made.

Knowledge and Experience. An element of demographic analysis concerned with the audience's understanding of and personal experience with the issues being discussed by the advocate.

Knowledge-Based Credibility. Image of a speaker as it is affected by his or her knowledge about the topic at hand.

Lay Testimony. Words that comes from individuals who have no specialized knowledge concerning the subject about which they are testifying. A form of outside support.

Listening. Affording others' communication careful attention, attending in particular to central elements of arguments and relational elements.

Logical Fallacies. Errors in formal reasoning. Often, fallacious arguments appear sound but close scrutiny reveals logical errors.

Middle Style. Communication style situated between the grand and plain styles. Usually authoritative but personalized. College lectures typically use a middle style.

Narrative Fidelity. Rhetorical narratives that are consistent with other related narratives with which the audience is aware.

Narrative Probability. The degree to which an account or argument is understood as coherent and plausible.

Narrative Rationality. Narratives possessing both narrative probability and narrative fidelity.

Narrator. The person presenting the story (rhetorical narrative).

Occasion. The reason an audience gathers. Generally one of three types: to (1) celebrate, (2) render a judgment, or (3) formulate a plan of action.

Opinion. A statement of judgment.

Outside Support. Evidence that does not originate with the advocate.

Peer Review. Scrutiny by individuals with expertise in a field involving review, critique, and/or suggested modifications before an item is published. Example: academic publications in field-specific journals.

Pivot. Changing the subject. The pivot received significant attention in the 2016 presidential race to describe candidates' tendency to skirt a direct question by responding with an attack on their opponents. Example: Q—Why haven't you released your tax returns? A—The real issue is, why hasn't my opponent released her e-mails?

Plain Style. Communication which is much less formal than the grand or middle styles, with word choices that are fairly basic and sentence structure that is relatively uncomplicated. Friendly interpersonal exchanges usually feature a plain style.

Plan. A stock issue in questions of policy. A plan is a specific proposal to correct the problems to which advocates have drawn attention.

Plot. A description of what happened. The story line.

Presumption. The notion that existing ideas, laws, etc., are assumed to be acceptable absent compelling reasons to believe otherwise.

Primary Source. The published reports from those who actually conducted the research. Firsthand accounts.

Problem. A stock issue for questions of policy. Establishes a need for policy revision by pointing out some undesirable condition that necessitates corrective action.

Qualifications. Words or phrases indicating the degree of confidence or certainty with which we hold a claim. A component of the Toulmin model.

Questions of Fact. Claims dealing with empirically verifiable issues. Example: John is six feet tall.

Questions of Policy. Claims that focus on taking a particular action. Example: The minimum wage should be raised.

Questions of Value. Claims which involve evaluation of the relative worth or importance of something. Example: John is trustworthy.

Reasons. Rationale or justification. See also: Grounds

Rebuttal. Identifying deficiencies in an advocate's position and offering counterclaims. Also a component of the Toulmin model which expresses instances in which a proposed claim will not be true.

Relational Cues in Argument. Three relationships are on display and play a substantial role in any argument situation. These are: (1) the other advocate's relationship with the topic, (2) your relationship with the topic, and (3) the relationship between you and the other advocate. Cues refer to the ways in which those relationships are revealed through an argument.

Representative Sample. A demographically sound selection of poll participants that allows for the generalization of findings to a larger population.

Rhetorical Narratives. Stories (narratives) designed to persuade an audience to think and act differently. Distinct from literary narratives, rhetorical narratives may not reach the formal stage of plot resolution. The audience interprets and completes the story. Rhetorical narratives are like literary narratives in that they feature rising action and turning points where characters must make important decisions.

Rhetorical Situations. Those situations that can be altered by communication. Considering the elements of the rhetorical situation (speaker, audience, occasion, constraints) helps advocates to determine how best to meet the expectations of the situation.

Sample Size. The number of people consulted or surveyed.

Scene. The setting in which an action takes place. Depictions of the setting help to create and convey the tone, feeling, and emotional content of the narrative.

Secondary Source. Someone else's account of an author's conclusions.

Selective Defense Mechanisms. The psychological process by which people manage information that is inconsistent with their beliefs.

Selective Exposure. Attending only to information that supports a preexisting point of view. Limiting attention to competing ideas.

Selective Perception. The tendency to reinterpret statements to make them fit preconceived notions.

Selective Recall. Strategic recollection in which ideas that are counter to existing beliefs are overlooked.

Statistics. Numerical representations often used as outside support.

Status. One's place in a social system (e.g., parent, child, teacher, student, etc.) and also an indication of relative prestige.

Status Quo. The current system.

Stock Issues. Issues that are central to a topic under dispute.

Structural Competition. Situations that by design (their structure) force mutually exclusive goal achievement.

Structural Inherency. Flaws in a system that prevent it from addressing a problem. Usually refers to law or rules.

Target Audience. The people who need to hear and accept a speaker's message in order for the speaker's goal to be achieved.

Testimony. Using the words of another to express or support a claim.

Transaction-Based Credibility. Image of a speaker as it is modified through interaction.

Trustworthiness. The extent to which listeners are willing to believe an advocate.

Unfamiliar Audiences. Listeners with whom the advocate does not have knowledge or a personal relationship. Example: public forums where the audience is likely to be both unfamiliar and diverse.

Warrant. A statement linking grounds to claim.

Zero Sum. Decision rules that demand win/lose decisions.

Notes

Chapter 1

1. Daniel J. O'Keefe, "Two Concepts of Argument," *Journal of the American Forensic Association* 13 (1976): 121–28.
2. "Zell Miller's Hardball Interview," nbcnews.com, last modified April 26, 2009, http://www.nbcnews.com/id/7644466/ns/msnbc-hardball_with_chris_matthews/t/zell-millers-hardball-interview/#.WLTcUG8rKM9.
3. Michelle Collins, "Cruise Uncontrollable," *You Can't Make It Up* (blog), June 24, 2005, http://youcantmakeitup.blogspot.com/2005/06/cruise-uncontrollable.html.
4. Alfie Kohn, *No Contest: The Case Against Competition* (Boston, MA: Houghton Mifflin, 1992), 3.
5. Ibid., 4.
6. Ibid., 5.
7. Morton Deutsch, *Distributive Justice: A Social-Psychological Perspective* (New Haven, CT: Yale University Press, 1985), 255–56, 265, quoted in Ibid., 156.
8. Chris Matthews provided another example of the limits of combat in an interview with Jon Stewart. Matthews is a political player and sees politics as an exercise in the acquisition and application of power to gain desired results. Matthews marvels at politicians who are able to strategically manipulate others. To promote his new book, *Life's a Campaign*, in which he urges readers to improve their personal lives by applying the lessons that can be gleaned from successful politicians, Matthews appeared on the *Daily Show* on October 2, 2007. Jon Stewart conducted the interview and began by questioning the book's basic assumptions. Calling the text a "prescription for sadness," Stewart questioned the value of leading a life motivated by a desire to manipulate others. Matthews suggested that we should look to successful politicians and "watch how far they get . . . you can learn from those methods." Matthews then pointed to the Clintons as examples of successful politicians who also think strategically, arguing that in college Bill Clinton got women to go to bed with him because he was a good listener who advised his buddies to do likewise (i.e., listen) because "it's flattering. It works." He further praised Hillary Clinton, whose political fortunes rose after she went on a "listening tour" during the Democratic primaries. While Stewart agreed listening was a good habit, he observed it is only really of value if one cares what others have to say and dismissed strategic listening as an example of "artifice" and a "contrivance." Stewart's reference to Matthews's work as "fundamentally wrong" and a "self-hurt book" elicited the response "you're trashing my book," a charge Stewart denied with the defense "I'm not trashing your book; I'm trashing your philosophy of life." Later, Stewart would elaborate by observing "there's nothing in this book about 'be good, be competent,'" noting that the basic formula seemed to be "do what you think will win, not do what you think is right." Matthews was clearly frustrated; he seemed to be on an entirely different wavelength than Stewart and, besides, this was not the way book promotion interviews were supposed to turn out. "This is the book interview from hell. This is the worst interview I've ever had in my life. This is the worst. You are the worst," said Matthews. *The Daily Show with Jon Stewart*, "Chris Matthews," October 2, 2007, http://www.cc.com/video-clips/dw4m4i/the-daily-show-with-jon-stewart-chris-matthews.
9. Nikola G. Swann, *Research Update: United States of America Long-Term Rating Lowered to "AA+" on Political Risks and Rising Debt Burden; Outlook Negative* (Standard and Poor's, August 5, 2011).

10. Richard Whatley, *Elements of Rhetoric*, ed. Douglas Ehninger (Carbondale: Southern Illinois University Press, 1963). The *Elements* was first published in 1828.

11. See Jeff Champion, *Pyrrhus of Epirus* (South Yorkshire, England: Pen and Sword Books, 2013).

Chapter 2

1. "Email to NBC News Staff About Brian Williams Suspension," *New York Times* (February 20, 2015), Media section, http://www.nytimes.com/2015/02/11/business/media/email-to-nbc-news-staff-about-brian-williams-suspension.html.

2. In late 1967, America found itself deeply involved in the Vietnam War. Although the *New York Times* and the *Washington Post* had been printing editorials criticizing U.S. involvement, it was legendary news anchor Walter Cronkite, widely referred to as "the most trusted man in America," who is credited with helping turn public opinion. After a visit to Vietnam, Cronkite concluded his February 27, 1968 news broadcast with an editorial that declared: "To say that we are mired in stalemate seems the only realistic, yet unsatisfactory, conclusion. . . . it is increasingly clear to this reporter that the only rational way out then will be to negotiate, not as victors, but as an honorable people who lived up to their pledge to defend democracy, and did the best they could" (Walter Cronkite, "Aftermath of TET: February 1968. 'We Are Mired in Stalemate'" in *Reporting Vietnam: Part One: American Journalism 1959–1969* compiled by Milton J. Bates et al., [New York, NY: Library of America, 1998]). Cronkite certainly wasn't the only public figure to suggest that the war was not winnable, but because of his credibility his opinions were influential. The U.S. military did not pull out of Vietnam for another 5 years, so concluding, as David Halberstam of the *New York Times* has, that "the Vietnam War was declared over by a television anchorman" seems slightly hyperbolistic (Daniel C. Hallin, *The Uncensored War* [Berkeley: University of California Press, 1986], 170). Still, Cronkite's place in public memory on this issue is testament to the importance the public places on speaker credibility, especially when people are looking for guidance on important decisions or on issues where their experience or knowledge is limited.

3. Aristotle, *Rhetoric*, trans. Lane Cooper (Englewood Cliffs, NJ: Prentice Hall, 1960), 8.

4. Stanley Milgram, *The Individual in a Social World: Essays and Experiments* (Reading, MA: Addison-Wesley, 1977).

5. Michael J. Fox., Testimony to the Senate Appropriations Subcommittee on Labor, Health and Human Services, and Education Hearing on Parkinson's Research and Treatment September 28, 1999, http://www.michaeljfoxdatabase.com/acting-career/writing/testimony-to-the-senate-appropriations-committee/.

6. Colin L. Powell, Remarks to the United Nations Security Council February 5, 2003, https://2001-2009.state.gov/secretary/former/powell/remarks/2003/17300.htm.

7. An excellent discussion of Quintilian's philosophy of a rhetorical education is provided by J. P. Ryan, "Quintilian's Message," in *Readings in Rhetoric* (Springfield, IL: Charles C Thomas, 1965), 193–202.

8. Rhetorical critic Kenneth Burke called alignment with the audience in some important way *identification*. Kenneth Burke, *A Grammar of Motives*, California edition (Berkeley: University of California Press, 1969).

9. David Corn, "SECRET VIDEO: Romney Tells Millionaire Donors What He REALLY Thinks of Obama Voters," motherjones.com, September 17, 2012, http://www.motherjones.com/politics/2012/09/secret-video-romney-private-fundraiser.

10. Warren E. Buffett, "Stop Coddling the Super-Rich," *New York Times*, August 14, 2011, http://www.nytimes.com/2011/08/15/opinion/stop-coddling-the-super-rich.html.

11. Chaim Perelman and Lucie Olbrechts-Tyteca, *The New Rhetoric: A Treatise on Argumentation*, trans. John Wilkinson and Purcell Weaver (Notre Dame, IN: University of Notre Dame, 1969), 318.

12. "Howard 'Dean Scream' 2004: Following the Iowan Caucuses, Howard Dean Delivers an Animated Speech," *ABC news.com*, http://abcnews.go.com/Archives/video/jan-19-2004-howard-dean-scream-9438051.

13. Dean appeared on David Letterman on January 21, 2004 to deliver "Top Ten Ways I, Howard Dean, Can Turn Things Around." Number one was, "Oh, I don't know—maybe fewer crazy, red-faced rants." "Top Ten Ways I, Howard Dean, Can Turn Things Around," *Late Show with David Letterman*, http://www.cbsnews.com/videos/deans-letterman-top-10/.

14. Jodi Wilgoren, "The 2004 Campaign: The Former Governor: On TV with His Wife, a Gentler, and Softer Dean," *New York Times*, January 23, 2004, http://www.nytimes.com/2004/01/23/us/2004-campaign-former-governor-tv-with-his-wife-gentler-softer-dean.html.

15. Wayne Brockriede, "Arguers as Lovers," *Philosophy and Rhetoric* 5(1) (1972): 1–11.

16. Brockriede uses the term *rapists*. We find the term *abusers* to be equally useful.

17. Brockriede, "Arguers as Lovers."

18. Ibid., 10.

Chapter 3

1. For a comprehensive discussion of the variables that constrain communication, see Eugene E. White, *The Context of Human Discourse: A Configurational Criticism of Rhetoric* (Columbia: University of South Carolina Press, 1992).

2. Stephen E. Toulmin, *The Uses of Argument* (Cambridge, England: Cambridge University Press, 1969).

3. We believe that a basic appreciation of fields is important if one wishes to engage different communities. The literature on fields is well worth your attention, especially if you envision a career path that is likely to require a thorough understanding of the conventions that will govern your chosen profession. Lawyers spend years learning about procedures and rules of evidence, and professors master not only a body of knowledge but learn presentational and research norms that prevail in academic circles. This knowledge is essential to success.

4. A complete accounting of the argument methods that characterize all of the diverse areas of human endeavor is not our central focus, as we are primarily concerned with the need for an appreciation of external constraints on how we argue.

5. Aristotle, *Rhetoric*, trans. Lane Cooper (Englewood Cliffs, NJ: Prentice Hall, 1960), 16–20.

6. Isocrates, "Helen," in *Isocrates III*, trans. LaRue Van Hook, ed. G. P. Gould (Cambridge, MA: Harvard University Press, 1986), 53–97.

7. John Berman and Calvin Lawrence Jr., "Blood Libel: Palin Admonishes Journalists, Pundits, Television," ABC News, January 10, 2011. Last accessed June 15, 2015. http://abcnews.go.com/Politics/sarah-palin-gabrielle-giffords-tucson-shooting-admonishes-journalists-pundits-blood-libel/story?id=12582457

8. Barack Obama, "Speech at the 'Together We Thrive: Tucson and America' Memorial" (University of Arizona, Tucson, January 2, 2011). Available for viewing on AmericanRhetoric.com at http://www.americanrhetoric.com/speeches/barackobama/barackobamatucsonmemorial.htm.

9. A similar backlash came after the memorial of liberal Democrat Paul Wellstone, a Minnesota senator who died in a plane crash 11 days before the election in which he was running for his third term in the Senate in 2002. As several speakers turned the audience's attention to attempting to preserve and advance the senator's political legacy (praise for the deceased is certainly expected), they were criticized for going too far in turning a memorial of Wellstone into a political rally. Some even believe that it contributed to the Democrat Walter Mondale's loss of the seat that Wellstone had held. Matthew Cooper, "Fallout from a Memorial," *Time,* November 9, 2002, http://content.time.com/time/nation/article/0,8599,388903,00.html.

10. This was the definition provided by Aristotle as one of the three types of rhetoric (the others being deliberative and epideictic/ceremonial).

Chapter 4

1. Jonathan Martin and Alan Rappeport, "Debbie Wasserman Schultz to Resign D.N.C. Post," nytimes.com, July 24, 2016.

2. Ibid. See also Ben Kamisar, "Wasserman Schultz Booed off Stage in Philadelphia," thehill.com, July 25, 2016, http://thehill.com/blogs/ballot-box/presidential-races/289059-wasserman-schultz-booed-off-stage-in-philadelphia, and David Catanese, "Debbie Wasserman Schultz Driven out of Chaotic Florida Democratic Breakfast: The Outgoing DNC Chair Was Roundly Booed and Heckled and Had to Be Escorted out by Security," usnews.com, July 25, 2016, https://www.usnews.com/news/articles/2016-07-25/debbie-wasserman-schultz-driven-out-of-chaotic-florida-democratic-breakfast.

3. During his failed bid for the presidency in 1988, Massachusetts Democrat Michael Dukakis addressed Iowa farmers and encouraged them to diversify by growing alternative crops like Belgian endive. While these remarks were a hit with the Belgian Endive Marketing Board, they fell flat with Iowa farmers (and midwestern farmers in general). Dukakis had forgotten one of the most essential rules of effective advocacy: understand and adapt to your audience. According to the *New York Times,* "when the laughter died down, the Republicans realized they had a ready-made issue in farm states to show that Mr. Dukakis was one of those out of touch Cambridge elitists who not only ate the stuff but knew little about the needs of farmers in the Midwest" (Alan Cooperman, "Salad Days: Dukakis Becomes Belgian Endive Marketers' Hero as U.S. Sales of 'White Gold' Sprout," latimes.com, April 23, 1989, http://articles.latimes.com/1989-04-23/news/mn-1757_1_flemish-michael-s-dukakis-salad-days) (Bernard Weinraub, "Campaign Trail; For Quayle, a Search for Belgian Endive," nytimes.com, Sept. 20, 1988, http://www.nytimes.com/1988/09/20/us/campaign-trail-for-quayle-a-search-for-belgian-endive.html). It mattered little that the proposal was impractical. The proclamation distanced Dukakis from midwestern voters and fed a larger narrative that portrayed Dukakis as aloof and out of touch. Indeed, Republican vice presidential contender Dan Quayle sent his staff on a frantic search for a Belgian endive (no easy task in the Midwest) so he could lug the lettuce around as a visual aid to ridicule his opponent while proclaiming "we need people to listen to agriculture not talk down to it" and suggesting "[h]is idea of farm production is growing flowers in Harvard Yard" (Eileen Putman, "Quayle Rips Dukakis on Belgian Endive and Waffle," apnewsarchive.com, http://apnewsarchive.com/1988/Quayle-Rips-Dukakis-On-Belgian-Endive-And-Waffle/id-4d16b5f492dbc41ff8bb18a5486d6520). To add insult to injury, *Saturday Night Live* aired a debate parody in which Jon Lovitz played Dukakis and proclaimed, "I have a vision for America . . . with direction, purpose, a little oil and vinegar and maybe some feta cheese, there is nothing we can't do" (*Saturday Night Live,* "Democratic Debate '88," snltranscripts.jt.org, http://snltranscripts.jt.org/87/87jdemocrats.phtml).

4. Richard Whatley, *The Elements of Rhetoric*, ed. by Douglas Ehninger (Carbondale: Southern Illinois University Press, 1963), 118–24.

5. Hear Morgan Freeman read the oration here: "Frederick Douglass Video," *History.com*, http://www.history.com/topics/black-history/frederick-douglass/videos.

6. Jon A. Krosnick and Duane F. Alwin, "Aging and Susceptibility to Attitude Change," *Journal of Personality and Social Psychology* 57(3) (1989): 416–25, doi:10.1037/0022-3514.57.3.416.

7. George A. Theodorson and Achilles G. Theodorson, *A Modern Dictionary of Sociology* (New York, NY: Harper & Row, 1969), 415–16.

8. Deborah Tannen, *Gender and Discourse* (New York, NY: Oxford Press, 1996).

Chapter 5

1. Chuck Barney, "Things We Learned from the People v. O. J. Simpson," *Detroit News*, April 2, 2016, http://www.detroitnews.com/story/entertainment/television/2016/04/02/people-vs-oj-simpson-television/82535550/.

2. Most of the attorneys who played a major role (and many who had no role) in the Simpson trial wrote books offering their analysis of the proceeding. For the defense narrative of a "rush to judgment" by a racist and incompetent police department, see defense attorneys Johnnie L. Cochran with Tim Rutten, *Journey to Justice* (New York, NY: Ballantine Books, 1996), and Robert L. Shapiro with Larkin Warren, *Search for Justice: A Defense Attorney's Brief on the O. J. Simpson Case* (New York, NY: Warner Books, 1996). The "mountain of evidence" narrative dominates the accounts of prosecuting attorneys Marcia Clark with Teresa Carpenter, *Without a Doubt* (New York, NY: Viking Penguin, 1997), and Christopher Darden with Jess Walter, *In Contempt* (New York, NY: HarperCollins, 1996).

3. John L. Lucaites and Celeste M. Condit, "Re-Constructing Narrative Theory: A Functional Perspective," *Journal of Communication* 35(4) (1985): 90–108.

4. Susan Mackey-Kallis, "Spectator Desire and Narrative Closure: The Reagan 18-Minute Political Film," *Southern Communication Journal* 56 (1991): 311.

5. Walter R. Fisher, *Human Communication as Narration: Toward a Philosophy of Reason, Value, and Action* (Columbia: University of South Carolina Press, 1987), 47.

6. Thomas A. Hollihan and Kevin T. Baaske, *Arguments and Arguing: The Products and Process of Human Decision Making* (New York, NY: St. Martin's Press, 1994), 44.

7. Gerald Prince, *Narratology: The Form and Functioning of Narrative* (New York, NY: Mouton, 1982), 71.

8. Walter R. Fisher, "Romantic Democracy, Ronald Reagan, and Presidential Heroes," *Western Journal of Speech Communication* 46 (1982): 301.

9. Will Brinson, "WATCH: Cam Newton Abruptly Leaves Super Bowl 50 Postgame Interview," CBSSports.com, February 8, 2016, http://www.cbssports.com/nfl/news/watch-cam-newton-abruptly-leaves-super-bowl-50-postgame-interview/.

10. Fisher, *Human Communication*, 47.

11. Robert C. Rowland, "The Value of the Rational World and Narrative Paradigms," *Communication Monographs* 39 (1988): 215.

12. Karyn Charles Rybacki and Donald J. Rybacki, *Communication Criticism: Approaches and Genres* (Belmont, CA: Wadsworth, 1991), 117.

13. David A. Ling, "A Pentadic Analysis of Senator Edward Kennedy's Address to the People of Massachusetts July 25, 1969," *Central States Speech Journal* 21 (1970): 84.

14. For a full discussion of this speech and its use of scene, see Ling, "A Pentadic Analysis," 81–86.

15. Robert L. Scott, "Narrative Theory and Communication Research," *The Quarterly Journal of Speech* 70 (1984): 197.

16. Phillip Swarts, "Ferguson Protesters Confront Jesse Jackson: 'When You Going to Stop Selling Us out?'" *Washington Times,* August 23, 2014, http://www.washingtontimes.com/news/2014/aug/23/ferguson-protesters-confront-jesse-jackson-when-yo/.

17. William L. Benoit, Katharina Hemmer, and Kevin Stein, "New York Times' Coverage of American Presidential Primary Campaigns, 1952–2004," *Human Communication* 13 (Winter 2010): 263.

18. Walter R. Fisher, "Toward a Logic of Good Reasons," *The Quarterly Journal of Speech* 64 (1987): 376–384.

19. Walter R. Fisher, "Narration as a Human Communication Paradigm: The Case of Public Moral Argument," *Communication Monographs,* 51 (March 1984), 8.

20. Fisher, *Human Communication,* 47.

21. Lucaites & Condit, "Re-Constructing Narrative Theory," 95.

22. Fisher, *Human Communication,* 47.

23. Fisher, "Narration," 7.

Chapter 6

1. B. Gil Horman, "8 Arguments for Concealed Carry on Campus," *Guns & Ammo,* last modified March 29, 2012, http://www.gunsandammo.com/galleries/8-reasons-for-concealed-carry-on-campus/.

2. Andy Pelosi and John Johnson, "The Important Work of Keeping Guns off Campus," *Public Purpose,* Spring 2014, http://www.aascu.org/WorkArea/DownloadAsset.aspx?id=8726.

3. "Guns on Campus: Overview," National Conference of State Legislatures, last modified October 5, 2015, http://www.ncsl.org/research/education/guns-on-campus-overview.aspx. Georgia has passed similar legislation, which was vetoed by the governor.

4. The four bills are HB1899, HB1910, SB589, and HB731. At this writing, none of the proposed bills had been passed by the legislature. The most efficient way to find and track the above-cited legislation is through LegiScan, available at https://legiscan.com/MO/legislation.

5. The use of stock issues is well established in the discipline of argumentation. Though scholars use different labels to identify stock issues, the content and direction are quite consistent across sources. The authors identified their use in the following representative texts: Austin Freeley and David Sternberg, *Argumentation and Debate: Critical Thinking for Reasoned Decision Making,* 12th ed. (Boston, MA: Wadsworth, 2009), 76; Karyn Charles Rybacki and Donald Jay Rybacki, *Advocacy and Opposition: An Introduction to Argumentation,* 6th ed. (Boston, MA: Pearson, 2008), 75–80.

6. James A. Herrick, *Critical Thinking: The Analysis of Arguments* (Scottsdale, AZ: Gorsuch Scarisbrick, 1991), 63–67.

7. Conspiracy theories abound on the Internet. The faked moon landing, the Kennedy assassination cover-up, and the 9/11 conspiracy are among the most colorful. In light of such minority opinions, it is safe to say that 100% agreement is not always required to consider an issue a matter of settled fact. We are more comfortable with a threshold of reasonableness or probability.

8. C. D. Fryar, Q. Gu, and C. L. Ogden, "Anthropometric Reference Data for Children and Adults: United States, 2007–2010," National Center for Health Statistics, *Vital Health Stat* 11 (252) (2012): 3, http://www.cdc.gov/nchs/data/series/sr_11/sr11_252.pdf.

9. The power of narratives is illustrated throughout the career of one of America's most colorful and successful attorneys, Gerry Spence, and in *How to Argue and Win Every Time* (New York,

NY: St. Martin's Press, 1995). According to Spence, "Every argument, in court and out, whether delivered over the supper table or made at coffee break, can be reduced to a story" (113). Notice the villains and victims in the following example: "In a recent case in which I sued an insurance company for its fraud against my quadriplegic client, a case in which I sought damages for his pain and suffering, I created a *theme* [italics in original, 'Human need versus corporate greed']. The jury responded with its human verdict: $33.5 million to which a human judge added interest amounting to another $10 million" (127).

10. The typical patterns for public speeches include problem/solution, cause/effect, topical, chronological, and motivated sequence. Consult any number of texts on public speaking for more information on each type of organizational pattern.

11. Michael D. Bartanen and David A. Frank, *Nonpolicy Debate* (Scottsdale, AZ: Gorsuch Scarisbrick, 1994), 39–50. This work is geared primarily to a contest debating environment, but their coverage of stock issues in value debate fits comfortably with the perspective advanced in this text.

12. Thomas A. Hollihan and Kevin T. Baaske, *Arguments and Arguing: The Products and Process of Human Decision Making*, 2nd ed. (Long Grove, IL: Waveland, 2005), 82–86.

13. Richard Whatley, *The Elements of Rhetoric*, ed. Douglas Ehninger (Carbondale: Southern Illinois University Press, 1963), 112–32.

14. Josh Sanburn, "These Are All the College Campus Shootings in 2015," *Time,* October 1, 2015, http://time.com/4058669/northern-arizona-university-school-shootings-2015/ (updated October 9, 2015).

15. Greg Bluestein, "Georgia Campus Gun Bill Puts Another Big Decision in Governor's Hands," *Atlanta Journal-Constitution,* May 1, 2016, http://www.myajc.com/news/news/state-regional-govt-politics/ georgia-campus-gun-bill-puts-another-big-decision-/nrD3Z/.

16. Kristina Torres, "Georgia Passes 'Campus Carry' Bill Legalizing Guns at Colleges," *Atlanta Journal-Constitution Online,* March 11, 2016, http://www.ajc.com/news/news/state-regional-govt-politics/georgia-passes-campus-carry-bill-legalizing-guns-a/nqjH4/. The governor vetoed the bill.

17. Ibid.

18. Ibid.

19. H.B. 859 (as passed by House and Senate), Sess. of 2016 (Georgia 2016), https://www.docu mentcloud.org/documents/2761664-HB-859.html.

20. "Common Arguments Against Concealed Carry," Students for Concealed Carry on Campus, http://concealedcampus.org/common-arguments/#1.

21. Karin Kiewra, "Guns and Suicide: A Fatal Link," *Harvard Public Health Magazine,* Spring 2008, http://www.hsph.harvard.edu/news/magazine/guns-and-suicide/.

22. "NSHE Arguments Against Concealed Weapons on Campus," *Legislator Fact Sheet: Nevada System of Higher Education,* 2015 Legislative Session, http://system.nevada.edu/Nshe/index .cfm/data-reports/legislative-reports1/legislative-fact-sheets/fact-sheet-concealed-weapons-on-campus/.

23. For a collection of related academic journal articles on the relationship between gun availability and suicide rates, see the Harvard School of Public Health, Harvard Injury Control Research Center/Firearms Research/Suicide, http://www.hsph.harvard.edu/hicrc/firearms-research/gun-ownership-and-use/.

24. This is a recurring narrative as liberals and conservatives debate government regulation, tax policy, environmental protection, minimum wage, and a host of other economic issues.

Chapter 7

1. You are encouraged to view a variety of websites to understand the controversy surrounding Santorum's comments since a variety of perspectives are offered. Two useful though arguably incomplete accounts are provided by Sandhya Somashekhar and David Nakamura, "Rick Santorum Takes Heat for 'Snob' Comment against President Obama," *Washingtonpost.com*, https://www.washingtonpost.com/politics/rick-santorum-takes-heat-for-snob-comment-against-president-obama/2012/02/27/gIQADiXteR_story.html?utm_term=.d00fd0432844. A bit more slanted, but informative, is: Lawrence O'Donnell, "Santorum: Obama a 'Snob' for Encouraging College," *The Last Word*, March 8, 2012, http://www.nbcnews.com/id/46686276/.

2. Austin J. Freeley and David Steinberg, *Argumentation and Debate: Critical Thinking for Reasoned Decision Making*, 12th ed. (Boston, MA: Wadsworth, 2009), 504.

3. Lorraine Mirabella, "Life after College: High Employment and Depressed Wages," BaltimoreSun.com, http://www.baltimoresun.com/business/bs-bz-jobs-college-grads-20120512-story.html; Titus M. Hamlett, "Students Trapped by High Debt, Low Wages," BaltimoreSun.com, http://www.baltimoresun.com/news/opinion/oped/bs-ed-student-debt-20121108-story.html.

4. O'Donnell, "Santorum."

5. Cicero, *Rhetorica Ad Herennium*, trans. Harry Caplan (Cambridge, MA: Harvard University Press, 1977).

6. *The Rhetoric of Aristotle*, trans. Lane Cooper (Englewood Cliffs, NJ: Prentice Hall, 1960).

7. For a discussion of levels of source quality, see Jack Perella, *The Debate Method of Critical Thinking: An Introduction to Argumentation* (Dubuque, IA: Kendall/Hart, 1986).

8. This controversy is discussed in Daniel Carlat, *Unhinged: The Trouble with Psychiatry—a Doctor's Revelations about a Profession in Crisis* (New York, NY: Free Press, 2010).

9. Terry Watkins, "Is Music Neutral?" n.d, http://www.av1611.org/neutral.html.

10. Linda Chalker-Scott, "The Myth of Absolute Science," n.d, https://puyallup.wsu.edu/wp-content/uploads/sites/403/2015/03/bad-science.pdf.

Chapter 8

1. Transcript: Vice President Gore on CNN's "Late Edition," *CNN.com*, last modified March 9, 1999, http://www.cnn.com/ALLPOLITICS/stories/1999/03/09/president.2000/transcript.gore/. A brief history of the incident is available at: Seth Finkelstein, "Al Gore 'Invented the Internet'—resources," http://www.sethf.com/gore/.

2. Matthew Ashton, "Great Mistakes in Politics (No. 10) Joe Biden Steals Neil Kinnock's Speech," *Dr. Matthew Ashton's Politics Blog*, January 14, 2011, http://drmatthewashton.com/2011/01/14great-mistakes-in-politics-no10-joe-biden-steals-neil-kinnocks-speech/.

3. John Reynolds and Jessica Letkemann, "Who First Said 'Born on Third,' Thinks He Got a Triple?" *two feet thick*, http://www.twofeetthick.com/2004/09/01/who-first-said-born-on-third-thinks-he-got-a-triple/.

4. See Steve Benen, "Political Animal," *washingtonmonthly.com*, http://www.washingtonmonthly.com/archives/individual/2011_04/028869.php. The fallout from the comment is described in: Jennifer Epstein, "Jon Kyl's 'Factual Statement' Flap Comes Full Circle," *POLITICO.com*, last modified April 14, 2011, http://www.politico.com/story/2011/04/kyls-flap-comes-full-circle-053214.

5. An interesting account of the manipulation of words to elicit a particular response as practiced for political manipulation can be found in the autobiographical account of Frank Luntz, *Words That Work: It's Not What You Say, It's What People Hear* (New York, NY: Hyperion, 2009).

6. There are a variety of resources available on the implications of the digital age. A good starting point would be Mark Bauerline, ed., *The Digital Divide? Arguments for and against Facebook, Google, Texting, and the Age of Social Networking* (New York, NY: Penguin, 2011); Nicholas Carr, *The Shallows: What the Internet Is Doing to Our Brains* (New York, NY: Norton, 2010); William Powers, *Hamlet's Blackberry: A Practical Philosophy for Building a Good Life in the Digital Age* (New York, NY: HarperCollins, 2010).

Chapter 9

1. See, for example, Rush Limbaugh. In one striking instance, Rush Limbaugh called Georgetown law student Sandra Fluke a slut because she testified about the importance of having birth control covered as a part of the Affordable Care Act for her and other women who had been denied such benefits at religiously based institutions. Obviously, Limbaugh, the most widely listened to right-wing political talk show host in the nation, was not trying to engage in rational dialogue to facilitate community decision making, and his combative and offensive style of engagement and incendiary use of language should not serve as a model for those who do. Limbaugh did spark national discussion, but most of it centered on the appropriateness of his characterization rather than the merit of expanded health care coverage.

2. For an enlightening discussion of the politics of polarization, see Matt Taibbi, *The Great Derangement: A Terrifying True Story of War, Politics, and Religion at the Twilight of the American Empire* (New York, NY: HarperCollins, 2008).

3. We do fear, however, the influence these models have on what advocates and audiences *believe* public argument does and should look like.

4. Trump took the opportunity during a debate in the 2016 Republican primary to respond to a comment that opponent Marco Rubio had made earlier in the week, that Trump had small hands. Trump (correctly) interpreted the comment as an attack on his "manhood," and replied that there was "no problem" with the size of his hands or "anything else." The shocking exchange seemed, to us, to be a new low in a forum that is often raucous but not crude. See a report of the incident and a clip on cnn.com. Gregory Krieg, "Donald Trump Defends Size of His Penis," cnn.com, March 4, 2016, http://www.cnn.com/2016/03/03/politics/donald-trump-small-hands-marco-rubio/.

5. Marcus Tullius Cicero, *Rhetorica Ad Herennium,* trans. Harry Caplan (Cambridge, MA: Harvard University Press, 1977), 253–69.

6. Ibid.

7. Known for his linguistic gaffes, Bush even used those to his advantage, going so far as to admit during a presidential debate that "We all make mistakes. I've been known to mangle a syllable or two myself," while purposefully mangling the word *syllable*. Bush v. Gore Debate, October 11, 2000, Debate Transcript, http://www.debates.org/?page=october-11-2000-debate-transcript.

8. The video is available on YouTube through PBS at: https://www.youtube.com/watch?v=4ZN WYqDU948.

9. Robert H. Gass and John S. Seiter, *Persuasion, Social Influence, and Compliance Gaining,* 4th ed. (Boston, MA: Pearson, 2011), 64.

10. HelpGuide.org, "Conflict Resolution Skills, Building the Skills That Can Turn Conflicts into Opportunities," https://www.helpguide.org/articles/relationships/conflict-resolution-skills .htm, 1.

11. Ibid., 2.

12. If you desire a refresher course, any basic text in nonverbal communication or public speaking should suffice. We suggest Mark Knapp, Judith Hall, and Terrence G. Horgan, *Nonverbal Communication in Human Interaction*, 8th ed. (Boston, MA: Wadsworth, 2014), and J. Michael Hogan, Patricia Hayes Andrews, James R. Williams, and Glen Williams, *Public Speaking and Civic Engagement*, 3rd ed. (New York, NY: Pearson, 2013).

13. "Table," *Merriam-Webster.com*, http://www.merriam-webster.com (July 31, 2016).

14. "Hot," *Historical Dictionary of American Slang*, http://www.alphadictionary.com/slang/H.html (July 31, 2016).

15. "Hot," *Urban Dictionary*, http://www.urbandictionary.com/define.php?term=HOT (July 31, 2016).

16. "Family," *The American Heritage Dictionary of the English Language*, 3rd ed. (Boston, MA: Houghton Mifflin, 1996), 659.

17. For additional background, see: W. Barnett Pearce, "The Coordinated Management of Meaning (CMM)," in *Theorizing about Intercultural Communication*, ed. William Gudykunst (Thousand Oaks, CA: Sage, 2004), 35–54.

18. Jon Breenberg, "War of Words: The Fight over 'Radical Islamic Terrorism,'" *Politico*, December 11, 2015, http://www.politifact.com/truth-o-meter/article/2015/dec/11/war-words-fight-over-radical-islamic-terrorism/.

19. Ibid.

20. Ibid.

21. Kenneth Burke, *Language as Symbolic Action* (Berkeley: University of California Press, 1966), 45. Consider another example. In 2002, the Bush White House pushed to replace the term *suicide bombers* with the term *homicide bombers* in cases where people died at the hands of bombers who killed themselves in the process. Proponents argued the term *suicide* focused attention on those who perpetrated the bombing, deflecting attention from the victims. Ultimately, only Fox News used the term on air (and continued to use it for years to come). President Bush dropped it a few months after the announcement, preferring to call the bombers *suiciders*. The new term proved too problematic and use of the original term too resistant to change. See for example: "With New Iraqi Government, Bush Turns Eye toward Military," *Associated Press*, May 23, 2006, http://www.foxnews.com/story/2006/05/23/with-new-iraqi-government-bush-turns-eye-toward-military/.

22. "Party on" was popularized by the classic film *Wayne's World*. We recommend its viewing.

23. Howard Giles, Nikolas Coupland, and Justine Coupland, "Accommodation Theory: Communication, Context, and Consequence," in *Contexts of Accommodation: Developments in Applied Sociolinguistics* (New York, NY: Cambridge University Press, 1991), 7–8.

24. Peter Jennings, "Bill Clinton in 1998: 'I Did Not Have Sexual Relations with That Woman,'" ABCNews.com, January 26, 1998, http://abcnews.go.com/Politics/video/bill-clinton-responds-monica-lewsinsky-affair-allegations-28406403.

Chapter 10

1. George A. Theodorson and Achilles Theodorson, *A Modern Dictionary of Sociology* (New York, NY: Harper & Row, 1969), 56–57, defines the cognitive dissonance hypothesis as "the hypothesis, developed by Leon Festinger, that when a **cognitive system** compromises inconsistent items of knowledge (that is, contradictory perceptions, beliefs, or other forms of information) about a person, object, situation, or event (a condition referred to as cognitive

dissonance) the individual experiences discomfort or tension that motivates him to reduce the dissonance by modifying one or more aspects of the system" (L. Festinger, *A Theory of Cognitive Dissonance* [Evanston, IL: Row, Peterson, 1957]). A general theory of dissonance can be found in Robert H. Gass and John S. Seiter, *Persuasion: Social Influence and Compliance Gaining*, 4th ed. (Boston: Allyn & Bacon, 2011), 60–66.

2. Travis Bradberry, "Multitasking Damages Your Brain and Career, New Studies Suggest," *Forbes Media LLCI*, October 8, 2014, https://www.forbes.com/sites/travisbradberry/2014/10/08/multitasking-damages-your-brain-and-career-new-studies-suggest/#4ee9ddb556ee.

3. For a brief but useful guide to listening, see: Regenerative Leadership Institute, "You're Not Listening to Me!" *Active Listening in Conflict Resolution* (blog), n.d., https://www.regenerative.com/conflict-resolution/conflict-resolution-listening.

4. Helpguide.org, "Conflict Resolution Skills," http://www.helpguide.org/articles/relationships/conflict-resolution-skills.htm.

5. Interruption is the most common expression of aggression in argument, but we can manifest our hostility in a variety of ways. It is a good idea to be familiar with the consequences of anger on communication. See Ryan Martin, "All the Rage: Commentary on the Scientific Study of Anger," *Psychology Today* (blog), https://www.psychologytoday.com/blog/all-the-rage, for a variety of highly readable essays on the subject of anger.

6. For a discussion of the various styles of facial expression, see Mark L. Knapp, Judith A. Hall, and Terrence G. Horgan, *Nonverbal Communication in Human Interaction*, 8th ed. (Boston, MA: Wadsworth, 2014), 362–68. They discuss the styles of the withholder, the revealer, the unwitting expressor, the blanked expressor, the substitute expressor, and the frozen affect expressor.

7. An account of the trial can be found in Jason Epstein, *The Great Conspiracy Trial* (New York, NY: Random House, 1970). An account of the Chicago protests, along with additional case studies, can be found in John W. Bowers, Donovan J. Ochs, Richard J. Jensen, and David P. Schulz, *The Rhetoric of Agitation and Control* (Long Grove, IL: Waveland Press, 2009). For a docudrama about the trial, see *Conspiracy: The Trial of the Chicago 8*, directed by Jeremy Kagan (Simitar Entertainment, 1998).

8. Kelly Kazek, "Behind the Amazeballs Lingo of Spring's Totes McGoats Commercial," AL.com, December 17, 2013, http://www.al.com/living/index.ssf/2013/12/behind_the_amazeballs_lingo_of.html.

9. Jane Blankenship, *A Sense of Style: An Introduction to Style for the Public Speaker* (Belmont, CA: Dickenson Publishing, 1968), 112–24.

Appendix A

1. The most comprehensive treatment of the parts of argument can be found in Stephen E. Toulmin, *The Uses of Argument* (Cambridge, England: Cambridge University Press, 1969).

2. Stephen Toulmin, Richard Rieke, and Allan Janik, *An Introduction to Reasoning*, 2nd ed. (New York, NY: Macmillan, 1984), 25.

3. Ibid., 85–90.

4. Ibid., 95–99.

5. Ibid., 26.

6. Ibid., 26.

7. Ibid., 26.

Appendix B

1. The Writing Center at UNC–Chapel Hill, "Fallacies," http://writingcenter.unc.edu/handouts/fallacies.
2. There are a number of sources that discuss logical fallacies. We recommend: Gary Layne Hatch, *Arguing in Communities* (Mountain View, CA: Mayfield, 1996), 173–76; Timothy W. Crusius and Carolyn E. Channell, *The Aims of Argument*, 8th ed. (New York, NY: McGraw Hill, 2011), 541–54; Douglas Walton, *Relevance in Argumentation* (Mahwah, NJ: Erlbaum, 2004), 214–46; Karyn Charles Rybacki and Donald J. Rybacki, *Advocacy and Opposition: An Introduction to Argumentation,* 6th ed. (Boston, MA: Pearson, 2008), 150–71; and Douglas Walton, *A Pragmatic Theory of Fallacy* (Tuscaloosa: The University of Alabama Press, 1995).
3. Mario Matthew Cuomo, "1984 Democratic National Convention Keynote Address," *American Rhetoric: Top 100 Speeches,* http://www.americanrhetoric.com/speeches/mariocuomo1984dnc.htm.
4. Another famous example comes from the 1968 political convention coverage. ABC News had only limited coverage of the Democratic and Republican nominating conventions and believed that by incorporating some drama and conflict into their coverage they would still be able to compete successfully for viewers. ABC featured a series of debates between arch conservative William F. Buckley and notorious liberal Gore Vidal reacting to the events that had taken place at the convention. In a memorable rejoinder, Vidal called Buckley a "crypto-Nazi." Buckley leaned aggressively toward Vidal and after making a derogatory comment on his sexual preferences vowed to "sock you in the *&#^%@ face." Both men were intelligent individuals who had much to contribute, but the thinly veiled contempt they had for each other was the story line most people recall. A review of the debates with commentary can be found in Harry Kloman, "Political Animals: Vidal, Buckley and the '68 Conventions," 2011, http://www.pit.edu-klomandebates/html. A film about the debates worth viewing is *Best of Enemies*, directed by Moran Neville and Robert Gordon (Dallas, TX: Magnolia Pictures, 2015), DVD.
5. This fallacy is also known as the "Camel's Nose" (Under the Tent) because if a camel gets its nose under the tent, it can't be stopped from fully coming in—and who wants a camel in their tent?
6. See, for example, Robert Klein Engler, "The Slippery Slope of Same-Sex Marriage: 'Robot Love' Next?" *American Thinker,* August 18, 2015, http://www.americanthinker.com/articles/2015/08/the_slippery_slope_of_samesex_marriage_robot_love_next.html.
7. "Red Herring," Merriam-Webster.com, accessed August 28, 2016, http://www.merriam-webster.com/dictionary/red herring.

Index

Note: Page numbers in *italic* refer to illustrations.

About the Authors

Larry Underberg is a professor of communication studies at Southeast Missouri State University. He received his BA from Northern Illinois University, MA from Auburn University, and PhD from Penn State University, all in rhetoric and public address. He has taught argumentation and debate for nearly 40 years, receiving the Lifetime Achievement Award from the National Educational Debate Association and the Outstanding Contribution to Argumentation Award from the Central States Communication Association Argumentation and Forensics Division. In addition to argumentation, he teaches political communication, persuasion and social movements, rock'n roll and rebellion, and nonverbal communication.

Heather Norton is an associate professor of communication studies and chair of the Department of English and Communication at Fontbonne University. She received her BS from Manchester University, MA from the University of South Dakota, and PhD from Penn State University, all in speech communication with a specialty in rhetoric. She has taught argumentation and debate at the college level for over 20 years and spent several years as a successful intercollegiate debate coach. She served several terms as an officer for the National Educational Debate Association, an organization dedicated to preparing public advocates through audience-centered intercollegiate debate experiences. She primarily teaches courses in argumentation, persuasion, rhetorical criticism, and political communication.